Upended is a beautiful reminder of the principles found in the "upside down" kingdom of God, in stark contrast to the values and motives prominent in today's culture. As followers of Jesus, we seek to share His love through our attitudes and actions. I highly recommend this book to anyone who sincerely desires to become an apprentice of Jesus Christ…better equipped to place their faith into tangible action in a hurting world.

—WESS STAFFORD
PRESIDENT, COMPASSION INTERNATIONAL

Upended does anyone who reads it a great service. It shows how an authentic, reflective, engaged faith—the revolutionary faith taught by Jesus—can result in a life of meaning, purpose, compassion, and significance.

—MICHAEL GERSON
COLUMNIST, *WASHINGTON POST*
FORMER CHIEF SPEECHWRITER FOR PRESIDENT GEORGE W. BUSH

From the mid-level manager to the busy mom, the rhythms of a day sometimes feel as glorious as a dirt clod. With grace and realism, *Upended* helps us recognize how small choices can have impact in the midst of ordinary moments. Most of all, *Upended* shows us how we can aspire to be more like Jesus in ways that infuse eternal significance into our daily life.

—KRISTEN HOWERTON
RAGE AGAINST THE MINIVAN

Remarkably, one of the hallmarks of expanded media connectivity is its superficiality. We have more communication but less of it is substantive; more relationships but fewer that are meaningful; more interaction but less intersection with anything significant or transcendent. Writing with uncommon clarity, Medefind and Lokkesmoe explain how the strength and depth of our relational influence flows from both authentic discipleship and choices in how we communicate.

—FRANK WRIGHT, PHD
PRESIDENT AND CEO, NATIONAL RELIGIOUS BROADCASTERS

Upended arrives at just the right time, in just the right tone. The reader is invited back to a simple yet sacrificial devotion to Jesus—in an area few ever think about: the way we connect with others. This is a must-read book for every leader who finds herself broken down, stressed out, and giving up.

—LORI WILHITE
FOUNDER, LEADINGANDLOVINGIT.COM

Upended delivers savvy and heart. Woven with story and insight, *Upended* is for anyone who wants to become a more skillful apprentice of Jesus Christ.

—DR. SCOTT TODD
LEAD ARCHITECT, 58: CAMPAIGN

Upended will help any leader's message penetrate the noise. As we all experience information bombardment, Medefind and Lokkesmoe break down the lessons every one of us must remember to have our voice be heard amidst the competition of busyness, social media, and information overload.

Following Jesus isn't a slow march through a haze of spi̶
ture. In fact, following Jesus wrecks your life, in all the ri̶

D1495504

and Erik Lokkesmoe capture the adventurous joy of Christ following. The book is, like following Jesus, deep and joyful. Read this and see where Jesus wants to upend your life.

—RUSSELL D. MOORE
DEAN, SOUTHERN BAPTIST THEOLOGICAL SEMINARY SCHOOL OF THEOLOGY
AUTHOR, *TEMPTED AND TRIED: TEMPTATION AND THE TRIUMPH OF CHRIST*

As we seek Jesus's kingdom, God's shalom takes tangible form where our influence is felt. This is the promise of which *Upended* reminds us. And then it shows us how. As an apprentice to Jesus, I need this book. So do you.

—GIDEON STRAUSS
EXECUTIVE DIRECTOR, MAX DE PREE CENTER FOR LEADERSHIP

Most of us know that the life we are living now is a full-size less than all that God has cut out for us. So, good for *Upended*, grabbing us where we live, knocking us on our religious assets, and pointing to the daily, right-sided revolution of grace Jesus always intended.

—GEOF MORIN
CHIEF COMMUNICATIONS OFFICER, AMERICAN BIBLE SOCIETY

Upended is an encouraging, thoughtful, and challenging read. If you are in need of a fresh look at Jesus Christ and what He came to do in and through your life, then you've found it. Jedd and Erik not only invite you into the greatest adventure a person can ever experience, but they also skillfully guide and equip you as you continue the journey. If you take *Upended* seriously, you are going to be a much better person because you read it.

—DR. DENNIS RAINEY
PRESIDENT, FAMILYLIFE
HOST, *FAMILYLIFE TODAY*

Most "leaders" never step on a stage, stand behind a podium or pulpit, sit on committees or run corporations. Rather, true leadership shows up in the small and subtle moments of life—in the daily grind where it equally matters. *Upend*ed gracefully elevates Jesus's love and lessons for those who live outside of the spotlight: the parents, friends, employees, seekers, and visitors. Erik and Jedd have created a timeless resource for the everyday leader.

—BRAD LOMENICK
EXECUTIVE DIRECTOR, CATALYST

Medefind and Lokkesmoe represent two highly important voices from the rising generation that will not be satisfied with mere talk. This younger generation has a new and fresh authenticity not seen in my generation. Whether you are a student, half-timer, or senior statesman, you will see that *Upended* crackles with insight and energy, offering a masterful exploration of the unparalleled ways of the Master—and what it looks like to learn as His apprentice.

—BOB BUFORD
FOUNDER, LEADERSHIP NETWORK
AUTHOR, *HALFTIME* AND *FINISHING WELL*

Right from the beginning I was struck by the heft of life experience in these pages. Jedd and Erik have been writing this book all of their lives. If culture is a rushing river, this book is a steady swim upstream or an encouragement to get started. I was refreshed in my desire to be fully congruent with the gospel of Jesus and to integrate, integrate, integrate His words and work into my daily words and my daily work. Apprenticing Jesus…brilliant!

—SARA GROVES
SINGER-SONGWRITER, WINNER OF *CHRISTIANITY TODAY*'S ALBUM OF THE YEAR

UPENDED

JEDD MEDEFIND & ERIK LOKKESMOE >>>>>

PASSIO

Most CHARISMA HOUSE BOOK GROUP products are available at special quantity discounts for bulk purchase for sales promotions, premiums, fund-raising, and educational needs. For details, write Charisma House Book Group, 600 Rinehart Road, Lake Mary, Florida 32746, or telephone (407) 333-0600.

UPENDED by Jedd Medefind and Erik Lokkesmoe
Published by Passio
Charisma Media/Charisma House Book Group
600 Rinehart Road
Lake Mary, Florida 32746
www.charismahouse.com

Unless otherwise noted, all Scripture quotations are from the Holy Bible, New International Version. Copyright © 1973, 1978, 1984, International Bible Society. Used by permission.

Scripture quotations marked NKJV are from the New King James Version of the Bible. Copyright © 1979, 1980, 1982 by Thomas Nelson, Inc., publishers. Used by permission.

Cover design by Justin Evans
Design Director: Bill Johnson

Visit the authors' website at www.upended.org.

Library of Congress Control Number: 2012903364
International Standard Book Number: 978-1-61638-605-4
E-book ISBN: 978-1-61638-722-8

Portions of this book were previously published as *The Revolutionary Communicator* by Relevant Books, ISBN 0-9746942-5-8, copyright © 2004.

While the authors have made every effort to provide accurate telephone numbers and Internet addresses at the time of publication, neither the publisher nor the authors assume any responsibility for errors or for changes that occur after publication.

12 13 14 15 16—9 8 7 6 5 4 3 2 1
Printed in the United States of America

DEDICATION

Jedd

To my children—Siena, Marin, Eden, Lincoln, and the "twinkle in Daddy's eye." May you love this Jesus most of all, making His grace touchable in a beautiful and hurting world.

Erik

To my kids—Kolton, Skylar, and Sydney—who remind me in their small and subtle ways that "Daddy" is the greatest title and that "I love you" are the greatest words.

CONTENTS

SECTION VII: LIFE THROUGH STORYTELLING

SECTION VIII: LIFE THROUGH QUESTIONS

SECTION IX: LIFE THROUGH TIME AWAY FROM THE CROWD

SECTION X: WHERE IT HAPPENS

ACKNOWLEDGMENTS

A VERY BIG THANKS TO: Jared and Jody Jones; Matt and Leah St. Pierre; Trey Sklar; Mike Peterson; Matt Kronberg; Marlene and Gary Van Brocklin; Danny and Emily Kapic; Maynard and Colleen Medefind; Roger and Janet Scalice; Craig and Nikki Miller; Tom and Leah Carpenter; Joel and Kate Harris; Gavin and Carrie Jones; Seth and Cory Medefind; Caleb and Lori Medefind; Grant Medefind; Jerry Loving; Tim and Patti Lokkesmoe; Mike and Kirsten Ayulo; Lou and Marilyn Baumeister; Gabe and Rebekah Lyons; Justin and Laura Christensen; Jay and Siobahn Harren; Lee and Betsy Norwood; Phillips and Lori McCarty; Glenn Hoburg; Corby Pons; Marshall Mitchell; and Justin Dillon.

HEARTFELT THANKS AS WELL TO: Barbara Dycus and the entire team at Charisma Media for their diligent and skillful labor from start to finish.

AND THE BIGGEST THANKS TO: Jedd's most skillful (and beautiful) editor, Rachel Medefind, and to Monica Lokkesmoe, who makes Erik want to be a better man by the way she lives and loves.

INTRODUCTION

The Scriptures define Jesus followers as a peculiar people, and rightly so, for we follow One who upends the world's assumptions and expectations at every turn.

→ Born to a teen mother in an insignificant town

→ Lived a tradesman's humble existence for thirty years

→ Challenged the religious and celebrated with outcasts

→ Rejected the demands of the crowd to seize earthly position and power

→ Told stories about the first as last...better to give than receive...losing life to find it

→ Went willingly to the cross to die unjustly as a criminal

→ Sprang up from the dead

 Up·end [*uhp–end*] verb (used with object): 1) to set on end, as a barrel or ship; 2) to affect drastically or radically, as tastes, opinions, reputations, or systems; 3) to defeat in competition, as in boxing or business.[1]

Jesus did more than turn tables in the temple; He turned all of life upside down. Yet even for many of us who claim to follow Him, our lives are not peculiar at all.

If anything, we are a rather predictable people.

We have settled into a routine of expectations and assumptions shaped by social mores and respectable habits. We are middle creatures—most comfortable in a space that demands neither too much nor too little. Church on Sunday, work on Monday. A percentage of our paychecks. A few minutes of prayer.

We follow an upside-down God yet live right-side-up lives.

Yes, we often hear pleas for more radical living. Sometimes we yearn for it. But often *radical* ends up being just an idea, a theme for talks and books, conferences and blog posts.[2] We are tempted to imagine we can put it on like a wristband or attain it by association with the right causes or leaders. We commit to grand goals, then wonder why we fail soon after.

The revolution Jesus sowed in human hearts was not a logo to wear or brand to cultivate. Nor did it hold much in common with the gleaming eyes of the zealot or the prophet's tangled beard. It was not a fist raised in the air or beret on the head, identifying its wearer as a *real* radical.

Following Jesus is usually subtler, less obvious…and often far more costly.

That's why this book isn't about big choices that make us radical. It's mostly about small choices that begin to mirror the life of One who was radical indeed.

QUESTIONS THAT BRING LIFE

Let's start with a few questions.

Becca graduated from college last year, hungry to harness her learning and live out her faith. She wanted to serve well, wherever she could be of most use in a hurting world. But a year after graduation, she shared that the gulf between her deepest convictions and her daily life seemed to be growing ever wider. She expressed in dismay, "You see all this pressing need and you hear, 'Do something!' But then you graduate and you think, 'How am I supposed to do something from a cubicle or while I'm doing pizza delivery because I can't get another job?'"

Many of us who are five or ten or fifty years down the road feel the same. No doubt we've heard that we can honor God amidst ordinary tasks. We affirm that it's not just preachers or missionaries who can build God's kingdom and that Christian conviction should invigorate all we do. But still, the lofty ideals of our faith often seem utterly disjointed from what wins our paychecks and fills our weekends. We yearn for a greater *integration* between eternal truth and daily life yet often feel the two remain largely disconnected.

We ask with some frustration, "Can discipleship to Jesus Christ really make something extraordinary out of ordinary life?"

A friend of ours set his sights on bringing God-honoring influence into Hollywood. After training at one of the world's best film schools, his skills and connections carried him ever deeper into Hollywood's inner circles. But even as his capacity for impact blossomed, his priorities became less and less distinguishable from the culture around him. As he took on a leadership post in a global advertising firm, the world's mold only squeezed more tightly around him. Small compromises led to big ones. Ultimately, the one-time Hollywood missionary landed on the front page of the *Wall Street Journal*, not as a winsome witness for Christ but in scandal and disgrace. Our friend's fall and the pain that followed ultimately led him homeward. He sought a restored relationship with his wife and God and reset his priorities. But he wishes with all his heart he'd been able to keep his faith and his professional life aligned at each step along the way.[3]

Stories like his are rewritten every day. As it is sometimes expressed in Washington DC, "He came to change the city, but the city changed him." Learning to be world shapers is no small thing, from local schools and churches to global institutions. But even tougher is to do so without being conformed into its shape ourselves. Some wonder if it is even possible to play significant roles in art or politics, education or commerce—yet also subvert the world's destructive patterns of false progress, soul-consuming technology, and empty success.

So we wisely question, "Can we powerfully influence our culture without being irreversibly influenced in turn?"

The London *Telegraph* broke the tragic story of Simone Back. At 10:53 p.m. on Christmas Day, the forty-two-year-old woman posted aching words on her Facebook page, "Took all my pills be dead soon bye bye everyone." Simone had 1,048 Facebook *friends*. Not one stopped by to knock on her door or even alerted the authorities. By the time Simone's mother heard about the note and called for help, it was too late.[4]

Perhaps few of us live with the isolation and despair Simone Back must have known. But the news reports of her death struck a chord across the UK and beyond. Readers seemed to sense that it said something not only about a lonely woman's lack of real community but our own as well.

Yes, we are more technologically connected than ever before. Just below the surface, however, lurks a vague feeling of disconnection. We long to know and be known, and have endless options for doing so. But amidst dizzying activity and interaction, there remains a grinding absence of real community. It feels a bit like an airport restaurant. Those diners are people who go places, get things done. They have clients and customers in far-off cities such as New York or Bangkok. But there they all are, eating alone.

And we wonder, "Will we ever know the sense of authentic relationship and community we hunger for?"

JESUS AS BOTH MASTER AND MASTERFUL

These questions may seem unrelated. Yet we write this book convinced that all three ultimately share a single answer. Or rather, that the solution is discovered along a singular road. For the two of us, it's a journey that continues to be the most daunting and exhilarating of our lives.

We've both held deep commitment to Christ as long as we can remember. He was our Savior and, we would have said, our Lord as well. Our conviction was sincere and its consequences significant. But we also must admit that often we viewed the abundant life Jesus offered as being mainly about eternity, not today.

Jesus's death and resurrection stood for us as the axis point of history, but somehow we missed that He was truly masterful at *all* that He did. We knew to the core that Jesus's words were true and good. Yet they just didn't translate that well into the daily tasks and activities that filled up nine-tenths of our time. So often, being a Christian looked like little more than being nice and assenting to the right truths.

It wasn't faith without works; it was faith that didn't seem to work.

What began to topple all this was not some *new* idea. Rather, we were newly struck by truths that should have been obvious all along. That Jesus is not only good but also smart. That a real disciple doesn't just attend lectures and do well on tests, but he also emulates the character of the Master. That, as 1 John puts it, "Whoever claims to live in him must walk as Jesus did."[5] That to see Jesus in action is to see the Father, and to be like Jesus in action is to be like the Father. That Jesus wasn't calling us only to affirm who He is and what He said but also to put it into practice.[6]

Piece by piece these thoughts came into focus around a central theme: *apprenticing to Jesus.*

What did that mean? We had only a shadowy sense at the time. But we knew it'd require more than lecture and exam learning alone. We'd need to fix our eyes on Jesus *Himself*: how He moved and taught and loved and led. We wanted to see His unparalleled character and ways penetrate every aspect of who we were. Not for any other reason or end, but simply because our hearts longed to know and love Jesus and to follow Him always, whatever that meant and wherever it led.

For this we'd need not just to learn more *about* Jesus but also *from* Him.

TO LOVE, LEAD, AND CONNECT

For us, it seemed that communication would have to be the first—and perhaps most important—aspect of apprenticing to the Master. For starters, communication had always been central to our careers. Most of what we did all day had at least something to do with it, from writing speeches to overseeing interns. It's that way for most people, whether teachers or managers or stay-at-home moms.

If we weren't learning to walk as Jesus throughout the workday, how could we call ourselves His apprentices?

Just as much we wanted Jesus to pervade our personal lives as well. It is no exaggeration to say that how people communicate colors every aspect of their lives: romance and marriage, parenting and friendship, leading small group studies and talking with a lonely student in a bar, interacting with an angry landlord or meeting a frail neighbor on the sidewalk. To become an apprentice to Jesus in communication touches and alters every aspect of life. It grows intimacy and authentic community. It unites our deepest convictions with daily tasks. It builds true character and lasting influence.

That's what we wanted, even if we sensed it'd be costly.

Our motivation wasn't to undertake some wearying new exercise toward religious excellence. It was not a vain attempt to earn God's grace. Nor was it about spiritual manipulation to *win friends and influence people*. Rather, we were compelled by the beauty and power of Jesus Himself, His wisdom and graciousness, humility and strength.

Really, shouldn't that be enough?

We'd observed and worked alongside some of the most skilled communicators in the world, from Washington to New York to Hollywood. In truth, none held a candle to Jesus. And as we looked closer, we found ourselves awed again and again by His way of entering the space of an audience, of embodying abstract concepts in touchable objects, of guiding listeners toward discovery with potent questions, of lavishing attention on people others ignored. It all was at once so needed and so lacking in even the best communicators we knew.

To become Jesus's apprentice in these things, we were certain, could turn life upside down.

In this book, Section I (chapters 1–2) lays a simple foundation for this vision. Although a bit more *big picture*, this section is the soil from which the rest of the book grows. From there, Section II begins the deeper, hands-on exploration of how to apprentice to Jesus. We focus on one particularly vital aspect of life: the way we communicate. It is learning to love and lead, influence and connect in the unparalleled ways of the Master.

A SMALL KIND OF RADICAL

When we first began exploring these questions, we lived on opposite coasts. Jedd worked as a chief of staff in the California legislature. Erik served as speechwriter to a member of the president's cabinet in Washington DC. Via phone, e-mail, and occasional visits, we reexplored the Gospels together, asking what it would really look like to apprentice ourselves to Jesus as communicators.

Much of what we found along that journey we included in the book *The Revolutionary Communicator*, which we wrote together in 2004. Some of those reflections are found here in this book too.

Yet much changes in seven years. In 2005 Jedd took a job in Washington DC. That year we both moved with our families into old row houses on Capitol Hill, just around the corner from each other. With our wives and children, we shared weekly meals, traded babysitting, and learned ways of loving our neighbors and our neighborhood. We walked together through the thrills of politics and their ugly underbelly, marital conflicts and joys, picnics on the Potomac, miscarriages, triumphs and frustrations at work, and much more.

Meanwhile, communication remained central in our respective jobs also. The two of us met weekly in the Cosi restaurant on Pennsylvania Avenue to continue exploring together what apprenticeship to Jesus meant for marriage, parenting, friendship, and our professions, day in and day out. It was among the richest seasons of our lives.

Today we again live on opposite coasts. Erik's work took him to New York, and Jedd returned in California. Our friendship continues to deepen, as does our ongoing learning together.

Through it all we've grown only more convinced of how potent it can be when a woman or man becomes an apprentice to Jesus as a communicator. In every situation, from presidential speeches and national marketing campaigns to loving our wives and nurturing the brood of young children with whom we're blessed, we grow ever more certain that apprenticing to Jesus is a road like none other.

To be clear, the choices it involves don't always maximize bottom line, sell product, or elect political leaders. Sometimes they do. Often they lead along a path in the opposite direction.

Nor will the one who follows Jesus always be easy to spot—at least initially. It's mostly the small choices that set the apprentice apart.

Meeting a true apprentice, others may at first note only that they felt especially well listened to or were helped to see an old truth with remarkable clarity. Over time, however, they may begin to sense that the apprentice is not quite like anyone they've ever encountered. Peculiar. Even radical. But not because of claims worn on the wrist or shirtsleeve, nor even grander things such as moving from the suburbs to the city or leading a nonprofit. Rather because of a quiet vibrancy that animates the apprentice's words and questions, listening and stories. Most of all the observer will likely conclude that he or she has never felt so loved by the communication of another.

That is our hope for our readers. No matter the stage or position, we invite everyone to journey along with us—frequent speakers and those who can't stand a microphone; musicians and farmers; bloggers and junior high Sunday school teachers. It's a road for *all* who want to know Jesus more deeply and to see His unparalleled ways indelibly color every facet of life.

Most steps along the way are little ones. But as we take them, life and leadership and love are inevitably upended—not always how we'd imagined, or even how we'd hoped, but always for the better. Much better.

Section I

APPRENTICING TO JESUS

Chapter 1

ETERNAL TRUTH AND
THE DAILY GRIND

Most of the genocides of the twentieth century—from Communist Russia to China to Cambodia—were led by avowedly atheist governments. Often, pastors and priests were among the first killed. But the story of Rwanda's genocide is more complex. Yes, many faithful Christian leaders were targeted for immediate death. But in 1994, when the horrific events of one hundred days took an estimated eight hundred thousand lives, roughly 90 percent of Rwandans claimed to be Christians.

Experiencing the pictures and stories of the genocide in the Kigali Memorial Centre today, a thoughtful Christian cannot help but question in anguish, "How is this possible in any nation, let alone one that was supposedly so Christian?"

Rwandan pastor Antoine Rutayisire has grappled with this question himself. He experienced the searing pain of the genocide firsthand. In both anger and grief he explored what enabled such a profound gulf between professed religion and what played out in practice.

At the heart of the matter Rutayisire has concluded that the Christianity of most Rwandans was totally divorced from their ordinary lives. It had to do with heaven, but not earth; abstract doctrines, but not daily choices. Rutayisire explains how traditional African religions always carried implications for virtually every task and interaction, from animal husbandry to cooking. The imported Christianity that took root in much of Rwanda, in contrast, was "a kind of catechism based on memory but not touching issues of daily life."

The issue was not simply that many Rwandans did not take religion seriously or didn't carry sincere religious beliefs. Most all Africans do. The issue was that their Christianity carried almost no consequence for the small choices they made every day. The missionaries had taught catechisms and rituals, but not how Jesus would want them to manage a business or interact with their neighbors.

Rutayisire explains, "The consequence was that many people got baptized and integrated into churches, but every time when they ran into problems, they fell back into traditional religion.... And in terms of conflict, they relied on what they had been taught by their fathers."[1]

It is easy to view the savagery of Rwanda's genocide and imagine it has nothing to do with us. But the simple truth is that the Christianity practiced by many self-described Christians worldwide is not all that different from the religion practiced by the many Rwandans who failed to stop, or who even participated in, the genocide. It is a religion of great truths and noble ideas that remain largely disconnected from daily choices.

Even those of us who take our faith *seriously* can fall into the same trap, allowing gaps to form between Christian conviction and the activities of daily life. We study and explore doctrinal truths, but we often feel at a loss to explain how they affect the way we converse with friends, serve our boss, or invest retirement funds. We lack practical *connection points* between Christianity's big ideas and what we do each day.

Like that of many Rwandans at the time of the genocide, our religion may feel real enough in the life of the mind. As Rutayisire would say, we have been baptized and integrated into churches. But we have not learned what it looks like to "walk as Jesus did."[2] So when practical decisions must be made, we fall back on habits and learning that really have little to do with the ways of Jesus. When tested, such religion disconnected from daily life is found profoundly lacking, whether in school or work, marriage or wider social engagement—just as it was in Rwanda.

THE FATAL SPLIT

Disconnecting Christian faith from daily experiences is not just unfortunate. It is deadly. We see its effects on a grand scale in the breathtaking evil of genocide, but just as surely in the withering of once-rich friendships, marriages grown cold, or children estranged.

Over a lifetime the disconnect becomes a trail of opportunities squandered. It is the possibility of living vibrantly, loving well, and leading in ways that leave lasting impact...lost forever.

At times even Christian teachers have encouraged this fatal split. They have elevated a *higher* realm of religious knowledge and activity above the *lower* realm of everyday life. But this view has no basis in Jesus or the apostles, nor the Old Testament either.[3] Rather it was Greek philosophers and Gnostics who tried to divorce the spiritual from the physical. For them abstract ideas were superior to the world around us. So spiritual progress required moving *away* from physical things. Their goal was to transcend the mess and muck of the ordinary.

In contrast, Christianity—like Judaism before it—affirmed that all God made was "very good."[4] Paul summed it up well to Timothy: "For everything God created is good, and nothing is to be rejected if it is received with thanksgiving."[5] This includes work and recreation, food and wine, sex and friendship.

Yes, sin has marred these things profoundly. But God's response is not to abandon or *transcend* ordinary, physical things. Rather, His plan from the start was to *enter* His creation in order to repair, renew, and restore.[6]

That same pattern is God's call to His people as well. We are to take His truth and vitality into each day's activities and interactions, just as Jesus did. Learning how to do so from Jesus is the lifelong adventure of the apprentice.

Though exceptional, there were many in Rwanda in 1994 who'd embraced this vision too. One was Celestin Musekura. As a pastor he'd sought both to teach and to live a practical, daily apprenticeship to Jesus. When the 1994 genocide began in his home country, he was completing his graduate studies in Kenya. While most everyone who could was rushing pell-mell out of Rwanda, Celestin headed in, risking his life to try to turn his fellow Hutu tribesmen from murder and to exhort Tutsis to resist the urge for revenge.

There were others too. As evil surged around them, they refused to participate or look the other way. Some hid neighbors in their homes. Others stared down machete-wielding mobs. Many died for their efforts to protect innocent life. But they'd learned long before how to weld together eternal truth and their daily choices—and they continued to do so, even at immense cost.

Today, with anguish from the genocide yet pungent in Rwanda, Celestin and others like him continue to live as apprentices to Jesus. Though still mourning profound loss, they forgive those who killed their dear friends, family members, and neighbors. Risking the hatred of their own tribes members, they build reconciliation in their communities and churches. Slowly they are reweaving the fabric of Rwanda.

Explains Celestin, "Amidst the bloody history of tribal hatred, Africa's only hope lies in a Christianity that pervades our lives down to the smallest things, when our identity in Christ supersedes our tribal identity. It is costly. But the alternative costs even more."[7]

CAN WE REALLY DO IT TODAY?

Living two thousand years away from Jesus's time on earth, it may seem overblown to speak of actually becoming an *apprentice* to Him. Looking closer, however, we realize that the experience of Jesus's first apprentices is not as different from ours as we might think.

Paul, like us, never walked with Jesus. Yes, the twelve disciples did have the privilege of observing Jesus in person. But it was only for three short years. And truth be told, they didn't do particularly well as apprentices while Jesus was still with them. It was only after Jesus's departure, when they were in much the same situation we are now, that they really began to look like His apprentices in their attitudes and actions.

For them and all who've followed since, the core of apprenticeship has always been the same. Responding to God's grace and empowered by His Spirit, the apprentice marks the words and ways of the Master—and then puts them into practice.

Follow Me, Jesus offers to us too. It is a summons to learn not just *about* Him but also *from* Him.

Personal Notes: Jedd

With college graduation nearing, law school seemed the next logical step for a guy who didn't have the prerequisites for any other graduate studies. But talking with many who'd walked that road gave me pause. So few loved what they did. The grinding hours at big firms brought fat paychecks but seemed to snuff out enthusiasm and purpose.

Three close friends of mine were grappling with similar thoughts. We each wanted badly to engage the world fully and experience Christ's *life to the full.* Just as much, we feared that the ladder of success might lead to far less than we hoped for out of life.

So, with a blend of hope and desperation, we put grad school and paychecks on hold. Instead, we'd spend the year living with and learning from committed Christians around the globe—people who served God and neighbor faithfully in their own native lands. Most of all, we hoped to taste life at its fullest...and learn how to keep that going for five or six decades.

The months ahead were indeed the adventure of a lifetime: from the Guatemalan highlands to Russia's frozen north, Africa's mountain kingdom to the endless rice fields of Bangladesh.

But there was a sobering element too. No matter how thrilling a place was when we first arrived, we were struck by how quickly *exciting* wears off. Adrenaline ebbs. Exotic becomes commonplace. We saw with dismal clarity that the *life to the full* we sought wouldn't be found in relentless adventure alone.

Yet alongside this realization, hope glimmered. It wasn't in the buzz of novelty or grand exploits but in a number of the local Christians we served alongside. Their work and relationships weren't *exotic* to them. Many had done what they were doing for years. They delivered medical care to Guatemalan peasants; taught wrestling and Jesus in Russian orphanages; created simple business opportunities for the poor in Thailand; led secret house churches in Communist Vietnam. Their work and daily choices were mostly quiet, steady. Some weren't in full-time ministry at all. Yet their days blazed with the kind of purpose and humble joy we hoped would fill ours to our last breath. With countless small choices to follow Jesus, they infused daily life with eternal life.

That journey taught us more than we could recount. But what I most pray will shape my choices is still that simple realization. Life to the full isn't found *out there*—in far-off adventure, or a much-anticipated change, or the next stage in life. Rather, it's found in ordinary places and daily choices to love and give and serve with abandon for Christ's sake.

NOT MERELY A HUMAN PURSUIT

We must know from the start that apprenticeship is not merely a human pursuit. Its wellspring is always response to God's grace. It is surrounded by faithful witnesses from every generation. It is engaged as part of a community, both local and global, called the church. It is nourished continually by God's living Word. It is undertaken with a continual sense of gift, never earning or merit.

Perhaps most importantly, Jesus promised His apprentices a mighty *Helper*. The Holy Spirit works continually, both within and alongside the true apprentice. He encourages, convicts, provokes, guides, enlightens. Apart from the Spirit, our labors become wearisome toil. But as we welcome *His* labor inside and around us, beauty and good fruit spring from even our most feeble efforts.

The fact that apprenticeship to Jesus is not *merely* a human pursuit, however, does not mean that it happens apart from the human choices that go into most any other form of apprenticeship. We would not imagine we could become an excellent chef or doctor or painter simply by waiting for it to happen to us. Nor can we if we desire to become like Jesus.

We must learn from Him how to do so via practical, daily, real-world decisions. Choice by choice we participate with the Holy Spirit in bringing our understanding, character, and daily actions into alignment with those of the Master.[8]

This book explores just one facet of this apprenticeship: how we communicate. Yet there may be no better place to begin. For we are all communicators, and how we do so shapes both the quality and outcomes of virtually everything we do. If we can become a true apprentice of Jesus in this, it will touch every relationship and undertaking.

The approach we will take together is straightforward. Like Jesus's apprentices in every age, we study the words and ways of the Master recorded in the Gospels and amplified in all of Scripture. We take special note of how He spoke and served through speech, how He listened and led, how He connected and conveyed. We consider carefully how what we see can be reflected in our daily choices. We learn from others too who have done the same before us.

All of this we offer frequently to God in prayer. We ask from Him more-than-human insight and perseverance. We invite the vivifying, guiding presence of the Holy Spirit. Then, ideally as part of a community that shares our commitment, we put what we see into practice.

If we are ever to connect the lofty convictions we claim with what we do day in and day out, this is where we must begin. Here we start to knit together eternal truth with our jobs and parenting, marriage and friendships. Over time every interaction increasingly reflects the heart the Master.

GRACE AND EFFORT

Personal Notes: Jedd

My dad was twenty-one when he first donned the flat-brimmed hat of a Yosemite ranger. Never had he wanted anything more. But learning the ropes in 1969 was nothing like the myriad classes and certifications that novice rangers undergo today. Instead, Dad was paired with a veteran ranger and sent out to learn in action.

He hadn't been on the force long when the old-timer he'd been paired with, Ranger Utterback, slid from their parked patrol car into the night. "We're seeing a lot of drugs used and sold in this camping area," explained Utterback. He held up his hand as Dad began to follow. "Leave the hat in the car. Too obvious."

Raucous laughter drew them through the darkness to a group gathered around a fire on the edge of camp. Dad followed as Utterback moved into a space shadowed by a large pine. Marijuana smoke hung dense in night air. In those days even possession of the drug was a felony.

As Utterback prepared to step into the firelight, Dad stopped him. "I've never made an arrest," he warned.

"Just watch what I do and do what I do," whispered Utterback.

That phrase became the theme of the summer, from serving arrest warrants to chasing break-in bears out of cabins. Dad watched, then replicated.

Looking back, he describes, "Rangers joining the force today have some advantages in all the formal training." However, he observes, "when you learned by putting on the uniform and following a veteran, you saw *how* to do it. The things you can't get from a book or a class. How to convince a hostile crowd to cooperate, calm down a hurt child, or scare off a bear without hurting it. If you have the desire, you absorb all of this from the veteran in the field in a way you just can't fully learn in a classroom."

Riding horse patrol one morning with another veteran ranger, Don Pimontel, Dad encountered one of the most beautiful scenes he'd ever laid eyes on. As the two men crested a mountain pass, the snow-laden peaks of Yosemite's vast north country rose ahead of them. Overhead, thunderheads billowed heavenward, painted with every shade of dark and light. Immediately below opened a meadow, fragrant and glowing purple in a sea of lupine flowers.

Dad sat on his horse, awash in wonder. Unexpectedly, tears began to fill his eyes. He pushed them back and set his jaw as he imagined a ranger ought. But when he glanced over at Ranger Pimontel, that illusion was banished forever. Pimontel's leathered face glistened, wet with tears.

"I didn't just learn from him there; I felt with him," Dad shared with me decades later, "I knew it was OK to *feel* the beauty. God's beauty."

Dad learned that summer not just as a student but as an apprentice. Facts and information were certainly part of the training. But the most important elements went deeper. The veteran rangers like Utterback and Pimontel provided what no classroom teacher could. This included habits and skills Dad had not possessed before, which increasingly became second nature. Perhaps even more significant, they conveyed new perspectives, commitments, and even intuition. The veterans' time-tested ways of protecting and serving could hardly be put into words; yet they were passed from one generation of rangers to another as Dad carefully observed and then put them into practice.

The intentionality and effort suggested by the term *apprentice* may make some Christians uncomfortable. Sometimes this discomfort is little more than a slumbering spirit; we may not *like* the idea of putting serious discipline into changing behavior and beliefs that we feel are *good enough*. Or there may also be another, more legitimate discomfort. Does an emphasis on *our* role and *our* disciplines of apprenticeship undercut His grace? Might it lead toward pride and "work-your-way-to-heaven" righteousness? Could desire to grow more like Jesus in action change our focus from gratitude at what God has done into a self-consumed bravado in what we are doing?

History reveals that there is, in fact, danger in that direction. Whole movements have grown up around efforts to earn the favor of both God and man by straining for spiritual attainment. Such quests can feed arrogance and self-centeredness as gasoline feeds a fire.

Grace is opposed to earning, not effort.
—DALLAS WILLARD

So we would do well to proceed with care. To imagine we could somehow *earn* God's favor is utter vanity. As Jesus portrays in story, it'd be like a household servant imagining he could pay off a debt equivalent to two hundred thousand years of wages.[9] God's grace alone is the wellspring of His favor and heaven's only door. We must never forget that.

Yet…

Despite the hazards, Jesus never watered down His call to apprenticeship. Rather, He urges us to hold two counter-weighted truths at the same time. On one side, joyous gratitude at God's unmerited forgiveness and love. On the other, a robust *response* to that gift expressed in obedient action.

As Dallas Willard puts it, "Grace is opposed to earning, not effort."[10] Jesus depicts this truth in story at the end of His Sermon on the Mount. Two builders are constructing homes. As the old Sunday school song describes, the wise man built his house upon the rock. The foolish man built his house upon the sand. The rains came down and the floods came up, and the house on the sand went splat.

What distinguished the two builders? Not abstract belief. Not identity as a Christian. As Jesus bluntly explains, "Everyone who hears these words of mine and *puts them into practice* is like a wise man who built his house upon the rock.… But everyone who hears these words of mine and *does not put them into practice* is like a foolish man who built his house on sand."[11]

This down-to-earth, put-it-into-practice vision was especially vivid on Jesus's last night with His disciples. Although unequivocally the Master, He strips Himself of His status both literally and figuratively. Wearing little but a towel, He kneels and scrubs dirt from between their toes. Then, rising and redressing, He puts the Master-apprentice relationship into words: "Now that I, your Lord and Teacher, have washed your feet, you also should wash one another's feet. I have set you an example that *you should do as I have done.*"[12]

A Champion of Gift and Diligence

Perhaps no living person has ever more fully celebrated the wonder of God's unmerited favor than that great apprentice to Jesus, the apostle Paul. Paul viewed everything as a *gift*, including the very inclination to follow as Jesus's apprentice. As he put it simply in 1 Corinthians, "What do you have that you did not receive?"[13]

Yet this same Paul described his own apprenticeship to Christ not only as receiving a gift but also as serious exertion. He knew better than any that grace saves us. Yet intense effort defined his pursuit of Christlikeness. "I press on to take hold of that for which Christ Jesus took hold of me....Forgetting what is behind and straining toward what is ahead, I press on toward the goal to win the prize."[14]

Every part of the Christian faith requires gripping two seemingly opposite realities at once.

→ Justice and mercy

→ Contrition and confidence

→ Gentleness and bold truth

→ A Savior who was fully God and fully man

In apprenticeship, we must do the same. We cling unyieldingly to the lavish, unmerited gift of grace. And we hold with equal passion to a vision for pursuing apprenticeship with abandon.

The outcome of holding this apparent contradiction together is a result worth longing for. Paul described himself as "the worst" of sinners.[15] Nevertheless, as an apprentice to Jesus, he could declare without flinching, "Whatever you have learned or received or heard from me, or seen in me—put it into practice. And the God of peace will be with you."[16]

How could Paul claim that God's peace would rest on those who practiced not just what he taught, but what they *saw him do*? Not simply because he'd become a "good man." Rather, Paul had come to mirror both the character and behavior of the Master. So he could say, "Follow my example, as I follow the example of Christ."[17]

What a breathtaking thing it would be to meet a person today who could, in humility, say the same. Imagine it being said of you, "Follow the way she speaks and listens, for she mirrors the example of Jesus." "Follow

the way he leads and loves, for he reflects the words and ways of Jesus."
Impossible? Not if we believe the Scriptures.

Yes, we will always struggle against sin. But we can have every reason for
confidence that in five or ten years from now (even one!) we will look more
like Jesus than we do today.

As we grow as Jesus's apprentices, our small choices and daily habits
increasingly reflect the Master's. As explored in the chapters ahead, we
become more fully *present* before others; the ideas we convey become more
tangible; our manner is recognized as more *authentic*; our *questions* guide
and inspire; we present not just facts, but set them in *stories* that give facts
meaning; our words carry greater *vision and weight.*

Choice by choice, small act by small act, we "are being transformed into
his likeness with ever-increasing glory."[18] Not just in theory, but also in the
visible, tangible actions that meld eternal truth with daily life. Praise be to
God that He never leaves us where we are.

Personal Notes: Erik

Apprenticeship demands humility. The very act of apprenticing to a master
is acknowledging your own inabilities. You know less. You need to learn.
You don't have what it takes yet. Maybe that is why so many of us are
reluctant to be an apprentice: it's hard to submit to others. That is my challenge, at least.

Early on in my career I served as a deputy for a senior speechwriter.
He would pass me the ceremonial events—the award ceremony for a top
employee, a ribbon cutting at the factory—and on a good week, he might
let me take a swing at a first draft of a major speech.

"Good start," he would say, and then inevitably hack away until only a
few of my original lines remained—and even then, he would take credit
for everything.

It was not humbling—it was humiliating.

"I'm better than him," I would think, especially after lunch when he would
kick up his feet on the desk, lean back in his chair, and sleep for two hours.

I had no interest in being his apprentice. Maybe that showed. Eventually,
my job became nothing more than printing speeches on 4 x 6 cards for
delivery to our boss.

It was a difficult season, but an important one. Looking back, I wasn't
ready. I needed to study great speeches, listen to the tone and cadence of
leaders, and perfect my craft.

I thought I had it all figured out, just as Simon did until Jesus approached
his boat.

The fifth chapter of Luke tells the story of Jesus teaching on the shoreline
of a lake. A crowd is pressing in, and Jesus pushes back in a boat to create space and to amplify His voice off the water. Professional fisherman are
nearby, cleaning nets after a dismal day of fishing.

"When he had finished speaking, he said to Simon, 'Put out into deep water, and let down the nets for a catch" (v. 4). Simon questions the Master, as all of us surely would and certainly do. *I am the professional. I know what I am doing. This is not a good spot or time to fish.* He relents, drops his nets. And the abundance of fish almost topples the boats and tears the nets. "They came and filled both boats so full that they began to sink" (v. 7).

Then Simon repents, Jesus calls him to a new life, and he leaves everything—even his boats and nets and crew—to follow the Master.

The simplicity of the story is beautiful. Jesus comes to you with an absurd request—*Erik, leave the professional stuff to Me*—and yet He is faithful and fulfilling, which leads to a humble repentance and a life renewed. Apprenticing Jesus isn't a hollow echo of Jesus's life and words. It's not a self-awareness or self-preserving. Its about a real submission to living under the audacious authority of Jesus, the Master who will ask for everything we have so He can give us everything we need. We come empty. Ready. Humble. Only then can He begin.

Chapter 2

THE KINGDOM VISION

The book *Lest Innocent Blood Be Shed* recounts the breathtaking true story of the town of Le Chambon during World War II.[1] Its inhabitants were Huguenots, committed French Protestants. Europe was descending into madness, and even respectable citizens found ways to justify collaboration with the Nazi invaders. But Le Chambon's residents held fast to Jesus and His ways, becoming an outpost of grace and self-sacrifice for thousands who'd been marked for death.

Written by a Jew, the book description reads:

> During the most terrible years of World War II, when inhumanity
> and political insanity held most of the world in their grip and the
> Nazi domination of Europe seemed irrevocable and unchallenged, a
> miraculous event took place in a small Protestant town in southern
> France called Le Chambon. There, quietly, peacefully, and in full
> view of the Vichy government and a nearby division of the Nazi SS,
> Le Chambon's villagers and their clergy organized to save thousands
> of Jewish children and adults from certain death.[2]

Under the leadership of local pastors André Trocmé and Edouard Theis, the people of Le Chambon labored together to protect fugitive Jews. For three years residents sheltered children and families, women and men in their own homes, nearby farms, and public buildings. They helped transport Jews to the safety of neutral Switzerland as well. Some paid dearly for their choices, including Reverend Trocmé's cousin, who was killed in the Maidanek concentration camp.

Why did the people of Le Chambon take such risks, give so boldly? No doubt, many factors played a part. But it's clear these choices flowed especially from an apprenticeship to Jesus that shaped their daily lives long before the war. For generations they'd withstood great struggle as a persecuted Protestant minority in France. They'd studied the Scriptures in small groups and families. They'd served and cared for one another in imperfect yet authentic Christian community.

When the town's residents were interviewed after the war, they seemed to see nothing spectacular in what they'd done. They had just followed Jesus's instructions when people needed help.

This is what we see when women and men align their ways with those of Jesus. The madness of the world rages all around, yet in the places and events influenced by the apprentice of Jesus, we see God's heart made visible.

When this becomes our goal, we dispel any thought that apprenticing ourselves to Jesus is just another form of self-actualization or personal development. Thankfully, the objective is more magnificent than that. Ultimately we seek first the *kingdom of God*. This was the unifying vision that knit together everything Jesus said and did.[3]

THE APPRENTICE'S ULTIMATE GOAL

As with the earthly king of Jesus's day, Caesar, a king's authority touches every facet of life. His law determines justice; his policies construct means of transportation, irrigation, and entertainment; his decrees depose leaders, dispense mercy, and can set whole populations traveling to register for a census. In a kingdom, the king's will is reflected in everything.

The Bible declares that God is king over all. His authority is complete in both heaven and earth.[4] In His love God delegated to humankind a certain authority on earth.[5] Thus each of us in a sense has a *kingdom*: a space in which our will shapes what happens.

For some this kingdom may be large, influencing the affairs of nations. For others it may require overseeing three children, all under age five. But however different, each is a kingdom, one carrying potential for great beauty and great sorrow.

When women and men choose to align their influence with God's will, the good that He intended for us from the beginning springs up. It's all that is conveyed in the Hebrew word *shalom*: not just absence of conflict, but also a profound wholeness both within us and in every relationship. This is what we seek when we pray, "Your kingdom come, your will be done on earth as it is in heaven."[6] It looks like loving marriages and rich friendships; working to bring grace through art or commerce or motherhood; delighting in amber waves of grain and the Golden Gate Bridge. Here righteousness and peace kiss each other.[7]

Personal Notes: Erik

My pastor in New York, Jon Tyson, often Tweets a simple line to his followers: "In New York as it is in heaven." That line alone shatters any purely abstract understanding or application of the Lord's Prayer. What does the kingdom look like amid the extremes of wealth and poverty on the Upper West Side? With our local merchants? With the homeless couple that sits outside of the Catholic Church on 71st? No one person can change New York City, but a group of friends could impact their city block. A group of like-minded influencers could reshape their industry—whether that is fashion, advertising, publishing, or hedge funds. The potential builds; *shalom* becomes possible—a restored wholeness in every relationship, every street corner, every merchant, every schoolyard, and every church building.

It's difficult, right? Since the fall of Adam, all of us are broken and bent, prone to not align with the graceful flow of God's will but to cut against it. We exercise our authority in ways marred by selfishness, pride, and greed. So battles and injustice, bitterness and greed, frequently displace the *shalom* God intended.

That's why our world often carries the feel of a war zone, like Le Chambon in occupied France. The Bible describes that we are, in fact, underneath the oppressive rule of an invader to God's good earth. The dark dominion seeks to bend and distort every human system and relationship in ways that replace *shalom* with selfish, aimless grasping. We collaborate with the enemy whenever we exercise our authority in line with this grasping, mistakenly imagining we will attain our own good in our own way.

Again Jesus steps into this. He aligned His will completely with God's. So in every place Jesus exercised His authority, what God's perfect will looks like—His kingdom!—was seen and felt. It was light cascading into a dark place, a bonfire banked high against a blinding blizzard.

Someday God's kingdom will cover all the earth with *shalom* "as the waters cover the sea."[8] For now it breaks forth wherever God's will is reflected in human action as it was by Jesus. That is why—even though Jesus pointed forward to a *future* kingdom of God—He also declared that His kingdom was also *among* those who experienced His work.[9] Whether in physical healing, release from mental illness, reconciled relationship, or restoration of industries, the kingdom of God took shape wherever Jesus was.

Amazingly the same is true of us as Jesus's apprentices. When we align our will with God's in the way Jesus did, the kingdom of God springs up, just as it did wherever Jesus was present. Our small, delegated kingdom becomes an outpost of the kingdom of God and a foretaste of what is to be. Broken relationships are reconciled. Shattered lives are restored. Long-cold eyes light up. Lost souls feel the weight of their God-given worth, and that of others too. We see this even, and sometimes especially, in the smallest choices: the person who gives genuine praise to others amidst a crowd of self-promoters; the executive who listens to interns as if they were equals; the friend who asks good questions when everyone else does nothing but talk.

This is what it means to seek first His kingdom. It's the ultimate goal of the apprentice. Our desires and actions become so fully like those of Jesus's that God's *shalom* takes tangible form wherever our influence is felt. As it does, others come to know and praise the goodness of God—they've experienced a small taste of His kingdom because we are in the room, in the neighborhood, in the school, and in the office.

Such outposts of the kingdom may be surrounded and hard pressed. But, small as they are, they glow with the grace and self-sacrifice of a Le Chambon, blooming amidst enemy territory.

Personal Notes: Jedd

India's streets pummeled my senses. The inescapable din of horns, hawkers, and whining motors. Moist, oppressive heat. Brilliant hues of women's saris and shanty homes. The blended smell of diesel, curry, and the garbage piled high on street corners. Everywhere, pressing crowds and grasping beggars. Life felt dirty and cheap.

Then, in a moment, it all disappeared. I passed through a high concrete wall into a space about the size of half a football field, somehow hidden there in the middle of the city of Calcutta. The tumult of the streets outside softened to a muffled hum. The even green of cut grass stretched before me, and cool shade beckoned beneath ancient trees.

This was Prem Dan, a home established by Mother Teresa to provide refuge and care for the dying of Calcutta's streets.

The sensation of *haven* wrapped around me. It came not only in the hush, cool, and orderliness. Nearby, Sisters of Charity cared for the ailing and maimed with strong arms and gentle touch. Yes, pain was evident here too. But matching it, blow for blow, was love. The city outside tossed the poor to the gutters. Here, there were attentive eyes and ears, tender hands, faces wholly present to the ailing until their last breath.

I watched a sister kneeling by a man on a low cot; from his throat came the rasping rattle of approaching death. She clasped both of his hands with both of hers. Her eyes caressed his face. She whispered softly to him and to God.

Prem Dan offered grace amidst a city that seemed to lack it. And though never in quite the same way, I've caught glimpses of this elsewhere too. Outposts of grace—not just places, but people.

I think of Tim, a state senator who made a practice of inviting his political enemies to lunch. No agenda. Just to get to know them and to convey he cared about them despite their disagreements. He'd become convinced that is how Jesus would approach politics.

I think of Donda, Tim's secretary. In the fierce, overbusy environment of the state legislature, people were drawn irresistibly to the chair opposite her desk. Donda listened. She'd ask good questions, inquiring about things that mattered, sometimes even praying for a visitor on the spot. Whether fellow secretaries or senior staff, lobbyists or even legislators, each knew that they—not their status or functional use as a *good contact*—mattered to Donda.

Encountering Tim or Donda felt a bit like coming off the streets of Calcutta to a cool, quiet, caring place. In small choices to apprentice to Jesus, they became a bit like Prem Dan—outposts of grace in a world that often seems to lack it.

THE APPRENTICE'S MEASURE OF SUCCESS

This vision of the kingdom provides the definition of success to guide our apprenticeship. For Jesus's apprentice, truly great communication is found in *serving others well through our communication*.[10] In God's kingdom—where much of what our broken world prizes is flipped on its head—true greatness is found not in glittering success, but in meeting the concrete needs of others.

> You know that those who are regarded as rulers of the Gentiles lord it over them, and their high officials exercise authority over them. Not so with you. Instead, whoever wants to become great among you must be your servant, and whoever wants to be first must be slave of all. [11]

That is our barometer, the measure of triumph. Have we met others' needs through our presence and words? Have we built them up? Have we nourished and encouraged and spurred them forward to love and good deeds? Are they better for the brief encounter, stronger for that conversation, empowered by what we have said and done?

THE ONE WELLSPRING

Serving others well. Aligning our kingdom with God's. Outposts of grace. True *shalom*. Perhaps these ideas sound inspiring. Well they should, for they lead deep into the heart of what we were made for. But here we must take caution. For *serving others well* is costly, sometimes profoundly so. The things that motivate much of the good people do—duty, guilt, idealism, or simply the desire to be admired—will ultimately prove inadequate for the long journey.

JT and Sara already had several children when they sensed God nudging them toward adoption. Both excited and daunted, they decided to move forward. The year ahead was heavy with paperwork, prayer, financial sacrifice—and waiting. Finally, they found themselves at the orphanage in China where little Grace lived, ready to take her home for good.

Their journey, however, was just beginning.

Like many children who've known little touch or affection, Grace had major developmental delays. Though eighteen months old, she still couldn't roll over or form a word. She had scars where she'd been tied to her crib. Grace greeted Sara and JT by screaming nonstop for hours.

Confident that love would overcome the challenges, JT and Sara returned home upbeat. But within weeks it became clear that Grace's wounds were deep. Fear seemed to grip her. When asleep, she would bolt upright at the slightest sound, then remain awake for hours. She seemed incapable of laughter. Worst of all, Grace rejected any hint of intimacy. If her parents held her too close or put their cheek against her skin, she would cry with such ferocity that her capillaries ruptured, leaving what looked like a rash all over her body.

As struggle piled on struggle, exhaustion shadowed JT and Sara's world. At times they felt disillusioned. In low moments, both wondered, "What have we done to our family? Will we ever be normal again?" By day, Grace was agitated, reactionary. And every night she woke again and again with shrieks from night terrors. "We trusted God," Sara expressed, "but it was hellish."

What carried them through the darkness was the same thing that had motivated them in the first place. It had not been a sense of duty or guilt or idealism driving JT and Sara to adopt. Yes, they'd wanted to give a family to an orphan. But even deeper, they were responding to what they knew of God's heart and what He'd done for them.

"God adopted us at profound cost to Himself," explained JT. "So adopting an orphan, even when very difficult, is just a small retelling of the Gospel. That story too includes suffering."

It took a year before JT and Sara began to notice Grace laugh often or smile readily. The sacrifices and tears preceding that milestone were innumerable, and many more were to follow. But bit by bit, small change by small change, Grace responded to her parents' love—just as they sought to love her in response to God's.

Recently, Sara shared with Jedd, "Grace is the snuggliest thing, the most tender, compassionate girl you can imagine. She's now nine. She brings so much joy to our family, to each and every person. We are all just crazy about her. It seems nearly every day when JT looks at Grace, sees a picture of her, or retells a story about something she has done, he remarks, 'I am a rich man!'"

Love has overcome, though not without great cost. Observed Sara, "If we'd adopted just for ourselves or only to rescue an orphan, I'm not sure we would have made it through. But we knew from the start that Christ had walked the kind of path we were taking long before we did. Our giving was just a reflection of His, and we knew His love would surround us—even if the outcome turned out to be not what we'd hoped. That kept us there, even in the most desperate moments."

Jesus calls His apprentices to the most exhilarating and sacrificial of journeys. But what He used to motivate was remarkably different than what most generals, nonprofit leaders, or pastors draw upon. Yes, He affirms that things such as self-interest, fear, and obligation are potent drivers. But ultimately, the wellspring Jesus points toward always goes deeper: *the loving character of His Father.* The final motivation Jesus provides for any instruction is never guilt, duty, or even idealism. Rather, it always returns to a vision of God's tenderness, grace, and provision.

> If that is how God clothes the grass of the field…will he not much more clothe you, O you of little faith?[12]

> Love your enemies and pray for those who persecute you, that you may be sons of your Father in heaven. He causes his sun to rise on the evil and the good.[13]

> Do not be afraid, little flock, for your Father has been pleased to give you the kingdom. Sell your possessions and give to the poor.[14]

It is God's character and care for us, not any other source, that serves as the fountainhead of apprenticeship. His love—especially as seen in Jesus— is both the motivation and the model. We serve others because God served us first. We adopt because we have been adopted. We forgive because we have been forgiven. We lay our lives down and build others up because He did this for us.

The same is true for every aspect of apprenticing to Jesus as a communicator. The way we give the gift of full presence, ask questions, tell stories, incarnate ideas, draw near to the vulnerable and outcast...*all* rise from long draughts of God's heart and action on our behalf.

Here pounds the pulsing heart of all Christian action: "We love because he first loved us."[15]

This is not abstract theology. It's the one, the *only* fuel that can nourish lifelong apprenticeship to Jesus. A gut-level grasp of the gospel is the only force potent enough to sustain and guide us for the long haul.

The apprentice's mission is to love others, but we need not strain to drum up affection for them. The mission is to obey God, but we need not struggle to grow feelings of guilt or duty or enthusiasm for Him. Rather, we turn toward God's heart, desiring first to see and savor the love revealed by His Gospel. Everything else grows from this as naturally as taste bud-tingling grapes from a healthy vine.

So we begin our journey as an apprentice praying most of all that we may "grasp how wide and long and high and deep is the love of Christ, and to know this love that surpasses knowledge—that [we] may be filled to the measure of all the fullness of God."[16]

With that as our passion, let's go deeper into what it looks like in daily life.

Section II

LIFE THROUGH PRESENCE

Upend a Life of Splintered Distraction

Chapter 3

THE GIFT OF PRESENCE

No question this was urgent. Death crept close to the beloved daughter of Jairus, an influential synagogue ruler. With the desperation only a father could know, Jairus begged Jesus to come—*quickly!*

The two men set off together at a rapid clip. A large crowd pressed close alongside, eager to catch a glimpse of what might happen at Jairus's home. With all of its noise and dust and anticipation, the procession seemed to blend tragic drama and carnival.

They'd covered some distance when—in the midst of it all—Jesus suddenly stopped. The whole convoy came to an off-balance halt. "Who touched me?" Jesus asked, gazing into the crowd. Eyebrows rose, and onlookers chuckled. Amid this throng, anyone could have touched Him. But Jesus searched on, face after face, seeking a telltale gesture or trace of emotion. As seconds ticked by, the futility of Jesus's inquiry seemed to be confirmed. But suddenly, from out of the crowd, a woman tumbled forward, her tear-streaked face weary and afraid. "It was me," she choked, "I grasped Your robe…"

The riddle was solved. People shrugged and began moving forward, anxious to get to the more pressing matter ahead. What more could she want? According to the Gospels, just touching the edge of Jesus's robe provided the physical healing she'd come for.

But Jesus knew better. So there, with a dying girl awaiting Him, a desperate father at His side, and a murmuring crowd willing Him forward, He turned His entire attention to the one friendless woman before Him. The world seemed to stand still. It was as if they were the only two people on earth.

And so she began, pouring out the story in detail for perhaps the first time: twelve long years of chronic bleeding, swindlers whose costly treatments accomplished nothing, medical bills sucking away the last of her resources, the burning loneliness of social rejection…

Her words flowed until there were no more. As Mark described, she "told him the whole truth."[1]

We can imagine her finally falling silent. She gazes at Jesus, and He smiles tenderly back. Then Jesus addresses her with a word we never see Him use again. *Daughter.* It conveys affection, but something beyond that too. We see even more clearly what His attentiveness to her meant: that she *belongs.* She is no stranger, not an outcast. She is precious and beloved, a true child of God and of the Jewish community. "Daughter, your faith has healed you. Go in peace." Only now would Jesus return to the urgent matter at hand.

In a story like this, it's the miraculous healing that inevitably takes the headlines. Not every day does touching a robe cure an intractable disease. Truth be told, the physical cure was probably all the woman came hoping for anyway. That's why what happened is so remarkable. What Jesus did *after* healing her body may be even more extraordinary than a medical miracle. After all, when was the last time you saw a super busy, ultra engaged, highly demanded-of individual choosing to shut out all competing noise to focus entirely on the person before him? That's what Jesus did, making Himself entirely present to the one.

Today, just as it was for Jesus on the way to Jairus's home, it seems that gravity itself pulls in every direction but the here and now. News and noise and tasks yank us continually away from the person before us. If we yield to this force, the bulk of our thoughts and attention will always be elsewhere. It can be almost a strain to do otherwise. But if we desire to be apprentices to Jesus, we must plant our attention here, in what George MacDonald called "the holy Present."[2] For this is where connection always begins.

OUR SPLINTERED ATTENTION

It was Halloween, and evening was fast approaching. Six eager children bounded around the kitchen, each in need of dinner and a costume before the night's festivities could begin. Anne—mother to half of the youngsters—stirred macaroni and played makeup artist on several small faces. The population of her home had doubled a few hours before with the arrival of some little-known relatives and their three kids, happy for the free accommodations amidst their family vacation.

Anne eyed Erica, the mother of the visiting family. They hadn't met before today. Erica seemed a decent enough person but had been on and off Facebook all afternoon, hardly asking a single question of Anne the entire visit. Even as Anne set mac and cheese out for the six kids, Erica seemed unable to tear herself from her laptop.

Finally, perhaps feeling a twinge of guilt, Erica glanced over her shoulder. "Are you on Facebook?" she asked.

Anne tried to keep irritation out of her voice. "Not really. Every now and then."

"You should," Erica responded with cheerful invitation, "We could chat. We could get to know each other."

Anne later recalled with a smile, "She hardly even looked up at me from her computer to say it."[3]

 The way we live is eroding our capacity for deep, sustained, perceptive attention—the building block of intimacy, wisdom, and cultural progress.[4]

—MAGGIE JACKSON

Most of us would admit to finding ourselves on both sides of that equation, perhaps frequently. We're frustrated by the distractedness of others and yet deeply distracted ourselves. Whether driven by busyness, worries, or just plain lack of focus, our minds drift in and out of the present. We trade away the moment and the people who share it with us, often in exchange for stimulation and interactions coming from anywhere but here.

Personal Notes: Jedd

On any given day, I may communicate online with friends and contacts on several continents, sometimes extensively. On any given day, I may catch only a glimpse of my neighbor as he drives into his garage. It's that way most days, actually.

I can't help wondering, "Is the heavy imbalance toward far-off friends over nearby neighbors ideal?"

Sure, linking with good friends and colaborers around the world is rewarding. With my work, it's often very purposeful too. And truth be told, I doubt my neighbor and I would ever be best buddies anyway.

But still, I know I experience only *part* of a full relationship when it mostly takes place online. That doesn't mean it is not meaningful. It's just that there are a lot of ways you *can't* love someone through technology. And some of those things are pretty significant—like sharing a meal, or praying side by side, or babysitting each other's kids.

My friends Trey and Kristina know how to be neighbors. They work at it. Trey likes to host BBQs. Kristina teaches free art lessons in their garage to kids living nearby. They offer to feed the animals or pick up mail when folks are out of town.

But most of all, Trey and Kristina are just present. They've made it clear that they are *there* for people when needed, whether for a listening ear or to help in a pinch.

Whenever I visit them, I see so clearly how that enriches life: for them; for their neighbors; for the whole neighborhood. I see too that loving others face-to-face in this way stretches and grows them in a way technology can't.

I'm trying to be more like Trey and Kristina. I'll probably always do a lot of communicating online, especially for work. But I'm seeking to shift at least a portion of time spent there to people closer to home. Even if they wouldn't always be my first pick for lifelong friends. Even if it is a bit less streamlined than online interaction. Because I see that I just can't listen…can't help…can't be present…in quite the same way from a distance as I can nearby.

Technology certainly isn't the only thief of presence. But it greatly multiplies potential for distraction. Most every acquaintance we've ever made, every business we've bought from, every song we've enjoyed is little more than a click away. They don't wait for us to seek them out, but they invade our consciousness through Facebook, Twitter, e-mail, and pop-ups.

As a result, we increasingly live in what is aptly called a state of "continuous partial attention."[5] Whether in church or lecture hall, on the phone or online, or even amidst the most intimate conversations, diversions continually nibble at our attention and draw us away from the person with whom we're interacting. A technology-loving teen quoted in the remarkable book *Distracted* put it bluntly: "Personally, I like talking to a lot of different people at one time. It kind of keeps you busy. It's kind of boring just talking to one person."[6] Even if we would not express it so directly, we can grasp what she meant.

There's no denying that innovations have vastly expanded our ability to gaze out at the world. We prospect the globe and others' lives with thoughtless finger taps and mouse clicks. But what honest observers increasingly see is that these connections rarely foster deep, meaningful relationships. Often, they seem to work in the opposite direction.

As Randall Bush has noted, we have not become global villages but "global voyeurs."[7] We peer with fascination through technological windows into others' lives but rarely gaze eye to eye in true friendship and understanding. We are the most connected generation in history yet feel more disconnected than ever before. The founder of the popular photo-sharing site Flickr, Caterina Fake, explains, "These technologies allow you to be much more broadly friendly, but you just spread yourself much more thinly over many more people."[8]

Danah Boyd, who studies and teaches on technology and social media at Harvard, enjoys an impressive number of online followers. But she admits it's "not the same as in a deep social relationship. I've been very, very sick lately, and I write about it on Twitter and my blog, and I get all these people who are writing to me telling me ways to work around the health-care system, or they're writing saying, 'Hey, I broke my neck!' And I'm like, 'You're being very nice and trying to help me, but though you feel like you know me, you don't.' They can *observe* you, but it's not the same as *knowing* you."[9]

We swim in a sea of information and entertainment. Opportunities to get linked in with others are ever before us. And always, worries and to-do lists nip at our heels like wild dogs. Amidst it all, less and less remains for the person in front of us. Perhaps if he or she got on Facebook, we could chat sometime.

THE GIFT OF PRESENCE

Jesus's way cuts in the opposite direction. It pushes back against noise and distraction to be deeply present to the person immediately before us. We should not miss that Jesus's response to the bleeding woman was as startling and difficult in His day as in ours. The demands on Jesus's time were every bit as fierce as those we face. No doubt Jairus and many in the crowd could not believe their eyes as Jesus stopped and gave such *time* and *focus* to that one woman. Yet for that moment, He was all hers.

We could call it *giving the gift of presence*. And this episode was not an exception. It was a recurring theme of Jesus's way with people, making Himself fully present to them regardless of their status or reputation.

We see this vividly in one of the most beloved stories of the Bible. Imagine a half-dozen young mothers like you sometimes see at the zoo or mall, a noisy tumult of small children like a cloud around them. Some of the little ones are balanced on the women's hips or strapped to their backs. Some cry; some squeal; some sneeze. With an eye for efficiency, and perhaps status, Jesus's disciples assumed this group shouldn't make the cut. Not the best use of time. No autographs, please.

Jesus's words of affirmation echo to this day, "Let the little children come to me…"[10] Those who would be His apprentices would do well not to miss *how* He affirmed them. See Him lifting them onto His lap. See Him taking the time to bless them, praying words of grace and protection over them. For that moment in time, the present, Jesus was wholly *there*. He was *with* the children and their mothers, entirely.

As we all know from experience, this gift of presence is most precious when presence includes not just the body and mind but the heart also. With Jesus it consistently did. Time and again the disciples noted His reaction to the ragtag crowds and hapless individuals who filled them. He did not hover above them with stoic reserve. He didn't analyze from a distance as most of us are prone to do when encountering deep need. Writing about it years later, the disciples consistently used the same word to describe Jesus's response: *compassion*. Jesus did not merely feel sorry for their need. In the literal meaning of the word *compassion* (co-passion), He felt and even *suffered with* them.[11]

At the tomb of Lazarus, Jesus displayed this quality with special poignancy. Although apparently having every intention of ending the cause of everyone's sadness, Jesus opened His heart to the ache of the moment and the anguish of those around Him. There was no hint of distant, above-the-fray scrutiny. It was the full attentiveness of compassion, suffering with. And Jesus wept.[12]

We glimpse Jesus's way of presence one last time upon the cross, amidst the most excruciating pain a man can feel. His hands and feet had been nailed to boards, His body lacerated with whips and thorns. Almost certainly the slow suffocation brought by crucifixion had begun. Yet Jesus again made Himself fully present to another. Perhaps unable even to turn His head, He yet focuses His attention upon the dangling man beside Him. The thief cries out, "Jesus, remember me when you come into your kingdom." Jesus is all there. "I tell you the truth, today you will be with me in paradise."[13]

WHAT PRESENCE GIVES

Sir William Osler is considered the father of modern medicine. He insisted that medical students learn by spending time with real patients. He urged doctors to pay close attention not only to their patient's illness but also to the patient himself, taking the time to hear his story, feelings, and background. "Listen to your patient," said Osler. "He is telling you the diagnosis."

Once in a hospital where he was serving, Osler noticed a little girl whom all the other children seemed to avoid. The head nurse explained to Osler that the girl's mother was dead and her father had visited only once, leaving the small dolly to which the girl clung in her loneliness. The nurse described that the children in the ward seemed to have concluded that since the girl had no visitors, she mattered little.

Osler entered the ward and said to the girl in a voice loud enough to be overheard, "May I sit down, please?"

She nodded shyly, and Osler sat. "I can't stay long on this visit, but I have wanted to see you so badly," he began. He asked question after question, listening carefully as the girl responded. He examined her dolly as well, his stethoscope placed carefully upon its chest. As he stood to depart, Osler declared in a whisper loud enough for most of the room to hear, "You won't forget our secret, will you? And mind you, don't tell anyone."[14]

Departing the room, Osler looked over his shoulder. A small crowd was already beginning to form around the girl. With a power that words alone could never carry, the doctor's small gift of presence had conveyed to the girl—and everyone else—that she was valued.

Presence conveys value to another like nothing else. It affirms that she, and not anything else in the universe, deserves your thoughts, gaze, and listening at that moment. Presence is the wellspring of influence, for it is the first step to loving well.

All truly great communication begins with presence. Until we are fully present to another, connection is thin or even impossible. Without presence we will fail to understand what the other person most needs and who he or she is. Only in being fully present can we come to know and be known.

Even addressing a large audience, presence undergirds connection. To be moved by a speaker, a crowd must feel that she is truly *with* them. They must sense that she understands them, knows them, even feels with them. And while this ultimately includes more than presence alone, it always starts there. For only a speaker who has indeed been present to her listeners or others like them can identify with an audience in this way.

On the day Martin Luther King Jr. was assassinated, Bobby Kennedy was scheduled to participate in a political rally in a black neighborhood of Indianapolis. When he arrived, the city's police chief urged him to cancel. Fears of riots and reprisal were thick across the country, and soon proved to be well founded. There was no telling what the reaction would be to a white leader breaking the news that King had been killed.

But Kennedy decided not to pull back. He wanted to be with those most grieving, even if it carried risk. His extemporaneous words were brief—announcing the tragic news, identifying with the anger the audience felt, and also urging toward compassion and healing. Yet it was not his words that were most powerful, but simply that he was there. Not just there in that neighborhood, but that he had been sincerely present to the black community in America for a long time before—listening, learning, empathizing, coming alongside. That night there were riots in 110 cities across America. But not in Indianapolis.

After King's funeral in Atlanta three days later, Bobby Kennedy gathered with some of King's closest friends in the civil rights movement. But instead of discussing political issues or his own bid for the presidency, Kennedy insisted it was a time only for being together and honoring King. Andrew Young, who would become the first black mayor of Atlanta, later observed, "You got the impression…well, that in a way, he was more sensitive to the situation than some of us were." Through this time together, Young came to believe that "white America does have someone in it who cares."[15]

Personal Notes: Erik

Admittedly, I struggle with being present. I pride myself, wrongly, in the ability to keep a dozen plates spinning at once. I am known to be in a conversation with a friend and be looking at my phone at the same time. I used to think it didn't really matter…"Everyone does it and I am busy," so I would justify, "You're only going to get what I am able to give." Most of the time I was there but not really *present*.

Then one day I was joking with a friend that my son, Kolton, will learn how to throw a ball with one hand on the ball and the other with his hand up to his ear, just like his daddy does. You see, many times when we were playing catch I was on a call, my cell to my ear as we threw it back and forth.

I realized that instead of teaching my son to play catch I was teaching him to never be fully present. He knew that I was neither fully with him nor fully with my caller; I was communicating superficiality, efficiency.

And that scared me. I doubt I will look back someday and say, "Man, I am so glad I took that phone call instead of playing with my kids!"

This year Monica and I introduced *No Screen Sundays* in our home. We've realized that if were not careful, any given Sunday can look a lot like any given Tuesday—laptops open, smart phones on, typing and texting, watching movies and sports.

So we're reserving a day for family and friends, music and reading, play and worship. We're starting with Sundays, then hoping it spills into Saturdays—and eventually into weekday evenings.

Our goal is simple: be present. Don't miss out on the gifts around us— each other, our kids, our friends, the wonders of God, and the needs of others. We all love getting attention. Now I'm trying to love by giving attention. All of it.

Chapter 4

ALL THERE

I believe in being fully present," Morrie states in *Tuesdays With Morrie*. Morrie is dying, and life and relationships have grown clearer to the ailing professor. He explains to the young man who sits beside his hospital bed, "That means you should be with the person you're with. When I am talking to you now, Mitch, I try to keep focused only on what is going on between us. I am not thinking about something we said last week. I am not thinking of what's coming up this Friday...I am talking to you. I am thinking about you."[1]

This kind of presence touches us to the core when we receive it from another. But giving it is no easy matter. Living in the present, it has been said, is as difficult as balancing on the head of a pin. Behind us lies the past; it calls to us with memories both sorrowful and sweet, urging us to savor triumph and gnaw upon regret. Ahead stands the future. Though veiled, it calls just as loudly with hope and worry, ambition and fear. Meanwhile, to the left and right shout myriad voices from today—urgent needs and entertainment, children and friends, in-boxes and to-do lists, technology for both labor and distraction.

To overcome these voices and attend to a person before us is no easy matter, even for a brief conversation. So although being present to others may seem passive, it is not. Presence is a gift we must *give*, often with much effort.

What most enables us to give this gift we could call *disciplines of silence*.

We live awash in noise—the sounds and motion around us, the pull of technology and responsibilities, the churning thoughts and voices inside us. So unless we *actively* shut it out, we will never be more than partially present to others. As Maggie Jackson, the author of *Distracted*, observes, "We have to be the gatekeeper for silence for our own attention, for our own ability to focus."[2]

The first discipline of silence is external: the background TV, incoming calls, newspaper on the table, text message alerts. They must be shut out, turned off. We turn our back to the computer when on the phone. We refuse to glance over the intern's shoulder for more important guests while talking with him at the staff party. If we wish to be present, we will take whatever steps necessary to do so.

Perhaps most importantly, this discipline requires that we confront our desire to multitask. Few would say multitasking is a sin. But as we all know deep down, if we're trying to do two significant things at once, neither will be done particularly well.

Many recent studies show the variety of ill effects of multitasking. They reveal that pairing a simple, repetitive task such as weeding or laundry with an activity that demands little concentration (like listening to music) generally seems to enrich both activities. But trying to do two things that both require concentration almost always diminishes both.

One Stanford study offered a surprising prognosis of what results with increased multitasking. Multitaskers were found to have diminished capacity to concentrate or carry on sustained activity. This is "likely due to reduced ability to filter out interference from the irrelevant task set."[3] In other words, multitasking makes us less able to silence all the things around us that keep us from being present in tasks or relationships.

Even more surprising, however, multitaskers also scored very poorly at multitasking itself. The habit of dividing attentions between multiple things seems to have made multitaskers worse at everything. "The huge finding is, the more media people use, the worse they are at using any media," expressed one of the study's researchers. "We were totally shocked."[4]

Jesus's apprentice, desiring to be present to others as He was, may well decide that multitasking is of such harm to presence that it must be killed.

THE SECOND DISCIPLINE OF SILENCE

As significant as this first discipline is, a second is even more so. To be present requires an *internal* silencing as well. Why? Even in a soundless room, if our minds are abuzz with worry and chatter, we will be no more present to a friend than if we had our iPods turned up full volume.

Addressing this challenge is not nearly as simple as external silence. There is no off switch to press. It is, as author Annie Dillard describes, a battle to "gag the commentator, to hush the noise of useless babble that keeps me from seeing just as surely as a newspaper dangled before my eyes. The effort is really a discipline requiring a lifetime of dedicated struggle."[5]

This struggle is not merely one of focus or concentration. It is a spiritual matter requiring practices of a spiritual nature. As Dietrich Bonhoeffer put it in *Life Together,* "Real silence, real stillness, really holding one's tongue comes only as the sober consequence of spiritual stillness."[6]

As we'll explore in Section IX, the regular practice of solitude and other time-tested Christian disciplines are vital in this process. Especially as we learn to quiet ourselves to attend to the "still, small voice" of God, we grow more able to quiet ourselves before others as well. The regular practice of solitude also helps us to order the clutter and calm the commotion of an overtaxed mind; this enables internal quiet in times with others.

Most importantly, this silence comes as a result of confidence that it is God—not our own frenzied straining—who will ultimately provide the good we most need. If we think otherwise, our minds *must* churn. We need to be continually planning and plotting to grasp at what we desire. Our thoughts boil with regrets from the past and worried ambitions for the future.

The assurance Jesus gives of God's provision is the only antidote:

> See how the lilies of the field grow. They do not labor or spin. Yet I tell you that not even Solomon in all his splendor was dressed like one of these. If that is how God clothes the grass of the field, which is here today and tomorrow is thrown into the fire, will he not much more clothe you, O you of little faith? So do not worry, saying, "What shall we eat?" or "What shall we drink?" or "What shall we wear?" For the pagans run after all these things, and your heavenly Father knows that you need them.[7]

In the end it is Jesus's vision of the Father that undergirds and enables the disciplines of silence. Left to fend for ourselves, there is simply no basis for peace from the noisome worry and self-consumed clanging in our heads. There is just too much to think about, too much to do. Nor can we rest from the relentless drive toward productivity and accomplishment, which morphs so easily from a healthy form of stewardship into life-dominating obsession. Only as we see Jesus's Father as our Father—concerned with our cares so that we do not have to be—can we become fully present to others.

Personal Notes: Jedd

I loved the efficiency that my first Blackberry gave me. Like a superpower, it filled every empty moment with productivity. But I soon began to see that it wasn't only previously *wasted* moments that the device invaded. It also crept into quality time, good conversations, and quiet moments alone that had once provided rare opportunity to think.

I felt keenly the significance of what was being lost. Yet my work carried an expectation of intense efficiency and near-immediate response to e-mails. Living without a Blackberry wasn't an option. So I decided to identify certain spaces of time and block them off from the Blackberry: my morning devotions, breakfast with the kids, dinner with my wife, Rachel, and all of Sunday. I created other simple rules as well, like stepping away from a table with others if I needed to check e-mail. These habits, which I still keep, made a great difference in enabling me to be more present to others...and also to myself.

I've realized more recently that it isn't just how I use my Blackberry while with others that impacts how present I am to them. What's going on in my mind is even more important. So now, for instance, I try never to do a "quick e-mail check" before going in to spend good-night time with the kids. After all, I'd not likely act immediately upon what I read anyway...but it certainly could dominate my thoughts while we're saying bedtime prayers or telling stories. Without some newly arrived message on my mind, I find myself entering and relishing those times more fully.

Urgent issues and *crises* have sometimes required me to be flexible with these rules, especially when I was working in the White House. But the need to make exceptions comes less often than I'd expected, and the reward of keeping to the practices has been far greater. Most of all, I stand more convinced now than ever that very few things deserve permission to steal our presence from those we're with.

PRESENCE AS A PRESENT TO OURSELVES

Presence is a gift given to others. To be truly present to another helps her feel the weight of her God-endowed worth. It heralds her value to others as well. Presence is love's first expression, for one who loves always longs to be with his beloved. To give presence not only claims but also *shows* our desire to know and be known.

As we become people who dwell naturally in the present, the gift returns to us many times over. Our connection to others and influence with them grows deep. We also awaken our own capacity to experience life. As we "rejoice with those who rejoice; mourn with those who mourn,"[8] we come to feel much more than before. We taste of both sorrow and joy more richly, almost as if new taste buds had been added to our tongue.

In fact, as we learn to live in the present, we see and feel all of creation more fully. God's gifts have always been there, of course. As the Psalms describe, "The heavens declare the glory of God."[9] Our senses "taste and see that the Lord is good."[10] As poet Gerard Manley Hopkins described: "All things…are charged with God and if we know how to touch them give off sparks and take fire, yield drops and flow, ring and tell of him."[11]

This glory, however, we must encounter in the present. Nowhere else do we taste and see it. So when our attention dwells elsewhere, the gifts are largely lost to us.

> Earth's crammed with heaven,
> And every common bush afire with God:
> But only he who sees, takes off his shoes.[12]

To dwell in the present is to see. As we do, we take off our shoes in praise of our Creator, even before a backyard berry bush. To dwell in the present is to hear. As the clamor around and within us quiets, we catch the breathtaking songs and stories of people and creation. To dwell in the present is to taste. We experience as never before God's goodness in herbs and bread, fruit and wine. To dwell in the present is to begin to experience what we were made for.

BE ALL THERE

Initially the feeling of *effort* in making ourselves present to others will be keen. Like pulling back on the chain of an overeager dog, we must repeatedly yank our attention back into the moment. We must drag our thoughts away from *everything else* that calls to us—and turn again to the person before us.

It will be hard. Voices and distraction will rise around us, much like the crowd that pressed upon Jesus when a lonely woman grasped at His robe. Trying to become more present to others may at first feel as futile as asking, "Who touched Me?" amidst a multitude. Slowing our frenetic motion may feel as irresponsible as letting the father of a dying girl wait. At first we may feel we've sacrificed efficiency and lessened our sense of stimulation in decreasing our multitasking. It all will indeed feel like discipline.

Over time, however, disciplines become habits and habits turn into character. What at first was a straining decision becomes second nature. Perhaps for the first time we begin to dwell in the present. And the gift we can give, the gift of presence, is precious indeed.

Professor Leo Buscaglia recounts the true story of a little boy whose neighbor's wife passed away. Seeing that the elderly man was heartbroken and grieving, the boy's mother warned her son not to bother the neighbor.

It wasn't long before the mother noticed the little boy crossing into the neighbor's yard and climbing up into the old man's lap. He remained there for some time, sitting quietly.

When the boy returned home, his mother met him with her hands on her hips. "I told you not to bother him," she gently scolded. "What were you doing?"

The little fellow shook his head. "I wasn't doing anything," he answered. "I was just helping him cry."

Connection, influence, and empowerment of others begin here. Not with words but with presence—even if we feel we have little else to offer. As communicators this is the single most important decision we will make. Everything else, from the questions we'll ask to the stories we'll tell, grows from this soil.

Missionary martyr Jim Elliot summed it up well. "Wherever you are, *be all there.*"[13]

LIFE THROUGH ATTENTIVENESS

Unend a Life Consumed With
Our Own Thoughts and Words

Chapter 5

OUR CULTURE'S RAREST COMMODITY

The book *Am I Making Myself Clear?* recounts findings from a study of teenage prostitutes in San Francisco. Most were runaways, venturing the world alone in a desperate quest to find what they'd not been given at home. They'd never felt loved, protected, cherished. But when asked specifically what they'd most lacked, the girls' often-tearful answers almost universally carried the same three words: "Someone to listen."[1]

Ironically a similar yearning can be glimpsed in the prostitute's patrons. As former call girl Roberta Victor shared with writer Studs Terkel, "When I was a call girl, men were not paying for sex. They were paying for something else." It was not uncommon, she expressed, for that "something else" to be nothing more than "paying for someone to listen to them."[2]

Climb up the ladder of influence, and the story remains much the same. As a senior legislative staffer in California's Capitol confided in Jedd, "Hardly anyone really listens around here. People act politely and nod at what you say, but they rarely really hear you. When someone does listen, it leaves a deep impression on me. I think to myself, 'Now *that* is a person I want to be around.'"

Even those who appear hopelessly hardened are often driven by the same need. The words of former President Jimmy Carter from a 1994 interview with *Rolling Stone* are telling. Speaking of his experiences negotiating with brutal dictators of small nations, he expressed, "Quite often...these little guys, who might be making atomic weapons or who might be guilty of some human rights violation...are looking for someone to listen to their problems and help them communicate."[3]

This yearning is universal—often felt as a grinding absence in the soul of young and old, rich and poor. It is the consequence of a world in which almost every person's thoughts turn reflexively upon their own interests and concerns. It is a world in which communication is mostly about *self-expression* of what is in us, not *seeking out* what is in others.

Rare though it may be, however, there is a potent opposite to this view of communication. The essence is captured in the word *attentive*, coming from the Latin *attendere*, meaning, "to *stretch* toward." Attentiveness builds from the gift of *presence* into active *pursuit*. In choosing to be present, we silence all distraction that could pull us away from the person before us. In choosing to be attentive, we begin to *stretch toward* them and draw them out.

The remarkable novel *The Listener* depicts the winding life journeys of fifteen individuals. From the doctor and the judge to the cleaning lady, each bears deep wounds. One by one, healing comes, but not from a psychologist's analysis, medical prescription, or self-help manual. The restoration each experiences flows from the attentive listening of a mysterious figure, the Listener, ultimately revealed to be Christ Himself.[4] In her preface to the novel, author Taylor Caldwell describes what she'd seen that prompted her to write it. "The most desperate need of men today is not a new vaccine for any disease.... Man does not need to go to the moon or other solar systems.... His real need, his most terrible need, is for someone to listen to him, not as a 'patient,' but as a human soul."[5]

STRETCHING TOWARD IN JERICHO

The throng poured out through the gates of Jericho, a whirlwind of noise and dust. At its ever-shifting center walked Jesus, the rabbi from Galilee. Even those watching from a distance could tell that each man, woman, and child wanted to press nearer to Him, hear His replies, see what He would do next.

Despite the crush of the crowd, Jesus kept remarkable composure, interacting with those fortunate enough to thrust themselves within earshot. People on the fringes scrambled along, hoping to catch just a glimpse or a phrase. A blind beggar seated on the roadside was not helping matters, shouting something in an unintelligible croak.

"Quiet, Bartimaeus!" a large stonemason grunted at the blind man. "I didn't leave the job site just to hear you barking."

The crowd brushed Bartimaeus by, offering only a mouthful of dust for his trouble. "Jesus, son of David," he called one last time.

"Don't waste your voice," someone shot back.

Suddenly a hush rippled through the crowd. Jesus had stopped. He was saying something. What? Two young men began clearing a path out from the middle, back toward Bartimaeus. The beggar's blanched eyeballs turned skyward, his body trembling as he heard his name. "Bartimaeus, Jesus is calling for you!" A half-dozen eager hands lifted him to his feet and tugged him forward, into the heart of the whispering crowd.

The hands fell away and, on instinct, Bartimaeus stopped. Silence. Then a voice. "What do you want Me to do for you?"

Bartimaeus's mind felt like it was tumbling down a hillside. *He's asking a question? To me? How did He hear me in the middle of all this?* His dusty mouth seemed to be full of wool. From the midst of a swirling crowd, the rabbi had somehow noticed him, a blind beggar, calling from the margins. Now Jesus stood here next to him waiting, listening. *"Does this great man really want me to answer, to hear from me?"* wondered Bartimaeus. The expectant silence made the answer clear.

This kind of encounter with Bartimaeus was replayed countless times in Jesus's interactions with others. He almost always provided the physical healing requested, as He did for Bartimaeus. But Jesus didn't stop there. He offered the focused attention that can cure an even deeper ailment.

Mother Teresa, who knew intimately the depths of physical illness, expressed, "As far as I'm concerned, the greatest suffering is to feel alone, unwanted, unloved. The greatest suffering is also having no one, forgetting what an intimate, truly human relationship is…"[6] For both rich and poor, this lack can carry anguish beyond words.

With His pursuing attentiveness, Jesus's healing touched this place too. Most often He focused toward people or details others overlooked, like Bartimaeus—the tossed out, the unlovely, the disease-ridden, the rejected. He was not only present to them; He stretched toward them. Not for what they could do for Him, but to give the healing grace that attentiveness uniquely provides.

As much as any modern man, Jesus was immersed in the sort of dizzying activity that can drown out all but the loudest voices. Yet somehow, in the grandness of His mission and purpose, in all the demands upon His time, in the seriousness of His words, the size of His following, Jesus never became consumed with His own concerns and thoughts. His attention was outward. He approached the seemingly irrelevant and expendable with a thoroughness that bestowed deep value and dignity. He emphasized the small and insignificant.

During another visit to Jericho, it was a diminutive man perched in a sycamore tree that became the center of Jesus's attention. Just as with

Bartimaeus and the bleeding woman, Jesus paused within a churning crowd to focus entirely upon a single soul—in this case a small, despised tax collector. You could say Jesus *stretched toward* him: "Zacchaeus, come down immediately. I must stay at your house today."

Everyone knew this man was a collaborator with the hated Roman overlords and thieved from his own oppressed people. Yet Jesus's attention, expressed especially in His willingness to enter the intimacy of a shared meal, confirmed to Zacchaeus and to everyone else that "he, too, is a son of Abraham." Zacchaeus's life was never the same, and the impact rippled outward from there to benefit the poor and those Zacchaeus had formerly cheated as well.[7]

In each of these interactions and countless others, what began with the gift of presence grew into full, active attentiveness.[8] Jesus stilled noise, activity, and others' expectations—and then turned His focus entirely upon the one. Jesus noticed them. He truly saw the woman or man in a way they may not have been seen in years, and then He stretched toward them.

ATTENTIVENESS IS POTENT

It was a Thursday afternoon, but the Sunday school classroom in the small urban church was full. Senator Tim Leslie's owlish eyes smiled out at the roomful of sharply dressed African Americans.

This was not familiar territory. Senator Leslie's home district was almost entirely white and rural. But several weeks before, as he pondered running for statewide office, his longtime friend Sam had challenged: "If you want to represent the whole state, Tim, you need to know folks from *my* community better." Tim accepted, and Sam arranged a chance for Tim to dialogue with a group of Sam's fellow pastors.

Receiving a nod from Sam, Tim began, "I appreciate you all coming to meet today. I've been looking forward to telling you a bit about my thoughts on what's right and what's wrong with our state, and what it needs…"

An hour later Tim was all smiles as he rounded the room, shaking hands with each pastor. He made it to the parking lot ahead of Sam and stood reviewing the experience. "Some great folks in there—and they seemed receptive to what I had to say." He glanced hopefully at Sam as they slid into their seats. "Well, Sam?"

"You really want to hear?"

Tim's grin dropped, but he nodded. Sam shook his head. "I don't know,

Tim. They appreciated you showing up, but…well, there wasn't much beyond that. I'm sorry."

"Me too," muttered Tim, deflated. Sam started the car, and they rode in silence for several miles before Tim turned back to him. "Could we give it another try?"

A month later Tim sat at the head of another gathering. "I appreciate you coming to meet today," he began. "Sam helped set this up because I'd like for us all to share together how we feel about our state and what it needs. So, we're going to go around the room, starting here on my left, sharing our thoughts on three questions…"

Nearly everyone had spoken, some extensively, when Sam nudged Tim and pointed to his watch. It was past time for their next commitment. "I haven't spoken yet," whispered Tim. Sam shrugged apologetically, "We've got to go."

Sam thanked the group for gathering, and the two men began toward the door. Tim did not get three steps before finding himself surrounded. Pastor after pastor gripped him on the shoulders and pumped his hand. A woman in a broad red hat squeezed the air from him with an unexpected bear hug. "This has been the best dialogue we've ever had!" she beamed. Voice after voice boomed the same thought.

Tim was nearly dizzy by the time he made it to the car. Sam looked over at him with a wry grin. "Now *that* went well."

Tim shook his head, grinning as well. "I got an education in there. But was that a *dialogue*? I didn't even speak."

"You *heard* what they had to say. I could tell you were really listening. They could too. You listened with your heart. That's not something these folks have seen much of—especially from legislator types like you."

Tim Leslie lost the statewide election by a narrow margin and returned to his post in the legislature. But he says now that listening brought even better rewards. He gained lasting friendships and a deepened appreciation for a once-distant community. Drawing from ideas shared in that discussion and others like it, he also helped form the California Community Renewal Project to support the work of urban churches and community groups in solving local needs.

Of course it is not only urban pastors who desire to be heard, to be noticed, to be focused upon. From the glittering top of the social pyramid to its gritty basement, all humans crave sincere attention.

A story is told of a woman who was taken to dinner by the great British prime minister William Gladstone. Not long after, the same lady dined with Gladstone's equally famous political nemesis, Benjamin Disraeli. Asked later about the impression the two prominent figures had made upon her, she explained, "When I left the dining room after sitting next to Mr. Gladstone, I thought he was the cleverest man in England. But after sitting next to Mr. Disraeli, I thought I was the cleverest woman in England."

What made the difference? We all know the answer. Attentiveness stirs us like nothing else in the world. It touches our deepest longings for connectedness and intimacy, our ache to feel valued, our need to be heard and known.

After the flashbulbs have exhausted themselves and the confetti is swept into a tidy pile, most people care little if you have built skyscrapers, scripted best sellers, or steered a Fortune 500 corporation. They want to know one thing: "Do you care about me?"

We are insecure and hungry, all of us, from the deaf janitor to the rock-jawed football coach. Frequently, the brighter a person's veneer of success and confidence, the more ravenous his hunger for affirmation. Pull back the façade just a bit, and we will find that each woman and man, no matter how polished or praised, is deep down a little girl longing to know that she is worthy and adored or a little boy eager to hear that he is strong and capable.

Of course this need can be manipulated. Frequently it is. Feigned attentiveness is a deadly weapon in the hands of ambitious ladder climbers, sexual predators, and other charlatans.

But sincere attentiveness is another path altogether. It conveys genuine respect, concern, and value more than any other communication decision. When a person receives another person's wholehearted attention, suddenly they matter; they have worth. In a very real sense, at that moment, they feel they have been brought into existence.

That is why people respond to attentiveness almost as if to magic. It is a kiss that really does transform frogs into royalty—changing behavior, opening hearts, and inspiring loyalty. The best teachers and parents, pastors and managers understand this and choose to build their connection and influence upon attentiveness.

Talkative Christianity

Potent as it is, real attentiveness is rare as snow in Phoenix. No doubt, this scarcity is one reason it is so desperately desired. As author Os Guinness observed, "The rarest commodity in America is attention."[9] The ill effects of this lack are legion, from broken marriages and teenage runaways to the affairs of nations.

Personal Notes: Erik

One Sunday, late in the fall, I parked my car in a Safeway lot. The store was as crowded as my mind—I was lost in confusing thoughts about who I was, what choices I was making, what kind of man I was and wanted to be. A recent break-up and a wallop in a political campaign didn't help—I was living a life devoted to one thing: me—no responsibilities or obligations, no memberships or accountabilities, exactly how I wanted it.

Just then, strangely, the car parked in front of me began to roll backward—with no one inside. As it picked up speed, I noticed two women talking near another car, directly in line of the rolling car and completely inattentive of the three thousand pounds of steel headed straight for them.

What did I do?

Nothing. I didn't jump out of my car or holler a warning. I just sat there, watching, unable to move—not out of fear but out of selfishness.

At the very last moment, they darted to the side as the car, in slow motion, crumpled the car by which they stood. They looked around, as if to say, "Where did that come from?"

A wave of shame crashed over me. I started my car and drove home.

To be attentive is to be active—it's not information or awareness. It's taking in to give out. Attentiveness, truly practiced, demands that we "attend to" others, despite our own desires or needs. It is Jesus stopping when a woman touches His garment. It is giving up an afternoon's plans when a friend needs someone to talk with. It is clearing your throat when asked why you live the way you live.

The selfish man sitting in his parked car still resides deep within me—when friendships become inconvenient, conversations drag, and near-by suffering pulls at my pant leg for help—and yet, this is what I am learning: life is in the rubble, the broken, the gritty, and the heartbreaking. Exactly where Jesus is.

William Easterly's landmark book on foreign aid, *The White Man's Burden*, explores the gargantuan failures seen in many global efforts to help the poor.[10] As Liberia's president, Ellen Johnson Sirleaf, observed in a 2008 speech, billions upon billions of foreign aid dollars have been spent in her country and worldwide "with shockingly little result."[11]

Why? Easterly explores the answer in example after painful example. Many carefully designed aid initiatives are yet plagued by a fatal problem: foreign aid planners are often neither *present* with the poor nor *attentive* to their actual desires, concerns, and priorities. Nor do planners pay much attention to feedback that would help them correct errors once programs are running. "Feedback only works if someone listens," reminds Easterly.[12]

As Mother Teresa observed, "Today it is very fashionable to talk about the poor. Unfortunately, it is not fashionable to talk with them."[13]

An independent review of a project funded by the Canadian government and the World Bank in Lesotho, Africa, explored in detail how inattentiveness in foreign aid can play out. The project nobly aimed to help residents improve their farming and sell what they produced for needed cash. Unfortunately no one seemed to understand that the intended beneficiaries weren't particularly interested in farming since they earned cash working as migrants in South Africa. Program planners also failed to foresee that their scientific plan for cattle management was incompatible with the way all land in Lesotho is publicly owned. Meanwhile, unanticipated weather patterns, crop diseases, and mismanagement actually led to reduced agricultural production, rather than the 300 percent increase promised.

In the end the project managers complained that the local people were "defeatist" and that they didn't "think of themselves as farmers"— probably because they weren't. The one lasting legacy of the project was the new roads. But these didn't boost exports; they helped bring South African grain *into* the region, driving what local farmers there had been out of business.[14]

The consequences of inattentiveness are indeed devastating. When Christians evidence this same human inclination, the outcomes are equally dismal. Actually, worse. For not only does our inattentiveness ensure failure, but in the process we also distort the vision of Christ the world sees through us.

No doubt novelist E. M. Forster had this kind of person in mind when he penned the damning description, "poor little talkative Christianity."[15]

If our communication leads first with words, we will rarely deserve better. We'll almost always fail to provide what is most needed—whether in global antipoverty efforts or serving a local youth group. Only when we begin with attentiveness do we show the world the heart of our Master— and begin to earn His followers a much better name.

Chapter 6

THE MINISTRY OF LISTENING

In poignant contrast to talkative Christianity, Dietrich Bonhoeffer writes as an apprentice to Jesus when he describes:

> The first service that one owes to others in the fellowship consists of listening to them. Just as love to God begins with listening to His Word, so the beginning of love for the brethren is learning to listen to them...Christians, especially ministers, so often think they must always contribute something when they are in the company of others, that this is the one service they have to render. They forget that listening can be a greater service than speaking.[1]

Of course this practice of attentiveness—of *stretching toward* others—is no easy undertaking. If it were, it would not be nearly so rare.

As a busy lawyer expressed, "I frequently find my *in*attentiveness due in large part to wanting to stay on schedule. Or I'm on the clock and want to keep my time productive. So I avoid or cut off personal conversations with clients and staff. Attentiveness requires sacrificing your goals, agenda, schedule, deadlines, and efficiency. It might mean your whole afternoon gets thrown off when you encounter someone starved for attention."

Following Jesus's pattern in this is subversive. To place such value on attention giving is an act of treason against values and habits that serve as pillars of our culture. Attentiveness upends efficiency, accomplishment, self-expression, and seeing days go just as planned.

So if we merely desire to increase our influence, the attentiveness we show will never reflect the kind Jesus modeled. We may feign interest or even ask sincere questions. But ultimately, the deep, ongoing, sacrificial attentiveness of Jesus will prove too costly. This is especially true when the recipient of our attention seems to have little to offer in return.

Given the cost, can we really hope to persevere in apprenticeship to Jesus here? Not if our motivation is mere reputation and influence. We need a deeper Source of motivation.

As with everything else Jesus modeled, it comes back to the character of the Father. Our listening springs from His. Bonhoeffer put it this way, "The ministry of listening has been committed to [us] by Him who is Himself the great listener...."[2]

From our exultant praise to gasped desperation, God delights to hear words spoken to Him from the heart. As Jesus described in a vivid parable, even the shame-bound sinner who calls out to God in brokenness will find a listening ear.[3] Our smallest worries, whispered questions, inarticulate hopes are all fair game. As the apostle Peter wrote, "Cast all your anxiety on him because he cares for you."[4]

Personal Notes: Jedd

A shrill scream split into my slumber. My wife, Rachel, and I were awake in a flash, but it took a moment to remember: our four-year-old daughter, Siena, had been having nightmares for weeks. This was the third tonight, splintering both her sleep and ours. But as I heard Siena's voice cry out again, still asleep and desperate, "Daddy! My Daddy!", I didn't *want* to stay in my bed. I wanted to charge to her side in a nanosecond, to know what she'd faced in her dream and be with her in her fear. I tossed back the covers and bounded from our room to hers. "I'm here, darling," I whispered, taking her head in my hands. "Daddy's here."

Slowly her rigid body relaxed, and, eyes still closed, her grimace softened. "My Daddy," she murmured from a dreamworld, the hint of a smile playing on her face. I knelt next to her for several minutes as her breathing slowed and steadied. In that moment I felt I'd be glad to wake a dozen times a night to attend to her like that again.

I don't think I could have fully understood that thought as a single guy. So perhaps it's no wonder that it is hard to grasp that God feels this same way toward us. As Jesus described in the well-known parable, while the prodigal son "was still a long way off, his father saw him and was filled with compassion for him; he ran to his son, threw his arms around him and kissed him."[5] Amazing. Such a desire to be near, to stretch toward His children is the heart of our God, even to the most undeserving. Even to me.

We see this most vibrantly in the way Jesus prayed. He spoke heavenward with utter confidence that God was near and listening, eager to hear and to respond. We get no hint from Jesus that when we call out, God glances up from a paper-strewn desk, hand on His forehead, trying to overcome His annoyance long enough to offer a halfhearted, "*Hmmm?*"

An image far closer to what Jesus conveyed would be that of an adoring father whose son has just toddled into the room. He kneels down next to him, hands holding the child's face, almost nose to nose. The little boy stumbles over the words, halting and imperfect. Yet it is clear the father desires nothing more in that moment than to know what is on his mind, "Yes, my precious son, what is it you want to tell me?"

If we can imagine ourselves reflecting even a glimmer of that kind of attentiveness to a colleague, a janitor, a lonely stranger, perhaps we are drawing nearer to the kind of attentiveness we have been shown. We give attention not because the recipient deserves it, or even because they may be changed as a result of it. Rather we listen—both to God's voice and to others'—because He first listens to us.

When apprentices to Jesus do so, it is beautiful to see. Workers at the CityTeam Ministries in San Francisco, California, seek to meet the homeless' physical needs as best they can. But the heart of their work is in striving to give their ragged, bleary-eyed patrons the personal notice they rarely receive. Volunteers even wash the feet of the homeless, listening carefully to their stories, doing all they can to draw out the human being before them. How a homeless man or woman will respond is never certain. But even the street-hardened or mentally ill often appear deeply touched by the focused attention they've long lived without.

Pastor Tim Keller models the same priority in a very different way through his book *The Reason for God*.[6] The field of apologetics sometimes embodies "talkative Christianity," dominated by answer-slinging logicians who can fire off chapter-and-verse responses before a doubting Thomas gets halfway through his question. Keller, in contrast, leads with listening. He is as insightful and principled as any. But Keller's tone, content, and story after story reveal he has spent a lifetime listening carefully to the questions, longings, and disillusionment of both saints and cynics. Before delivering answers, he articulates the skeptic's claims in its most compelling form, not the simplistic "straw man" that some apologists create and then knock down. He affirms legitimate counter arguments and reasons for criticisms rather than attacking the critic. Only then does he begin to lay out in clear but gracious form a potent defense of the faith.

The DVD series created to complement the book is perhaps even more revealing. It bears no hint of the "I've-got-all-the-answers" monologue one might expect. Rather Keller invites a group of sincere skeptics to discuss in an honest, unscripted format some of the most difficult critiques of Christianity. *How could a loving God send people to hell? How can Christians make such exclusivist claims? Hasn't science disproved the Bible?*

For those expecting traditional apologetics, it is almost jarring to observe Keller asking hard questions and then listening far more than he talks.

Jedd recently led an adult Sunday school class through the book and DVD series. In the final class he asked which of Keller's thoughts they'd found most compelling. The answers varied, but one was repeated more than any other. Beyond any new idea or insight, what the class had been most struck by was the way Keller listened so openly and intently in the videos. "Keller knows so much more than me," said one student, "and yet I felt myself continually itching to fire off some answer at the group he was dialoguing with. But I could see him holding himself back again and again to show his interest in them, and love and respect by listening. His ideas were amazing, but I think that way of listening was even more powerful."

GROWING ATTENTIVENESS

Even when we've committed ourselves to attentiveness, living it out can feel like an internal tug-of-war. Tasks, worries, and even shallow distraction pull viciously at our concentration. Amid even the most enjoyable conversations, self-interested thoughts can chatter on within our heads: "How will this affect my plans? What will I do when this conversation is over...next week...for my vacation?" Attentiveness can't happen without being genuinely *present* to others. When our lives are abuzz with noisy distraction—either external or internal—our attention to others will be partial at best. So the disciplines of silence described in chapter 4 form the foundation for growing attentiveness.

Personal Notes: Jedd

I love the eagerness and fresh eyes interns bring. But in the midst of a busy day, I often feel I have time for little more than the briefest interactions: giving a quick greeting or succinct directions. There may be times when that's all I can give. But I've come to realize that attentiveness to interns is one of the watershed choices I make daily between living as an apprentice to Jesus and self-centeredness.

I can still see interns from the past—Jeff, Rachel, Mike—popping their head into my office. "Do you have a moment to talk?" they asked. Sometimes I really didn't have a moment. But usually I did. So I had to decide, would I give that moment in attentiveness or hold it tight? Usually all that was needed was a few minutes and a listening ear. Sometimes we'd reconvene over a planned lunch or coffee. But regardless of the time involved, almost never have I regretted opting to attend in focused listening and conversation. Often I receive even better gifts in return: insight into the struggle a colleague had been facing; a fresh perspective on how to improve office operations; the privilege of making a difference in a key life decision; best of all, lasting friendship.

That said, a large part of learning to *stretch toward* others is simply choosing to make it a priority. Understanding the significance of attentiveness and the premium Jesus placed on it can grow into an *intention*. This intention, remembered amidst daily interactions, can begin to shape behavior, then habits. Often simply recalling that *this small decision to be attentive is a central aspect of serving others through my communication* can be enough to pull us back from distracted thoughts in order to really attend to the person we're with.

A number of practices can help us act upon this intention.

Make question-asking an art.

Jesus often anchored His communication in thoughtful questions. Prior to interactions, think through questions you can ask to dig beneath trite exchanges and into meaningful discussion. Try viewing yourself like a reporter, seeking to draw out significant thoughts and experiences from others.

Sacrifice distractions.

Concentrating technology-soaked senses on a single person involves strenuous effort. Simple but difficult choices are critical: shut off phones and TV, close the computer, place the newspaper on the ground when a child wants to talk, and turn away from the computer while on the phone. We may imagine no one will notice, but multitasking *always* diminishes attentiveness.

Involve the whole body.

Physical stance has a surprising impact on interactions. Consider how kneeling for prayer, although not necessary, can orient us toward humility and receptiveness. In much the same way, posture can prepare us for attentiveness—setting shoulders square toward the other, leaning forward. Most of all, force your eyes not to rove. These physical actions express interest and help us remain focused and engaged.

Confirm your perceptions.

Even the most discerning observer can misconstrue what she hears or sees. Simple inquiries—"You look frustrated. Are you down?"—can help clarify perceptions. Communication experts call this practice "active listening." By asking for confirmation ("Do you mean…?") or repeating back a form of what you think you heard ("So you're telling me…?"), we can ensure we understand what is being said and also convey to others that we care about what they are saying.

Take special note of people on the margins.

Jesus directed His attentiveness especially toward the *invisible* men and women of His day: the poor, ostracized, and chronically ill. The apprentice to Jesus gives special attention to people others overlook—yard workers, janitors, the disabled, or homeless.

Learn more in order to see more.

A boy who has no knowledge of forests will likely *see* nothing on a mountainside except "a bunch of trees." With a little study, though, suddenly every pine, cedar, and dogwood grows distinct. Now he can't help but see them. The same is true as we learn about the culture, family, or life story of an individual. Whether gained through books, classes, or conversations, new learning increases our ability to see.

Express what you observe.

Pulitzer Prize–winning writer Annie Dillard observes, "Seeing is of course very much a matter of verbalization. Unless I call my attention to what passes before my eyes, I simply won't see it."[7] The practice of articulating things we've noticed—like thanking a waitress's manager for her effort or mentioning a talent you perceive in a friend—makes what we've seen more real for us, and also can be a gift to others as well.

Alongside these practices, one spiritual discipline is particularly vital to increasing attentiveness toward others: praying for them. Perhaps this is because attentiveness requires escaping the self-absorption we're all so naturally inclined to. Attentiveness is a key part of what it looks like to "look not only to your own interests, but also to the interests of others."[8] When we pray for others, this is just what we're doing: we *look to* the interests of others in conversation with God. Prayer is a way of stretching toward others from a distance.

"There is nothing that makes us love a man so much as praying for him," wrote William Law in the mid 1700s. "This was the ancient friendship of Christians, uniting and cementing their hearts, not by worldly considerations or human passions, but by the mutual communication of spiritual blessings, by prayers and thanksgivings to God for one another."[9]

So it is that when we learn to stretch toward others in prayer from afar, we grow both more able and more eager to do so when together—even amidst myriad distractions. Although we've been apart, our *affection* for them has grown. We've been thinking about them, so we *remember* things they've told us. We've learned how to *concentrate* on them even when not physically present.

Thus, as with all spiritual disciplines, prayer for others *trains* us. Like an athlete running wind sprints in the off season, we exercise in times when we *don't need to* so as to grow more able to do a particular thing when we *most want to*. Praying for others grows a heart and character of attentiveness toward them while we are apart that becomes visible when we're together.

This is true not only of prayer for individuals but also for groups, just as when Jesus prayed for all those who would come to believe in Him.[10] When we pray for an intended audience—whether a crowd at a conference or even the anonymous readers of a blog post—we grow more attuned to *their* interests and needs, not focused only on *delivering* our message. When we do, we become far more likely to connect and leave lasting influence, whatever the medium of communication.

Personal Notes: Erik

Andy is on the road. Again. His beaten-down Honda is on Highway 40 or Interstate 95, on back roads to small colleges and coffee shops, where he sings melodies and sells merchandise, packs up, and is off to the next gig. His latest album, *Jealous Hands*, features a song written for his wife: "Gracious Woman." Indeed, she is, enduring Andy's long stretches away from home.

"What happens if five people show up at your show," I asked him a few years back. I was being curious, not cynical, which he understood. For him it was not a theoretical question; playing before small crowds is part of the artist's life.

"I play the same as I do for a packed house," he replied. It may sound predictable if you don't know Andy or if you haven't seen one of his shows. Sure, every artists *says* that, but no one really *means* it or actually *does* it. You cut sets short. You go through the motions. You hold back for the bigger shows.

Not Andy.

He's been around long enough to know that every fan counts. If those five fans tell five friends, that is twenty-five at the next show. If marketing pro Seth Godin is correct, it takes only one thousand true fans to make a living. And it's worked. Every year Andy's fan base grows. His shows are bigger. His fans more passionate. His albums more successful.

I believe its all because he was attentive to the small crowds. And that is not a strategy or a tactic; it's a way of loving people well.

THE REWARDS OF ATTENTIVENESS

The cost of attentiveness amidst a busy life is great; its rewards are even greater. Alongside the deepened connection and influence it brings, attentiveness enriches virtually every aspect of how we experience the world.

> I keep six honest serving men
> (They taught me all I knew);
> Their names are What and Why and When
> And How and Where and Who.[11]
>
> —RUDYARD KIPLING

When attentive, we continually learn from almost every person we encounter. Each individual is a trove of insight into *something*; we just must be willing to put in the effort to draw it out. If we're attentive, the astronomer can gift to us a new vision of the night sky. The immigrant plumber offers the best way to keep drains unplugged or shares his mother's recipe for *chile relleno*. The child enables us to see again, as if for the first time, what strange and wonderful creatures cows are.

The natural world too teems with gifts of beauty and knowledge. As we grow in attentiveness toward others, we grow more attentive to God's gifts in creation as well. That's why individuals who tend to notice and enjoy other people are often those who most notice and enjoy sunsets and daffodils also.

Finally, as we learn attentiveness toward people, we grow more attentive to God. The converse of this is true too: we'll often attend to others more as we learn to attend to God's voice. But as described in 1 John, it's usually easier for humans to begin by listening to others "whom they have seen" as a way to learn to listen to God "whom they have not seen."[12]

These rich gifts of learning, appreciation, and spiritual hearing ensure the attentive person will never grow stagnant. Instead of trite truisms and tired assumptions, his or her words vibrate with insight and freshness. Indeed the person grows into an artist. For attentiveness is the lifeblood of any art, from songwriting or sculpture to well-crafted blog posts.

The greatness of the masters—Da Vinci, Bach, Bronte, Frost—came in large part from their deep attentiveness. People and creation fascinated them, and their senses remained continually open and alert. Don Postema, who served as chaplain at the University of Michigan for thirty-four years, expresses this insight well. To be truly great as creators and communicators, he observes, artists "need this kind of awareness to write, or paint, or draw with any authenticity. They need to *pay attention*.... They must take time to penetrate below the surface of things, to rediscover the world with an eye of love, and to 'see' into reality. Being an artist involves 'grasping life in its depth,' as the sensitive artist Vincent Van Gogh once wrote."[13] Supplied in this way by the wellspring of attentiveness, words reverberate with creativity and life.

Through their attentiveness, apprentices to Jesus thus live amidst a continual giving and receiving. They learn from others, take delight in God's creation, and hear His guiding instruction. Meanwhile, they reach always beyond their self-absorbed thoughts, stretching toward others with the rare and precious offering of attentiveness. For such a person, the world is rich with discovery and relationships are rich with deep connection. It is a pursuit worthy of sacrifice.

LIFE THROUGH INCARNATION

Upend a Life Limited to Our Comfortable Spaces

Chapter 7

DRAWING NEAR

Moloka'i. The island's name was pronounced bitterly, with loathing and fear. Between 1866 and 1873 nearly eight hundred lepers were quarantined there on an isolated peninsula. Towering volcanic cliffs hemmed them in on three sides, and crashing surf on the fourth. It was a prison, a netherworld made all the more surreal by its pacific beauty.

Abandoned without law or hope, the lepers gave themselves alternately to despair and to what pleasures they could grasp. Robbery and drunkenness, sexual orgies and anarchy marked their lives. When finally, after a tortuous descent, the lepers succumbed to their disease, their already-decayed bodies often became food for pigs and wild dogs.

Father Damien first came to Hawaii in 1864. He had been born in Europe, the sturdily built son of a well-to-do Belgian farmer. When his brother fell ill and could not travel to his post at Hawaii's Sacred Hearts Mission, Damien asked to take his place.

For a decade Damien served at the mission. During that time many of his parishioners were forced away to Moloka'i. Their memory remained wedged in his mind, slowly building into a fearsome emotion. He yearned to go to the lepers and to convey love to them where they lived. In April of 1873, Father Damien wrote to his superiors, asking for permission. A month later he stood on the beaches of the dread isle.

Damien steeled himself for the worst, but the sights and smells of Moloka'i left him gasping. One of his first encounters was with a young girl, her body already half-eaten by worms. Damien set out to meet them all, one by one. Carefully avoiding physical contact, he confronted their rotting bodies, putrid breath, and the ever-present rasped coughing.

Damien's first desire was to remind the lepers of their inherent dignity as children of God. To demonstrate the value of their lives, he honored their deaths—constructing coffins, digging graves, protecting the cemetery from scavenging animals, and ensuring a ceremony for every passing.

As the days went by, however, Damien began to feel that he could not fully convey all that he wished to share without drawing even nearer. He began timidly to touch the lepers. He ate with them and hugged them. Over time he even began to clean and wrap their oozing sores. Everything Damien did, he did with the lepers. Together they built coffins and chapels, cottages and roads. He taught them how to farm, raise animals, and even sing despite their mangled vocal cords. One report described him teaching two lepers to play the organ with the ten fingers they still had between them.

Damien sought to draw near to the lepers in his words as well, even speaking of "*we* lepers." Writing to his brother in Europe, he explained, "I make myself a leper with the lepers to gain all to Jesus Christ. That is why, in preaching, I say 'we lepers'; not 'my brethren…'"

It was eleven years after Damien's arrival on Moloka'i that he spilled boiling water on his leg. He watched with horror as his feet blistered—yet felt no pain. His efforts to draw ever nearer to the lepers was complete. Now he would meet them in their disease as well.

The final five years of his life Damien served the lepers of Moloka'i as a leper priest. The days passed with both joy and suffering. Outpourings of international support arrived at the island, and also several helpers. Alongside the blessings, however, came physical pain and times of loneliness and even depression. Finally, on April 15, 1889, Damien breathed his last. He was laid to rest among the thousands of lepers he had helped to bury in what he called his "garden of the dead."

In 1936, at the request of the Belgian government, Father Damien's body was returned to his birthplace. Years later the people of Moloka'i pleaded that at least part of their beloved father be returned to them. What they finally received, with joy, was Damien's right hand—the hand that had touched and soothed and embraced them, even when everyone else had done all they could to keep the lepers far away.

COMMUNICATION IS COMMUNION

Communication. Community. Compassion. Communion. As is easy to see, these words grow with their roots entwined. All of them spring from the Latin term *com*, together. The word *communication* is itself from the Latin *communicare*, meaning, "to share together," or, more literally, "to make common."

To our loss we often define it otherwise. Many textbooks present communication as little more than the transmission of information. With such an emphasis, all that matters is the data we are working to insert into others' brains and the reaction we hope to create. The issue of connectedness fades to the background, valued only as a tool to be exploited. Viewed in this way, communication becomes an impersonal exchange of messages, a one-way street where, as author Margaret Miller described, "conversations are simply monologues delivered in the presence of a witness."[1]

True communication, however, is never monologue; it is dialogue, the *coming together* of two living beings, even when separated by chasms of culture and language, age and distance, opinion and race.

This connection, just as with electric lines, is the fundamental necessity of communication. Without connection, exchange is impossible, no matter how high the voltage. But when the wires touch, energy crackles and life begins to flow.

Whether on the mass scale or the most personal, communication is born as two human beings draw close and touch. Great communicators, before anything else, seek means of connection. To begin, the communicator must come near.

Father Damien did just that. He came near to the lepers, in every way he knew how. He dwelt in their space, spoke their language, addressed their most pressing needs, and even tasted their pain. To the fullest extent possible he entered their turf and dealt in their terms.

As these connection points between Damien and the lepers sparked, the love and ideas he wished to convey surged into them, just as the energy within a live wire passes to a grounded object the moment they touch.

This work of coming near for the sake of connection is the foundation of all fruitful communication.

For the apprentice to Jesus, it is also far more—the very epicenter of Christian faith. As the apostle John described of Jesus's life, "The Word became flesh and dwelt among us."[2] That which was far off, removed, and distinct came near. He dwelt in our space, spoke human language, addressed our most pressing needs, and even tasted our pain.

 Outrushing the fall of man is the height of the fall of God.[3]
—G. K. CHESTERTON, *GLORIA IN PROFUNDIS*

From His newborn cries in barnyard air to His last pain-wracked gasps on the cross, Jesus's life was continually a work of entering the space of those He sought to reach. His every act of communication, whether verbal or otherwise, was anchored in choices to connect with His audience—always moving *toward*, reaching *into*, drawing *from* their daily experiences. Simple, descriptive phrases from the Gospels capture this approach, startling only for their ordinariness:

→ Jesus went throughout Galilee, teaching in their synagogues.

→ While Jesus was having dinner at Matthew's house, many tax collectors and sinners came and ate with Him.

→ Jesus reached out His hand and touched the leper.

→ When Jesus came into Peter's house, He saw Peter's mother-in-law lying in bed with a fever. He touched her hand.

→ Jesus entered the ruler's house.

→ Jesus went through all the towns and villages.

→ Jesus went through the grainfields.

→ Jesus walked beside the Sea of Galilee.

→ Coming to His hometown, Jesus began teaching the people in their synagogue.[4]

He dined with the wealthy as a guest at their feasts. He conversed with religious leaders in their synagogues and temples. The poor He sought out on lonely hillsides and fetid gathering places, the destitute on their sickbeds. Even the outcasts and the immoral encountered Jesus at their sides, by their watering holes, at their tables.

The residue of Palestine's dusty roads coated Jesus's feet. He breathed the sour odors of the crowds. Fishing boats and hillsides served as His platform as often as pulpits or podiums. The unlovely received His gaze; the untouchable felt His hands.

Even His words were distinctly *near* to His audiences. He spoke not with ivory tower phrases and abstract doctrines. Instead He painted vivid word pictures that could be touched and tasted and smelled: baking yeast, a field of wheat, sheep and goats, salt, light, and falling towers. And, always, He returned to stories—a form as accessible to children and the illiterate as to the educated elite.

No matter what audience, Jesus continually conveyed His message in their terms on their turf.

Can we do it like Him? Absolutely. But be warned—it will require risk and even loss. Modern communication operates under the assumption that our words will be most potent when delivered from a position of power. Even when we recognize that making a connection is necessary, we seek it without releasing our grip on status, reputation, and comfort. No need to get too close, we believe. No need to lower ourselves. We seek impact without involvement, like a busy executive sending an assistant to pick up his sick child from school.

Real connection is never so safe or cost-free.

TO COME NEAR

"I may be compelled to face danger, but never fear it, and while our soldiers can stand and fight, I can stand and feed and nurse them." So vowed Clara Barton, the "angel in the battlefield" who joined fallen Civil War soldiers at the front lines to tend their wounds and whisper words of peace.[5]

Adorned in her trademark bonnet, red bow, and dark skirt, Clara arrived at the northern edge of Antietam's infamous "Cornfield" just after noon. Only days before the field had been lush with towering stalks; now bodies crisscrossed the land amid the matted corn.

Nearby, harried surgeons wrapped soldiers' wounds with cornhusks. The army's medical supply wagons had been left far behind by the rapid march of the soldiers. Urged on by Clara, however, her own wagon had driven all night to get closer to the front of the line. Surgeons voiced their gratitude as she handed them the bandages and other medical supplies she had personally gathered over the past year.

Soon Clara herself was wading out into the field. Between the whistle of bullets and thunder of cannons, feeble voices called out for death. Kneeling over a disoriented soldier, she cut back his wool pants to reveal an oozing wound. She lifted his head with her hand and offered him drink from a canteen, the only pain reliever she could offer as she prepared to operate.

Feeling something brush by her arm, Clara glanced down. A bullet had ripped through her sleeve. The weight of the man's head increased in her hand, and she realized the slug had pierced him, ending his life.

The hours passed quickly as Clara and her assistants moved from one man to the next. Again and again she stood, wiping caked blood and mud from her hands against her skirt, calling out for a stretcher.

As night fell, the fading light began to slow the work of the surgeons.

From her wagon, Clara produced lanterns. As soldiers returned to their campfires, she remained with the wounded, working through the night.

Within a few days, more medical supplies finally arrived. Exhausted, Barton collapsed from lack of sleep and an emerging case of typhoid fever. She was laid in the back of a wagon for the journey back to Washington. It was not long, however, before she regained her strength and returned to the battlefields of the Civil War.

Clara Barton later became the first president of the Red Cross. Throughout her life her focus remained with the people suffering at the front lines of wars and disasters. Coming into the troubled space of the desperate with aid and mercy was the hallmark of her life.

Personal Notes: Jedd

Tom Carpenter is one of my best friends, and also a fellow father of daughters. Last year Tom approached some of the older men he most admires, inviting their advice on fatherhood. One man, Jimmy, has the kind of relationship with his adult daughters Tom and I pray we'll someday enjoy with ours. Tom told me, "I grew up with Jimmy's girls and saw how special their relationship with their dad was, always respectful yet so tender. Even through the toughest years of high school and college they remained very close. They still are."

Jimmy's advice to a young father of daughters was straightforward. Praying for the girls fervently and spending significant time with them topped his list. But he went on to share precisely how: "Go where they are, every day," urged Jimmy. He explained that meant not waiting for them to come to him, but seeking his daughters out in their space—on the floor, playing dolls, in their room, reading a book.

Jimmy's advice has stuck with both Tom and me. It reminds and nudges us, especially when we might prefer just to unwind on the couch after work or get a jump on chores Saturday morning. For me, it most often invites me to the corner of our backyard. There, my three girls have turned an abandoned shed into their *house*. Its fine décor features construction paper curtains, a cardboard box table (with a real tablecloth that can double as a blanket), and a small bed made from a faded bench cushion.

"Have you come to visit our house, Daddy?" they declare, lighting up as I approach as if the president had come to town. And soon I find myself awash in the hospitality of the seven-, five-, and two-year-old hostesses. We dine on bits of wild mint that they've plucked from the yard, washing it down with a glass of captured rainwater. "You can sleep now, Daddy," says one, and I lay on a bench-cushion bed that smells of mildew, covered tenderly with a cozy tablecloth.

These are small, daily choices. But Tom got a glimmer of what they can mean over a lifetime from Jimmy's daughter Sarah. "He loved me like crazy," described Sarah. "He always seemed like he was enthralled with me."

Tom dug deeper, asking, "What did your dad do to make you feel loved and cherished?" Sarah's first words put it simply, "He came to me. Met me where I was."

Sarah went on to give specifics. "He brought himself to within a few feet of me and noticed me, loved me, asked me questions about me, played with me." More than two decades later she could gave example after example of things—often little ones—that her dad did to come near. Jumping on the trampoline with her. Sitting on the back porch to play games. Using an old chalkboard for pretend school. Often, coming near involved no more than Jimmy waking Sarah in the morning and taking a few minutes to "sit on the edge of my bed with his coffee (sipping it loudly just to be obnoxious) and tap my back and just sort of talk to me."

In a hundred small choices Jimmy drew near to his daughters—making both his love and God's love tangible to them. I pray that my Siena, Marin, Eden, and Lincoln will someday say the same.

Before anything else, connection requires *drawing near*, through whatever means available.

This was Jesus's way. "The Word became flesh and *dwelt among us*." The term "dwelt" literally means "to pitch a tent." Jesus was not a commuter, coasting in from distant suburbs to a downtown job site or a once-a-week ministry in the inner city. Like Barton, He set up camp, pitched His tent right smack dab in the middle of the people He desired to reach.

Whatever the cost, this quest to *draw near* marks all who effectively connect.

It was Mother Teresa, dressing herself in the white sari of the poor and taking up residence in the slums of Calcutta and even becoming a citizen of India.

It was Bobby Kennedy, choosing to go beyond the boundaries most "respectable" politicians kept to at the time by marching with Martin Luther King Jr.

It was George W. Bush, flying into embattled Baghdad to serve Thanksgiving meals to the troops stationed there.

It is the men and women at the inner-city Harambee Center in southern California, who have moved from the suburbs to live and raise their families in the tough urban neighborhood where they minister.

It is an aged man folding his legs beneath a child's table to enjoy tea with his granddaughter, a foreman who pounds nails with the day laborers, a doctor who makes house calls, a teacher who has lunch with students in the cafeteria, a friend who sits next to us as we bite our nails in the hospital waiting room. Nothing starts us along the path to connection like this coming near.

COMING NEAR IN WORD TOO

The effort to draw near marked not only Jesus's actions; it defined His words as well. Jesus continually worked to bring His communication into the place of those He addressed. Four qualities in particular accomplished this:

1. *Narrative.* Love for stories is universal. Says writer A. S. Byatt, "Narration is as much a part of human nature as breath and the circulation of the blood."[6] Jesus harnessed stories as His primary means of communication, telling tales of kindly Samaritans and forgiving fathers, buried treasure and mouth-watering feasts. Whether Galilean farmers or jaded American teens, *everyone* delights in a tale well told. The stories Jesus told in virtually every encounter were parables: literally, *para* (near) *ballo* (to bring)—"near-bringers." A *paraballo* is any story or phrase that connects a distant, hard-to-visualize thought or concept with something vivid and familiar. Jesus never forced His listeners to wade off into the realm of abstract principles and doctrines. Instead, He brought the ideas He wished to convey close to them. Using these "near-bringers," He imbedded lofty ideas and principles into the dust and grime of the people's workaday lives.

2. *Simplicity.* Jesus's themes were grand and expansive. But He always offered truth in bite-size chunks even illiterate laborers could digest. His language was never bookish or thick with theological jargon. Granted, sometimes even Jesus's disciples were so wrapped up in worn-out assumptions that they missed His points. Many still do today. Even so, multitudes of poor laborers, lowly peasants, and children gathered to listen to Jesus for days on end. Those who sincerely desired to learn never left empty handed.[7,8]

3. *Familiarity.* Jesus's communication was consistently fashioned from the stuff of His listeners' everyday lives.

He drew from their history, their Scriptures, their daily experiences, and from current events with which almost every listener would certainly have been familiar. People feel comfortable and connected when they hear references to things they recognize and interact with regularly.

4. *Concreteness.* As explored more in Section V, Jesus always connected the lofty ideas He shared to concrete examples and objects. He translated each concept into vivid images: a man plucking out his eyes, moths and rust devouring horded wealth, pigs trampling pearls. When possible, He involved nearby physical things as well—a small child, a coin, a man with a withered hand. Jesus made everything He spoke about real and tangible.

Communication that is simple, familiar, concrete, and makes ample use of stories—whether addressed to a large stadium or the junior higher next door—brings us *near* to our listeners. It connects us to them and their world.

Chapter 8

TAKING ON FLESH

Drawing near is the first step toward rich connection. Proximity alone, however, is rarely enough. Incarnation yet goes further. As John described, Jesus not only drew near; He also *became flesh*.

Becoming flesh. Putting on skin. Wrapping elusive truth with cartilage and muscle, tendons, and veins. This is the Christian faith's grandest enigma and wonder. Shockingly, an infinite God chose to speak not with lightning-bolt edicts or thundered commands. Instead He enmeshed the transcendent *Word* in a human body. What had been distant and abstract was made outrageously tangible.

The goal was clear. No medium could possibly be more accessible and familiar to humans than humanness. To communicate, God wrapped all that He desired to convey into physical, touchable flesh.

Such an act is a great mystery indeed. Yet this putting of flesh upon the far-off and hard-to-grasp is required of all communicators. Without it our words remain no more capable of touching others than a ghost would be.

So how do we do this? How does our communication become an act of enfleshment? How do we *incarnate* the things we wish to express in a way that can be touched and handled by our friends or spouses, students or employees?

Both the communicator and the communication must *take on flesh*.

INCARNATION IN SHARED EXPERIENCE

Nothing allows a communicator to "take on flesh" like shared experience. Soldiers who have fought together, an athletic team at the end of a season, or even a collection of strangers who have endured a long, hard bus ride together feel an almost mystical connection. Individuals who have had similar experiences in the past—having faced poverty, grown up overseas, or fought cancer—often share special bonds.

These connections allow for rich communication. This is because most of us assume, usually correctly, that those who have "walked a mile in our shoes" will understand us and care about the same things we do. So we tend to listen more readily and add weight to their words.

McDonald's Corporation requires individuals who wish to become franchise owners to spend time working the front lines of a restaurant's operations. Not only does this practice give would-be investors a better sense of how to manage their future business, but it also provides a basis for understanding and connecting to the people who will work for them.

Likewise a pastor in a small town spends a day every week or two at the work of one of his parishioners. He joins in as best he can, from a police ride-along to kneading bread dough at the local bakery at 4:00 a.m. These simple shared experiences give him a fuller grasp of his congregation's daily lives, and conveys his interest in them as well.

Whenever possible, good communicators do the same—choosing to engage in activities that will give them a point of connection and shared experience.

INCARNATION IN CULTURE AND CUSTOM

Sharing experiences is the fullest form of incarnation, but it is not always possible or realistic. A wealthy New Yorker will likely never fully know the taste of urban poverty or what it was like to grow up in rural Iowa. Yet despite this, communicators can still take on others' flesh by adopting some of their customs or symbols. By honoring the things others value, we convey that we desire to connect with them and respect them as individuals.

Hudson Taylor, founder of China Inland Mission, remade Christian missions through his decisions to incarnate himself in this way. Most missionaries of his day wore English suits, retained Western ways, and lived in residences that replicated homes back in England or America. After beginning much the same way, Taylor realized he could connect far more with the Chinese if he took on their culture. In addition to becoming fluent in Mandarin and a second local dialect, Taylor adopted the robe and satin shoes worn by Chinese teachers. He shaved the hair on the front of his head and grew the rest into the standard queue. He even allowed his fingernails to grow long, as other Chinese teachers did to show that they were scholars. It is said that literally millions of Chinese today trace their Christian faith back to this slight, humble man. Rather than communicating from the position of power and superior status expected by most

British citizens, Taylor chose to follow Jesus's pattern in the way he incarnated himself into Chinese culture.

Of course if we adopt symbols or customs merely as tools of influence, with little sincerity or concern for the people involved, it may well backfire. Some say Michael Dukakis cost himself the 1988 presidential election when he tried to appear pro-military by riding in a tank dressed in soldier's gear. Images of Dukakis bouncing around with his helmet hanging down over his eyes suggested to both the military and the American people little but opportunism. Similarly, a youth group leader desperately trying to be young and hip only invites contempt. Incarnation is anything but pretending to be something you are not. People disdain fakes and despise panderers.

Sincere efforts though, even if awkward, will ultimately bear fruit. A young American with plans to work someday in the Middle East has decided to give up pork and alcohol, grow a beard, and take other small-seeming actions to honor the traditions of the Islamic world. Even while living in California, his simple choices have drawn appreciation from Muslim acquaintances and opened opportunities for much deeper friendship.

INCARNATION IN SELF-DISCLOSURE

Despite the unavoidable differences between any two people, our deeper parts are knit of the same material. Most of us readily find pieces of our own story in the tales of Helen of Troy, Lancelot, King David, or Abigail Adams. Is it not certain, then, that we can discover at least as many points of commonality with the people living around us today? As Frederick Buechner wrote, "The story of any one of us is in some measure the story of us all."[1]

Seeking out and revealing this commonality is a work of incarnation. And it is often as simple as sharing honestly from our own lives and stories, especially when we speak with transparency about our hopes and failures, rough edges and desires. As we offer glimpses of the fact that we too experience these realities, we take on flesh in our audience's eyes. As some would say, we are showing our human side. This revealing of humanness brings us nearer, creating commonality and connection.

A brief anecdote is often all that is needed to connect in this way. The account need not be a war story, even if speaking with a veteran. It is enough to describe what it felt like when you failed your first high school exam, or how you lay beside your German shepherd when it was hit by a car. A simple, personal story or a moment of vulnerable honesty can quickly turn you from a shadowy and distant figure into a flesh-and-blood companion with shared hopes and struggles.

INCARNATION IN HEART LANGUAGE

The film *The Mission* opens as a Jesuit priest is being bound to a crude cross by South American natives and thrown into a river. The man bumps and spins helplessly through turgid, chocolate waters, finally plunging to his death over roaring falls.

Learning of what has occurred, the priest's superior, Father Gabriel, pledges to venture up into the dense jungle above the falls. He will seek out this tribe, the Guarani, and attempt to reach out to them with the grace of Christ.

An arduous journey brings Gabriel and two companions to the foot of the falls, where they build a monument to their slain brother. Then Gabriel proceeds alone, scraping his way upward beside the crushing flow of water.

Cresting the top of the falls, Gabriel knows the danger has only begun. It is Guarani territory, and the mottled green around him will soon glint with dark eyes and arrow points. Gabriel does not speak a word of the tribe's dialect, so he must find some other means of connection. Failure guarantees death.

He sits on a large stone and removes the cloth from a slender parcel he had slung over his shoulder, an oboe. Fingers trembling, Gabriel brings it to his lips. One note, then another. A haunting tune rises into the jungle canopy and filters out over tangled trails.

The eyes and gleaming blades Gabriel has expected soon appear in the shadows. A moment later the squat, dark-skinned men emerge, their black hair painted with stripes of maroon—the Guarani. It is clear they find the sound pleasing, mesmerizing. As Gabriel well knows, the native people of the region delight in music.

One stocky Guarani steps forward, his face twisted in a scowl. He grabs the oboe as if it were a viper, then breaks it over his knee. Fear tightens Gabriel's face. A moment later, however, another native picks the broken instrument from the ground. He places its broken ends together and hands it to the priest, motioning for him to play. Gabriel blows into the end, but only a faint whistle emerges. He shakes his head.

The other tribesmen, however, smile. One reaches for Gabriel's hand and lifts him to his feet. In the midst of the warriors, he is led into the village, welcomed.

Gabriel had discovered the heart language *of the Guarani.*

Each of us holds unique heart languages. These are the activities, symbols, or even objects in which we find special pleasure and delight.

Our words and ideas become incarnate when they are delivered in the heart language of another.

Sometimes a heart language is a literal language—Russian, Mandarin, or Spanish. If you've ever seen the glow on the face of an immigrant who is addressed unexpectedly in her native tongue, you know how meaningful such incarnation can be.

Just as often, however, what is required to learn another's heart language is subtler than study of a foreign dialect.

Law enforcement experts working with youth gangs report that effective interaction with young gang members requires learning to speak their heart language: *respect*. If a street cop can learn to speak this *language*, he will build rapport and gain respect for himself as well. Experts advise, for instance, never asking questions or dictating orders to a large group. Instead, inquire as to who is the gang's leader, and take him aside. Explain your concerns and what you are asking him to do. More often than not, he will honor the request and bring the group into agreement also. Most of the other young men will value your decision to use their currency as well.

Perhaps more than anywhere else, heart languages are critical in expressing love.

Marriage counselor Dr. Gary Chapman has suggested that spouses, lovers, and friends use five distinct *love languages* to give and receive affection. Each individual, he argues, experiences love most fully through only one of the five—physical touch, gifts, quality time, affirmation, or acts of service. Typically, individuals attempt to convey love the way they like to receive it: through their own primary love language. But no matter how sincere, these efforts can fall flat. If we are to truly communicate love to another, concludes Dr. Chapman, we must learn to speak love to them using *their* primary language rather than our own.[2]

The fullest connections always require us to move beyond our own native language. We must learn the unique words, images, symbols, and means that carry gut-level meaning for those we seek to serve, their heart language.

Jesus did this continually. For example, although He was a builder by trade, only a handful of Jesus's examples came from carpentry. Instead, most were drawn from the daily labors of the farmers, fishermen, and homemakers who filled His audiences: fields ripe for harvest, fish being separated at the end of the day, or yeast in a batch of dough.

Today this same decision may mean a husband learning to give gifts at unexpected times—even if he experiences love more fully through physical touch. For a parent, it's becoming familiar with a teenager's favorite bands. A heart language could involve a new sport or hobby, sign language, ethnic food, or old books. Whatever it may be, discovering another person's heart language—and learning to speak it—will incarnate our words like nothing else.

THE COST OF INCARNATION—AND REWARDS

It is said that British statesman and financier Cecil Rhodes was always flawlessly dressed. One evening a young man who had been invited to dine with Rhodes arrived late. The fellow's train had just pulled into town, and he had no chance to change his wrinkled, travel-stained clothes. Rhodes's other guests were already present, dressed with a precision worthy of their host. The young man joined the group, cringing internally with every glance that fell upon his clothing. Rhodes appeared later than expected. He was not dressed in his always-impressive evening attire, but in a dingy old blue suit. Later, the young man discovered that Rhodes had been wearing evening clothes but, hearing what had occurred, changed into the old suit to put his young guest at ease.

Even more than learning and effort, the active ingredient in incarnation is humility. If our own image and priorities remain paramount, we will never take off our tuxedo and put on the old blue suit. Nor will we bother to learn the heart language of the Guarani, move to Moloka'i, or even spend the time necessary to really understand others. Pride will always seek to communicate from a position of power—above, distant, superior, strong.

> This generation will never believe our gospel that God can be their father unless we are willing to step into their fatherlessness with the same intimacy that Christ stepped into our world at the incarnation.[3]
> —JOHN SOWERS, EXECUTIVE DIRECTOR OF
> THE MENTORING PROJECT

The best communicators, however, those like Jesus, will always bend down, just as He did when He wrapped a servant's towel around His waist and knelt to wash the feet of His students.

The costs of this communication can be high. To connect with the Chinese, Hudson Taylor hazarded the loss of respect from Westerners, and even a lower status in the eyes of many Chinese. Drawing near to wounded soldiers meant Clara Barton would not wait in safety for them to be brought to her. For Father Damien, it meant Moloka'i.

Yet this reckless journey of incarnation is the invitation made to every apprentice of Jesus. In the apostle Paul's stirring words:

> Your attitude should be the same as that of Christ Jesus: Who, being in very nature God, did not consider equality with God something to be grasped, but made himself nothing, taking the very nature of a servant, being made in human likeness. And being found in appearance as a man, he humbled himself and became obedient to death—even death on a cross! Therefore God exalted him to the highest place and gave him the name that is above every name.[4]

Even in much less dramatic situations there are still risks and costs. We will make mistakes, bumbling in a new language or culture. Our motives may be misunderstood. And the effort will almost certainly take far too much of our precious time.

Personal Notes: Jedd

There have been times while traveling in Asia or Africa or Central America that I rarely strayed from Western hotels, comfortable meeting rooms, and tourist sites. At others, I've lived in the homes of local people for weeks or longer: listening to their stories and songs, eating from their dishes, catching glimpses of life through their lens. Can you guess which kind of travel one tends to remember the most?

Truth be told, the closer I get to real people, the less convenient and comfortable the experience usually is…and the better too. It's a bit like the difference between crossing India by train in first class or third class. First class puts you in your own little air-conditioned box, quiet and comfortable. The countryside rolls by through a small window, as distant as a show on the Discovery Channel. Third class puts you out with the crowds, jostling for space amidst odors, noise, and kaleidoscopic colors. It's tougher, but you see more, learn more, are challenged and enriched more.

There have certainly been times while traveling when I've been oh so thankful for quiet and clean space, a hot shower, an American burger. But ultimately, whether traveling for work, study, or otherwise, it is always far richer when I choose to be nearer to others, open, and engaged. More of them stays with me, and more of me stays with them.

I can't say I'd choose a third-class train berth every time, but I know life is almost always fuller when I makes choices that draw me (sometimes force me) nearer to people.

But if we wish to connect—to *communicare*—there is no alternative.

And as we do, we come to see that the rewards far outweigh the costs. We will not only increasingly impact others; we will find ourselves changed as well. For the act of incarnation teaches us, even as we seek to teach others. It opens our eyes to things we'd never have seen from a distance; wakes new emotions; expands our experience of both sorrow and joy.

This is why the Book of Hebrews makes much of the fact that Jesus, although carrying all of the fullness of God, was yet somehow "made perfect" through the suffering He experienced in His incarnation.[5] Because of the incarnation, Hebrews explains, our Lord is not "unable to sympathize with our weaknesses, but... has been tempted in every way, just as we are..."[6] If God somehow enriched Himself through the incarnation—mysterious though this is—we have good reason to suspect that even our small choices to follow Jesus in this will leave us richer as well.

Esther Havens is a humanitarian photographer, capturing breathtaking images of people and situations around the globe. She shares that when she first began as a photojournalist, she was taught that it was necessary—even a moral obligation—to remain utterly detached from the scenes she captured: famine, disease, death. And she's seen it all.

But one day in Africa, Esther caught sight of a pathos-rich image: a small boy, severely malnourished, his belly distended. On autopilot, she aimed her camera and snapped a shot. "Great picture," she thought as she tromped away. But suddenly it struck her. "I didn't even bother to speak with him. I didn't even ask his name."

Something in Esther changed that day. She realized she'd been using people in poverty for her own gain. It'd been about her portfolio, her great photo or recognition. But no more. From now on she would work to make her art about the people she photographed—capturing their stories in ways that could help and honor them. She would no longer remain aloof. She would draw near to them, seeking to love the individual and see through *their* eyes.

To do this, Esther set new rules that have guided her work ever since. "Always put myself in their shoes before taking the picture. Ask myself, 'How does God see this person?' Ask myself, 'Am I taking this picture for myself or for them?' Connect with the person I'm photographing."

Now whenever possible, before taking a photo, Esther asks people if she can tell their story. She asks if she can partner with them to speak to the world. Admittedly, she snaps fewer of the gripping candid images she once did. But even a glance over Esther's photos makes it hard not to feel that what she captures now is far more powerful. For Esther has learned, and her photos *show*, that "who we are is not our circumstance, however difficult that may be."[7] Esther's subjects are mostly people the world would consider the lowly and destitute. But her photos tell a deeper story, capturing beauty, strength, and joy amidst great brokenness. They offer a glimpse of the glory in each person that is the *Imago Dei*.[8]

THE KISS

In *Mortal Lessons: Notes on the Art of Surgery*, Dr. Richard Selzer describes a scene he observed in a hospital room following an operation:

> I stand by the bed where a young woman lies, her face postoperative, her mouth twisted in a palsy, clownish. A tiny twig of a facial nerve, the one to the muscles of her mouth, has been severed. She will be thus from now on. The surgeon had followed with religious fervor the curve of her flesh; I promise you that. Nevertheless, to remove the tumor in her cheek, I had to cut the little nerve.
>
> Her husband is in the room. He stands on the opposite side of the bed, and together, they seem to dwell in the evening lamplight. Isolated from me, private. Who are they, I ask myself, he and this wry-mouth I have made, who gaze at each other, and touch each other generously, greedily?
>
> The young woman speaks. "Will I always be like this?" she asks. "Yes," I say. "It is because the nerve was cut." She nods and is silent. But the young man smiles. "I like it," he says. "It's kind of cute."
>
> All at once I know who he is. I understand, and I lower my gaze. One is not bold in an encounter with a god. Unmindful, he bends to kiss her crooked mouth, and I am so close I can see how he twists his own lips to accommodate hers, to show that their kiss still works. I remember that the gods appeared in ancient Greece as mortals, and I hold my breath and let the wonder in.[9]

Yes, *this* is incarnation: conforming our lips to the distortions of another…drawing near…taking on flesh…meeting on their turf and in their terms.

In every such act, real communication is born. *Communicare*. Community. Compassion. Communion. In a flickered reflection of the Incarnation, what once was far apart draws near. We come close and touch. And as we do, the electricity of life, thought, ideas, and intimacy flows between us.

Section V

LIFE THROUGH
AUTHENTICITY

Upend a Life of Image and Spin

Chapter 9

A DROUGHT OF THE REAL

Whatever else may be said of people today, it is safe to assume they're thirsty. Most all of us are. We'd pay just about any price for even a few refreshing droplets of something real, lasting, and true. We long for *authenticity*.

Authenticity itself has become a buzzword. "I love to be my authentic self," declared Katie Couric. "I believe in being as authentic as possible," Hillary Clinton expressed to *Glamour* magazine. "In everything I've done, I've always tried to just be authentic and real," newsman Anderson Cooper told the *Vancouver Sun*.[1]

Yet deep down, it's hard not to suspect that so much talk about authenticity is most of all a tribute to its absence.

Assembly lines and TV studios can mass produce just about anything else. But not this. Instead, they must offer an endless stream of all-too-unreal *reality shows* and products carefully manufactured by the thousands to appear as one of a kind.

And so we wander in a desert of spin, hype, and well-manicured impressions. It's the mirages painted by advertising, the wax-figure smile of the woman in the pew next to us.

No wonder we're thirsty.

But though it may seem impossible, refreshment lies near at hand. Apprentices to Jesus find ways to drill down and draw it up. They strive to allow others to experience things as they are. It is this *encounter with the real* that can give our communication that rare, thirst-slaking quality that people are panting for: authenticity.

THE RAGGED-EDGED REAL

The pious clergyman stood at his favorite spot in the temple courtyard for prayer. It was just far enough from the gate to be unobtrusive but still easily noticed. People needed to see a good example, he knew. His silvering hair appeared dry and tangled—he had not run any oil through it today, a clear indication that he was again fasting. His eyes swept the court-yard, narrowing slightly as he caught sight of one of those insufferable tax collectors huddled in the far corner.

Raising his face to the sky, the clergyman began, words well enunciated, just loud enough for passersby to hear—"I thank You, God. Yes, I *thank* You. I am no thief, no doer of injustice, no thinker of lustful thought. I am nothing like such men. Twice a week, I go without eating so I can devote myself to prayer. I faithfully give generously of my wealth to You. Yes, I thank You…"

His eyes closed for a blissful moment as he finished. He then began toward the exit, slowly. Beneath his beard, a smile played upon his lips. He could feel admiring eyes upon his back.

Though nearby, the tax collector had not noticed the clergyman's prayer. He bent low, his lips pressed hard against a clinched hand. An anguished sigh slipped from his lips. He knew his guilt—bribing officials, extorting extra fees from business owners, even squeezing extra pennies out of the widow. Oh, how he now desired to change! What could he say? He choked back the tears, finally stuttering, "Have mercy on me, God, a sinner."

The sun was casting long shadows when the tax collector finally rose. No one seemed to observe as he passed quickly from the courtyard, his eyes moist but bright with relief.

As Jesus explained at the end of this parable, the clergyman's prayer failed entirely to impress God.[2] Even if his behavior was as spotless as he let on, his pride and smugness soured it all. The tax collector's simple words, however, were different. Despite his past failings and inarticulate sput-tering, God received the humble honesty with welcome.

God is not, of course, the only one who feels this way. For most of us presentations that smack of self-importance or insincerity, even if impec-cably delivered, produce little but annoyance. In contrast, words flowing from the heart in truthful humility wake our warmth and interest.

For most of us, even a pinch of heart and soul can outweigh a boatload of Toastmasters' savvy.

Personal Notes: Erik

There are three things you'll rarely hear in politics:

1. I was wrong (confessing before you're caught).
2. That's a good point (validating an opponent's argument).
3. I don't know (admitting you don't have *all* the answers).

Jedd and I have spent the majority of our careers in politics, and with my prompting, I hope he will return someday soon; Lord willing, I hope I am done with it forever—at least as a paid staffer.

There's an old saying on "The Hill" that "sunshine is the best disinfectant," and it's true, really. The light of day is healthy and healing, especially in politics. Press secretaries (yes, I am guilty) and speechwriters (yes, guilty again) shape the images and ideas of today's leaders. Decisions are tested by polls and focus groups. Spin and crisis management are a daily occurrence. The stakes are far too high to show weakness, indecision, or failings.

It was interesting, then, when a group of consultants approached my boss one day with an idea. The year was 1999, and my boss, a newly elected member of Congress, had come from the advertising world where he marketed products such as St. Pauli Girl beer. The party was looking for a message, and leaders thought he could help.

Several members and their staffs lined the walls as the consultants pushed play on the video tape. The images and voiceover were typical. Proudly patriotic. A list of accomplishments. A heralding of bills passed and ideas advanced. Eyes rolled in the room. We'd seen similar ads before.

But then came the tag line:

Republicans in Congress. Not perfect, but getting the job done.

I loved it. But no one seemed to agree. And that was that. The ad never saw the light of day.

No one imagines that political leaders are perfect. But any admission otherwise is read as a mistake. And there lies the problem—more so now than thirteen years ago. We perceive transparency as weakness, not honesty.

I still have the video. I'm still waiting for someone to stand at the podium and, when asked by a vulturistic media, "What is your biggest mistake?", for the man or woman to tell us the truth.

To finally admit publicly what we all know to be true: that we're not perfect

WHY DO WE HIDE?

Deep down most of us know that our relationships will be shallow and our influence tepid if we shun authenticity. So then why is it so rare?

Very simply, because we fear.

We fear the deflation of our image and diminishment in the eyes of those who respect us. We fear rejection. We fear we will undermine the causes we believe in or the faith we want others to embrace. We fear our longings will be mocked and our dreams dismissed. We fear followers will no longer follow, our children will no longer respect us, students will no longer listen, and admirers will no longer admire.

So we remain no more transparent than canal water, revealing a shadowed outline here or there, but leaving our deeper thoughts, fears, failings, and hopes hidden beneath the murk.

We glide past each other...because we never dare to give ourselves.[3]

—DAG HAMMARSKJÖLD

John Eldredge sums it up well in *Wild at Heart*, comparing the way we veil our true selves to how Adam and Eve concealed themselves behind the foliage in the Garden of Eden: "We are hiding, every last one of us. Well aware that we, too, are not what we were meant to be, desperately afraid of exposure, terrified of being seen for what we are and *are not*, we have run off into the bushes. We hide in our office, at the gym, behind the newspaper and mostly *behind our personality*. Most of what you encounter when you meet a man is a façade, an elaborate fig leaf, a brilliant disguise."[4]

It is not hard to see why we feel our persona must be nearly flawless. After all, everyone else is, it seems—at least, everyone who matters.

Consider the fact that for every alluring photo included in *Sports Illustrated*'s yearly swimsuit edition, roughly twenty-five thousand photographs are taken and discarded. And that is *after* starting with statuesque models who likely have undergone intense dieting, rigorous exercise, and scores of cosmetic surgeries—not to mention the lights, makeup, and exotic settings. Tragically, countless women hold such photos as the standard for beauty, with devastating consequences for their health, confidence, and sense of priorities.

Of course beauty is not the only measuring stick. We are just as easily drawn toward elusive ideals in professional success, family life, popularity, or general having-it-all-togetherness. If we wish to influence or even be accepted by others, we feel we had best keep our all too real shortcomings submerged.

But what type of person influences you? Only the flawless? What is it that draws *you* up on your tiptoes to listen? What tugs at not just your eyes but also your heart? Certainly, carefully crafted images of beauty, power, and success are alluring. But do they leave lasting impact or merely fade as quickly as they are replaced?

The truth is, we are drawn to the ragged-edged real, even over the sleek and the smooth.

AN ENCOUNTER WITH THE REAL

Jesus's way of communicating continually led toward authenticity, an encounter with the real. He wove His very self into His communication, presenting not only concepts and instructions but also His personhood, as

He truly was. This startling approach cowed His enemies and stirred the crowds to awe.

Three qualities in particular made Jesus's communication authentic.

1. Jesus exhibited extraordinary vulnerability.

It would be hard to find a greater contrast than Jesus to today's model communicator. Plenty of successful politicians and TV personalities embody it: slick, polished, and unflappable, glimmering smiles with whitened teeth. In sharp contrast, Jesus made no attempt to bury the messy edges of life and tangled emotions that most of us keep carefully tucked away in our back pockets. Distress and elation, dependence and affection, anguish and need were all threads within Jesus's communication—just as they form the fabric of life.

When students Jesus had sent out returned glowing with success, Jesus gushed with thankfulness to God.[5] Facing a band of arrogant clergy, His face darkened with frustration at their indifference to human suffering.[6] When many of His followers were abandoning Him, Jesus turned to the disciples, His words gentle and exposed: "You do not want to leave too, do you?" He asked.[7] Arriving in Jerusalem to the songs of adoring crowds, Jesus wept in their midst at the hard-heartedness that had marked many inhabitants of that city in every generation.[8] Again and again Jesus's disciples took note of His overflowing tenderness toward the hapless masses.[9]

Even as He sensed His death approaching, Jesus did not grow silent or distant as one might expect. Despite His steely determination, He bared His heart to His friends and begged them to remain near. "My soul is overwhelmed with sorrow to the point of death. Stay here and keep watch with me."[10]

From first to last Jesus allowed His true self to radiate through His communication—even those elements that might seem to diminish stature or nobility. This vulnerability did not dull His impact or blunt His influence; it only made them brighter and sharper.

2. Jesus spoke with a startling forthrightness.

It is easy to imagine Jesus as the Sunday school cutout figure, smiling demurely with a lamb slung over His shoulders. And no wonder. Bright-eyed children delighted in Jesus's presence, and His companions marveled at the grace and mercy He consistently conveyed.

Even so, Jesus did not hesitate to deliver hard words that needed to be heard. His language could strike like brass knuckles when necessary—condemning injustice, exposing half-truths, or confronting double standards.

Significantly, Jesus directed His harshest words toward those who embodied the *opposite* of authenticity. To the strutting spiritual leaders who disguised their flaws behind façades of perfection, Jesus gave the label *hypocrites*—literally, "actors." He took a sledgehammer to their stony hearts. "You are blind guides," He declared. "A brood of vipers. Whitewashed tombs full of dead men's bones."[11]

Jesus did not attempt to soft sell the life He was offering either. Today, effective salespersons turn prospective buyers' focus away from costs and onto benefits—"Just imagine how good it will feel to get behind the wheel." Jesus did the opposite. "If you buy what I am selling," He warned, "it will involve death to self, the loss of many things you think you most want; consider the cost carefully before you begin."

Personal Notes: Jedd

There may be no theme more praised and pursued in Christian books, conferences, and discussion than *being relevant*. We want it. Badly.

I'll admit that's often the case for me, at least since sixth grade. That summer I decided it was time I finally caught up with current fashion. The first day of school I arrived with an upturned collar on a blue candy-striped shirt, a white cloth belt, and pegged pants rolled up to my ankles. It took just five minutes (and a few mocking words from an eighth grader) to realize I was parroting the style of the *prior* year, not the current one. At the first opportunity, I changed into my PE uniform for the rest of the day.

There's much to be said for relevance. I agree with a friend who suggests that faithful Christians should be reading the Scriptures in one hand and the *Wall Street Journal* in the other. We need to understand our culture and speak its language in order to engage it.

But much of what is viewed as relevance in the church today is little more than skill at *mirroring the broader culture*. When this happens, we soon have little to offer to society that it doesn't already have—including its prejudices, excesses, and mistaken assumptions.

And here's the simple truth that is hard for me to swallow: what the world needs most is *not* my relevance.

Nor has it in any age. Many of the most vibrant moments of Christian history came as believers accepted a bold, prophetic role—even to the loss of perceived relevance. These were the counter-cultural Christ-followers who called for an end to Rome's gladiator blood fests; argued against the progressive *eugenics* programs of the 1930s; fought the caste system in India; stood with steadfast Christian witnesses behind the Iron Curtain.

Yes, I'm inspired by these examples. But I realize my eagerness to speak and live in the bold manner of Jesus starts to ebb when it might decrease my perceived relevance. I want badly to be liked, respected, wanted in the room. I get excited when the *New York Times* calls for an interview.

But if I'm serious about being an authentic reflection of Jesus, I need to be willing to say and live what's good and true... perhaps especially when it's out of sync with the spirit of the age. Even if that means not getting quoted in the *Times* or asked to speak at conferences.

3. Jesus made Himself surprisingly accessible.

Conventional wisdom notes that familiarity breeds contempt. Those who wish to be revered, therefore, make their appearances short and tightly controlled. Many celebrities, politicians, and circuit speakers operate with the same basic plan: deliver what you have to say, shake a few hands, and then head for the door.

Jesus's approach could not have been more different. He made His place continually *with* the people, walking their streets, teaching on familiar hillsides and lakeshores, sharing meals in their homes. Children crawled up into His lap, the sick grasped at His clothing, and a prostitute washed His feet in her tears.

Jesus offered Himself even more freely to His primary students. As the Gospel of Mark describes, He set apart twelve disciples, "that they might *be with* him."[12] And they were, continuously—traveling, eating, sleeping, struggling, celebrating—always together. As professor Robert Coleman noted in his insightful study of Jesus's teaching methods, "Amazing as it may seem, all Jesus did to teach these men his way was to draw them close to himself. He was his own school and curriculum.... Knowledge was not communicated by the Master in terms of laws and dogmas, but in the living personality of One who walked among them."[13]

JESUS'S AUTHENTICITY MIRRORED BY HIS DISCIPLES

The consistent authenticity of Jesus's communication was not lost on His disciples. Years down the road, as Matthew, John, Peter, and others helped put the accounts of their experiences with Jesus into written form, they embraced the same principle.

It would have been tempting to do otherwise. After all, these men had by now become esteemed leaders of the burgeoning community of Christian believers. One could easily have argued that the success of the movement depended heavily upon carefully cultivating their own reputation and status.

But like their master, they chose vulnerable truth-telling over burnished image.

The disciples, as presented by their own writings, are anything but larger-than-life heroes. In fact, the Gospels portray their authors as just the opposite: painfully unperceptive and slow to learn, feeble in faith, given to superstition and fear, continually asking dull questions and expressing timid doubts, and scattering at the first hints of danger.

Even at their final meal with Jesus, they squabble over who would be the greatest among them. As their master sweats blood in anticipation of His death, they fall asleep, just yards away. When a band of brigands arrives to arrest Him, they disappear into the darkness, some denying they ever knew Him.

Describing their experiences with Jesus, these men faithfully offer readers of the Gospels nothing less than an encounter with the real. They present themselves not as towers of virtue or saintly heroes, but as they really were: a ragtag collection of stragglers, doubters, and screwups whom Jesus chose to embrace.

Yet this authenticity did not diminish their ability to communicate with power. If anything, it only increased it. And the books they wrote? They are the most-read texts of all time.

AUTHENTICITY REVIVES

Samuel Taylor Coleridge's famous tale, "The Rime of the Ancient Mariner," describes sailors dying of thirst. The seamen's ship is stranded in windless seas, battered by a merciless sun. The poem's most famous line—"Water, water everywhere, [but not a] drop to drink"[14]—is descriptive of our culture as well. All around are seas promising refreshing authenticity. But it seems the deeper we drink of them, the thirstier we grow.

When authenticity is lacking, relationships wither. Community is desiccated. But like soft rain falling on parched sailors, our decisions to grow more authentic in our words and presence bring new life.

First, from authenticity faded trust begins to grow anew.

Public trust seems to slide ever lower, driven by the never-ending parade of baseless advertising claims, campaign mudslinging, and corporate scandals. The results of a *New York Times*/CBS News poll indicated nearly two-thirds of respondents believed that in dealing with "most people," you simply "can't be too careful." Interestingly, however, the same study also showed that the respondents believed that of the people they "know personally," a full 85 percent would "try to be fair."[15]

Other studies reveal a similar reality: when people feel that they know us, they are far more likely to view us and our words as honest, fair, and well intentioned. By opening our lives and inviting others in, authentic communication builds that sort of trust. With even a basic familiarity, others become more willing to receive what we have to say. As it becomes apparent that we are willing to reveal the *whole* truth—our limitations and weaknesses, the "other side" of an issue, shortcomings of our plan—this effect only grows.

Authentic communication goes beyond merely avoiding lies. Communication becomes authentic as it reveals the whole truth—awkward, vulnerable, and inconvenient as it may be. It is a home seller disclosing an issue no one would have noticed, a researcher pointing out potential flaws in her findings, or an apologist for the faith acknowledging questions he doesn't know how to answer. Choosing this path builds trust and adds a weight to our words that no mere technique could ever buy.

In a tribute to the great author and media theorist Neil Postman, a former student attributed Postman's fabled effectiveness as a teacher to this sort of authenticity. Although his reputation as a thinker was legend, Postman made his claims with an authentic humility, always "[acknowledging] the possibility that he may be mistaken." This, noted the student, "was the essence of what made him such a great force in teaching. He felt things strongly, and articulated them wisely—often with a wink and a smile—but was always willing to concede the possibility that his feelings were stronger than his facts, which made us all the more likely to agree with him."[16]

Authenticity presents our messy situations, flawed selves, and fallible conclusions as they really are—messy, flawed, and fallible. And so it builds confidence and trust like nothing else.

A second sweet fruit grows from authenticity as well: the refreshment of reconciliation.

No matter how well articulated, words inevitably arrive stillborn when delivered into an environment of suspicion, anger, fear, or bitterness. In such circumstances, to speak the whole truth with authenticity is often the first and most necessary balm.

Personal Notes: Jedd

Three close friends and I wrote the book *Four Souls* together, weaving the true tales and reflections from our shared journey around the globe.

Our intent was to write with transparency, holding nothing back. Along with our brighter and braver moments, we would lay bare our blunders, quarrels, and insecurities.

I see now that our authenticity in the book was only partial. As much as we desired to communicate with transparency, the deep-down inclination to preserve image remains tenacious. We did *want* to be transparent, but perhaps not always to the extent that readers would think much less of us..

Despite this, some of the stories did come through with transparency, giving honest glimpses into things we might have preferred to hide. Painful struggle with faith and doubt. Intense conflicts spurred by my selfishness. An embarrassingly self-absorbed crush I had for a Russian girl. My way-over-the-top competitiveness in a soccer game with orphans.

Hearing from people who've read the book, it's struck me that these are the stories they tend to bring up. What most sparked their interest and sense of personal connection were the same accounts I'd have most wanted to leave out.

When readers do mention our "brighter" moments, those also are mostly accounts that touch deep-down things that weren't easy to share. How four young men, despite our conflicts, sincerely loved each other. The almost-desperate yearning to live wholeheartedly for Christ that had brought us together in the first place. Our practice of reconciling each night over any hurts we'd done to one another.

It was these more raw and honest expressions—not our nobler moments nor the more adventurous tales—that readers found most meaningful. The places of greatest vulnerability are often the places of greatest connection.[17]

Tom Tarrants, who served as the director of the respected C. S. Lewis Institute, was once feared across America as a terrorist with the White Knights of the Ku Klux Klan. His crimes, particularly violence against African Americans, landed his name on the FBI's most wanted list.

When asked if African Americans are willing to receive him now, Tarrants shared that he often feels more welcomed by the black community than anywhere else. Why? He explains that when he speaks, he always comes clean with his past bigotry and the wrongs he has done. In a community that often feels a subtle racism from even many enlightened whites, Tarrants's openness about matters that usually remain beneath the surface is a salve to deep wounds. It enables forgiveness and healing to begin. Authenticity is always the first step in reconciliation.

Finally, authenticity yields its highest blessing: the rich kinship of intimacy.

We are often inclined to feel we have nothing in common with certain people. Such a thought is always mistaken. Although often far beneath the surface, our deepest human experiences and emotions share far more than they differ.

This territory is the realm of weakness and aspiration, our failures and hopes, fears and passions. When we dare to enter that land with others by sharing with honesty, we inevitably find our listeners already there, ahead of us. For every person we encounter knows more sorrow and more joy than we assume at first glance.

To meet another in this humble place almost always involves an invigorating discovery. Suddenly we are no longer alone. Someone else has experienced *it* too. The sensation is akin to finding an aloof office mate seated next to you in a hospital waiting room, his hair disheveled and eyes redrimmed. Or like a child seeing her second-grade teacher at the grocery store in swim trunks and a T-shirt. Once encountered in such a way, the person never seems quite so distant. With excitement we discover new connections and common ground.

In the book *A Severe Mercy*, writer Sheldon Vanauken offers a breathtaking look into his own heart and the story of his romance, love, and ultimate loss to cancer of his wife, Davy. He allows the reader to gaze in upon his deepest hopes and anguish, failures and pride, desperate love, and tragic loss.

Vanauken reported that soon after his book was published, the flood of letters, phone calls, and visitors began. Many readers expressed feeling as if they and they alone had been penetrated to the depths of their being. They sensed that a deep and mysterious kinship had grown between themselves and the author. Vanauken agreed, but reminded that the kinship they felt was much broader than any of them knew.

He explained, "It is, I think, that we are all so alone in what lies deepest in our souls, so unable to find the words and perhaps the courage to speak with unlocked hearts, that we do not know at all that it is the same with others. And since I had been compelled, somewhat reluctantly, to go beyond reticence, readers were moved to kinship with one they felt to be the only other being who also knew."[18]

Those like Vanauken who are committed to authentic communication consistently *give name* to the feelings, sensations, and experiences others have known but have never uttered. Inevitably, such sharing touches both hearts and minds, knitting us to others with an intimacy we may have never before experienced.

Chapter 10

A DRAUGHT OF THE REAL

Erik is reminded almost daily that the entertainment industry isn't the first place to go searching for authenticity. It's the land of make-believe, of suspended disbelief, of smoke-and-mirrors, of special effects and auto-tune. The world pays Hollywood for a certain inauthenticity.

The inauthenticity is especially palpable behind the scenes, where the currency of the industry is perception and momentum. Who is today's hot item? What movies are performing best at the box office this weekend? What artist is selling out shows? The answers determine what high-level executives decide to put on the air, green light for production, and make a Q4 priority.

No wonder the out-of-work producer drives the new BMW and wears the Tom Ford suit. It's why movie billboards line the streets most driven by studio executives. It's why once-hot stars live in fear of the dictum, "You are only as good as your last project."

Perception matters. There are times, however, when authenticity takes the stage.

Two years ago the music of Owl City became a top priority for Universal Music. Adam Young, the singer, had emerged from his basement with a new sound and an explosive online fan base. His first publicized concerts sold out in hours—his first public performances ever! Soon his songs were rocketing up the charts around the globe. It was the dream of every artist: label priority, sold-out shows, and millions of fans who clamored for more.

Typically, artists start taking risks after a few double platinum albums. It's easier to do the unexpected, go off script when you are a legend, when you know fans will stick with you through your political rants or your quirky new album. Not Owl City. Adam took a risk early on, and his choice astonished many. It reflected the authentic heart of an artist who dared to speak from his platform with the passion of his soul.

On his blog he wrote:

> I'm twenty four years old, yet something about this song makes me
> bawl like a baby....If I were to count on one hand, the number of
> songs that have ever deeply moved me, this one would take the cake.
> Last night I probably spent more time actually crying at the piano
> than I did recording it. Such are the secret confessions of a shy boy
> from Minnesota.

The song? "In Christ Alone" by Keith Getty and Stuart Townend.
Adam finished his blog with:

> As I'm so often reminded what a priceless gift my life is, I ache with
> everything in me to make it count, so that when I finally cross the
> finish line, I'll hear the words, *"Well done, good and faithful servant."*
> To me, there is no greater reward.
>
> Of course, all of this weighs heavily on the spiritual scale, so
> allow me to be completely honest and say none of it is intended to
> be "crammed down the throat," if you will. That is not my intention.
> This is what I wholeheartedly believe, and to that belief, I remain
> steadfast until He returns or calls me home.[1]

Astonishing authenticity.

FAUX AUTHENTIC

Becoming an authentic communicator is not as simple as some imagine.
Shortcuts are everywhere. They promise of easy intimacy, or trying to
appear rugged and real without the risk.

Perhaps because it is so easy to exhibit our dirty laundry before the
world via blog post or Facebook update, *authenticity* is often confused with
letting it all hang out. Snarky comments or admissions of (typically forgiv-
able) flaws are offered up as proof of how remarkably real we are. But such
shortcuts offer only a little more honesty than the everything-is-marvelous
shallowness they seem to reject. *Both* are carefully managed to cultivate an
image, often one that hides as much as it reveals.

Real authenticity is not earned so easily. It cannot be grasped just by
throwing off restraint or verbal streaking, or by being crass or rude. All
these, in fact, are often just ways to avoid authenticity—boisterously
drawing attention away from one's own broken and hurting soul.

Nor is authenticity found by grasping for unearned intimacy by exposing our souls to others cheaply, before it is time. *Hooking up*, whether via casual sex or emotionally charged conversation, knows little of authenticity. Frequently it is its opposite, acting as a means to cover for insecurity and desperate need. Such choices exchange the hard and humbling process of building true intimacy for something thin and synthetic. Such closeness will be lost as quickly as it is gained.

Flawed as they are, these forms of faux authenticity are often affirmed in the stories told by Hollywood. From *The Bridges of Madison County* to *The Ugly Truth*, movies routinely present an uninhibited, *be yourself at any cost* authenticity as the highest of all values. It is exalted above traditional virtues such as self-sacrifice, kindness, or fidelity. The only unpardonable sin is failing to *listen to your heart*—even when doing so requires profound selfishness or disloyalty. The hope of growth and changing for the better is replaced by the ethic that *when all is known, all is forgiven*.

All of these imitations distort our sense of real authenticity and exalt cheap replacements. Baring our souls is equated with enlarging our souls. A willingness to show is confused with something worth seeing. And the mere act of revealing is mistaken for real character. Such approaches may be stimulating or create the illusion of authenticity. But they do not take us to places of lasting trust and real intimacy.

THE HARD WORK OF CARVING AUTHENTICITY

Personal Notes: Jedd

Coming from the wrong person, the words might have seemed shallow or self-congratulatory. But I sensed that Pastor Bob was the real deal. He'd come from retirement to help out when our pastor died suddenly. His head was bald as a bowling ball, but he glowed with vigor and sober joy.

"I'm a stumbler still," Bob shared one Sunday morning. "But I'm also very different than I was thirty years ago. I was a Christian then too, but God keeps growing me. Ask my wife, she'll tell you. I'm gentler than I was. Less likely to get angry. More giving. Think less about myself and more of others. Listen, I don't say that to highlight myself. I just want you to know that making the hard choices to follow Jesus has an impact. It *can* change you."

Those words moved me. "That's what I want," I thought. It struck me that I'd heard countless speakers share of their struggles. But virtually none seemed willing to speak personally of growth and change too. It was as if they felt humility required them only to confess the bad, not the good.

Bob was so compelling because he spoke of both. Like Paul, he saw himself as a chief of sinners. Yet he also was willing to let us know that he was pressing on toward the goal, that he was indeed being transformed to reflect the likeness of Christ.[2]

> Bob hadn't been with us long when an aggressive cancer took root in his body. We all hurt together as Bob atrophied before our eyes. But we could also see clearly: though outwardly he was wasting away, fresh life continued to spring from inside. Until his last breath, Bob's words and face reflected the spirit of Jesus.
>
> It was that rare combination that was so breathtaking. Not the shiny-happy Christianity on one side. Nor only the *I'm nothing but a worm* hand-wringing on the other. Like Jesus, Paul, and the Psalms, Bob's authenticity rang with both beauty and brokenness, honestly told.

Dr. Stephen Covey made a remarkable discovery in his landmark research into American success literature written from 1776 to 1976. For the first one hundred fifty years the literature emphasized development of character and abilities as the sure path to success. Covey labeled this approach the *character ethic.* The subsequent fifty years of success literature, in contrast, focused heavily on the use of surface level techniques and personality skills to portray a successful image—whether or not this image coincided with underlying reality. Covey called this the *personality ethic.* He has noted that despite lip service to the contrary, this focus on image and personality has become even more pronounced over recent decades.

The personality ethic is hard to resist. Everyone wants to be well received. We desire to impress, if only the small circle of friends at the dinner party. The personality ethic is the easy way, requiring only cosmetic self-improvement and easily attained skills.

Growing character is the harder road. Impression settles for a quick coat of cheerful paint over rotted boards; character repairs with lumber, nails, and sweat. Impression seeks a slim waist using diet pills or a cinched-up corset; character relies on exercise and vegetables. Impression seeks to impress others with a power suit and firm handshake; character always pairs such externals with real competence in one's role and genuine interest in others.

In the end the way of character is the only route to the authenticity Jesus possessed—a *oneness* between what lay within and what others saw. This kind of integrity permits no gap between *persona* and true self. It lives out the desire expressed well by Plato: "May the inner and the outer person meet."[3] In Jesus, it always did. His apprentices put a premium on doing the same.

Jesus's way rejects the many forms of faux authenticity. Like most pathways worth taking, it is a hard and sometimes costly road. There is no once-for-all commitment we can make. Rather, real authenticity requires a *repeated choosing.* When it comes to our words, three decisions in particular confront us daily. Each response either shapes us into increasingly authentic communicators or leads in the opposite direction.

1. The decision to tell of both beauty and brokenness

Russian dissident Aleksandr Solzhenitsyn experienced firsthand the horror of Joseph Stalin's murder of millions of Soviet citizens. Solzhenitsyn spent years behind the barbed wire of Siberian prison camps, and his family and close friends numbered among the dead. Yet looking back upon the evil Stalin worked, Solzhenitsyn made a shocking admission. He said that if he were placed in a situation identical to Stalin's, he may well have carried out the same atrocities. Pointing to himself he acknowledged, "The line dividing good and evil cuts through the heart of every human being."[4]

If we're honest with ourselves, we too know the vastly divergent qualities inhabiting every heart, including our own—good and evil, certainty and doubt, humility and ego, compassion and apathy. As French mathematician and philosoper Blaise Pascal observed in his *Pensées*, each one of us is marked by both wretchedness and greatness; at the same time we are both angel and beast. The world beyond us is equally bipolar. It is full of dancing fireflies, grandmother's kisses, and peaceful Sunday afternoons but also car accidents, Alzheimer's disease, and disintegrating marriages.

If we refuse to acknowledge *both* sides of this reality, we will inevitably abandon truthfulness, somehow imagining that a brushed-up picture will accomplish more than unvarnished truth.

Of course, it is easy for us to nod in affirmation of truth-telling. Still, we must beware: the lies we are most tempted to tell are not statements that could be proven false in a courtroom. They are subtler, usually sufficiently so to fool the one telling them—faint shadings, slight distortions, and positive *spin*. Justifying ourselves, we point out that we did not speak the half-truths to benefit ourselves but to help the good cause advance, the company expand, or the faith be embraced.

Personal Notes: Erik

Nothing compares to life's raw and unscripted moments, when all our polish and pretense disappear in an instant. The cheers of a first-time father at the sight of his newborn. The words of a man and woman exchanging vows on their wedding day. The tears of a couple upon hearing a doctor diagnose stage 4 cancer.

It was morning when my best friend called. His voice was unusually slow and solemn. "Lily died last night."

Lily was three months old, the healthy and cheery daughter of our close friends, when she died from SIDs in her crib.

I've never experienced a grief like that before. It was beyond tears. The hundreds of friends and family *groaned* together during the memorial service. The sight of the tiny casket. The bold hymns sung by mourners. The trembling of a pastor clinging to a promise that victory remains at the cross. The honesty of the parents attempting to make sense of it all. It overwhelmed us, broke us.

I'd always admired the authentic life of Lily's father during our early years as political staffers and later as roommates and colleagues. He was steady, optimistic, and genuine. I knew that with him it was true: he lived intimately with Christ.

Then he lost his daughter.

No surprise that the authenticity carried on. He was despondent, desperate. He was angry and confused—at life, at himself, and at his Father. He wanted nothing to do with his faith. He had no patience for quaint religious comforts that fit a Hallmark card but not a daddy who misses his baby girl.

And I loved him even more for that.

Authenticity, it is easy to think, is a skill or habit. But I saw from my friend that it's neither. Authenticity begins with honesty and humility, then moves to rest and grace, and finally to confidence and character. It comes from living a short distance from *the mess*—the raw material of people and places, of events and experiences that are unsafe and unstable.

And it's contagious. The hard months that followed little Lily's funeral also came with repentance and renewal as friends gathered to pray, to serve, to shoulder life together. It bound us together. No one cared about jobs or houses or what we looked like or how funny we sounded. We were raw and messy.

And amidst all the pain, it was beautiful.

Truly great communicators choose a different path. Their words carry a penetrating honesty about the world and themselves, glistening with both beauty and brokenness.

This kind of vivid honesty sings and weeps, celebrates and groans from the Psalms. "Taste and see that the Lord is good."[5] "For I eat ashes as my food and mingle my drink with tears."[6] "The earth is the Lord's and everything in it."[7] "You have taken my companions and loved ones from me; the darkness is my only friend."[8]

Jesus's words were just as delightful and disturbing.

He reminded of the beauty of the lilies and God's concern for even the sparrow. Yet He also spoke just as vividly of the costs of discipleship, of death to self, of the troubles His followers were guaranteed to face.

On the cross, this juxtaposition is breathtaking. The thief beside Jesus hears words as beautiful as can be uttered, "Today you will be with me in paradise."[9] Yet a moment later, Jesus cries out in the words of Psalm 22,

"My God, my God, why have you forsaken me?"[10] This expression, as New Testament scholar Bill Lane observes, carries a "ruthless authenticity."[11]

If we desire to become such communicators, says writer Frederick Buechner, we must "use words and images that help make the surface of our lives transparent to the truth that lies deep within...speaking forth not only the light and the hope of it but the darkness as well." If we are brave enough to tell this deeper truth, Buechner assures, we will "set echoes going the way a choir in a great cathedral does."[12]

2. The decision to offer what we have, rather than what we wish we could give

A series of Gallup polls and studies from 2001 to 2003 examined thousands of businesses worldwide with a central, driving question: *What makes successful companies successful?*

In response it became clear that one factor played an especially large role in separating the most effective enterprises from the rest of the pack: how they addressed their employees' strengths and weaknesses. Mediocre companies tend to focus on *fixing* employees' deficiencies so workers will better fit their job descriptions. In contrast, superior businesses focus on strengths, cultivating each employee's natural abilities and building job descriptions around an individual's unique gifts. Over time, the review concluded, the first route leads to subpar outcomes, the second to envied success.[13]

We face this crossroads in our own communication as well. Trying to fake strengths we imagine others expect of us will lead to uninspiring results. In contrast, communicators who employ their natural talents, however modest, rarely fail to leave an impact.

The great composer Beethoven was not known for social grace. Being deaf, he found conversation difficult and even humiliating. When he heard of the death of a friend's son, Beethoven hurried to the house, overcome with grief. He had no words of comfort to offer, but there in the room he found a piano. For the next half hour he played, pouring out his emotions in the most eloquent way he could. When he finished playing, he left. The friend later remarked that no one else's visit had meant so much.

This commitment does not mean avoiding areas where we are weak. Growth often requires stretching ourselves. But we must also accept that not everyone is funny, imposing, or charismatic, and there is no need to strive endlessly to be something we are not. Jesus apparently did not feel compelled to write books, create music, or even be particularly humorous. He operated almost exclusively through thoughtful verbal instruction and example.

Each of us has been uniquely equipped to give one-of-a-kind gifts, and we have every reason to make the most of what we have to give. In the movie *Chariots of Fire* Olympic gold medal sprinter Eric Liddle expresses, "God made me fast. And when I run, I feel His pleasure."[14] We must seek out where we are fast, and then run.

3. The decision to break from expectations, cliché, and pat answers when they distort reality

Convention and habit pervade our lives like the air we breathe. We learn by osmosis how to greet an acquaintance, the appropriate distance to keep during conversation, and which subjects are unacceptable in polite company. These unspoken rules are mostly benign. If left unexamined, however, they can deform truth-telling.

Whenever necessary Jesus smashed these molds. While respectable men avoided interacting with females in public, Jesus routinely engaged women in earnest conversation. Although other popular teachers included fasting in their students' regimen, Jesus did not immediately do so, evoking critical inquiry as to why. And while upstanding citizens gave wide berth to the morally dubious, Jesus chose to share meals—one of the most intimate expressions of friendship in Jewish culture—with prostitutes and drunkards.

Jesus was not merely shaking His fist at his culture. In fact, the vast majority of the things Jesus said and did *affirmed* the Jewish heritage into which He had been born. He wore Jewish prayer tassels, urged Peter to pay the temple tax, traveled to Jerusalem for Passover, and attended synagogue on the Sabbath. It was simply that Jesus would not allow expectations, habits, or cliché to distort His messages.

Following Jesus in this makes our communication more genuine, crisp, and impactful. Consider your own response to detours from the expected: a battle-hardened general lets a tear slip down his cheek; a CEO admits a major planning error; a scientist explains a concept with simple, homey words. As professor of anthropology Dr. Charles Kraft has observed, when a communicator "acts according to our prediction—the communication impact of whatever that person says or does is very low. If, on the other hand, that person acts or speaks in a way that is unexpected in terms of the stereotype, the communicational impact is much greater."[15]

The decisions required of us will often be less obvious. We must especially work to root out phrases that have lost their freshness—and much of their meaning—due to frequent use. An American missionary in Russia spoke often of a "relationship with God" until an inquisitive young woman asked, "Exactly what *is* a relationship with God?" The phrase did carry meaning for the young man, but he was struck by how much he stumbled in trying to explain what he meant by the cliché. We all do the same, frequently building our communication upon phrases that we have not bothered to define for ourselves in years.

To avoid this trap, we must relentlessly seek words that really mean what we say. Authenticity will be lost if our words and actions are consistently squeezed into the mold of thoughtless custom and tired truisms. What do we mean, after all, by saying we "felt led" by God or want to be "more radical"? What are we talking about, really, in promoting "greater collaboration" or "both-and not either-or"? These are all significant ideas, of course. But we must flesh them out in practical explanation and example frequently, or they will dissolve into abstraction.

Personal Notes: Jedd

In his 2003 State of the Union Address, President Bush launched the Mentoring Children of Prisoners (MCP) initiative. It works with community and faith-based groups nationwide to match caring mentors with children whose parents are incarcerated. When MCP reached the target the president had set of 100,000 mentor matches, we traveled together to visit a small mentoring program in North Carolina to celebrate the milestone.

As planned, we took our seats at a simple table with the local nonprofit director and three children and their mentors. The room was packed with reporters, and the president delivered brief remarks. Then he indicated he wanted a chance for us to talk with the kids and mentors in private, and the room was soon cleared.

I was always deeply impressed by the consistency between President Bush in public and the man behind the scenes. His sense of respect for the office he held, resolve to protect the country, and concern for the downtrodden never depended upon whether or not there was a camera in the room. In unseen moments like these, I felt, he was often at his best.

The president turned first to a shy African American boy. Although bright, the boy seemed to have little confidence, repeatedly deflecting the president's praise of his progress in school. "No, I ain't advanced," he mumbled.

The president repeated his conclusion, "A boy doing what you're doing in school? You must be advanced!"

After a third denial, the president attempted to hide his smile under a stern glance, "Son, if the president of the United States says you're advanced, then you're advanced." The boy's sober face broke into a grin, and he couldn't help joining the president and the rest of us in laughter.

The president drew out the story of a teen girl too. When he asked softly if she sometimes felt angry at her parents for having both gone to prison, a tear slipped down her cheek. "I want you to know something," the president said, his voice firm yet tender. "There's hope for anyone. See, I used to have a drinking problem. If I hadn't quit, I wouldn't just not be president now—I probably wouldn't even be married. But you know what happened? The good Lord entered, or reentered, my life. I hope you know what that means someday."

Her misty eyes lit up. There he was, the most powerful man in the world sitting next to a girl most of the world had forgotten, sharing honestly from his own struggles. I know she'll never forget that moment. Neither will I.

THE RELEASE TO GIVE WHAT NO ONE ELSE CAN

Do you recall what it felt like as a child when, after telling a lie, you had to carry it around for weeks? You strained beneath the vigilance required to preserve the deception, and guilt nibbled at your conscience. It could ruin even a day at the beach.

The way out would have been so simple.

As grown-ups our reasons for deception have changed. The way out, however, remains much the same. Authenticity offers release—the unburdened, school-is-out-for-the-summer freedom that only honesty can bring.

Many of us live with the continual, wearying effort required to try to get others to believe in something that does not exist: the only partially accurate image of ourselves we like to present. Dallas Willard explains, "'Growing up' is largely a matter of learning to hide our spirit behind our face, eyes, and language so that we can evade and manage others to achieve what we want and avoid what we fear."[16]

Sometimes they buy it, sometimes they don't. But the always-on caution, the constant guard keeping, the spin control, and image management can be as emotionally draining as living in a war zone.

The opposite, Willard observes, is childlike openness and transparency. "The child's face is a constant epiphany because it doesn't yet know how to do this.... Those who have attained considerable spiritual stature are frequently noted for their 'childlikeness.' What this really means is that they do not use their face and body to hide their spiritual reality. In their body they are genuinely present to those around them."[17]

Only this kind of authenticity cuts us free from the terrible weight of impression making and image building.

Yes, the hazards of authenticity are real. Our image may be tarnished when others see that we too are broken and needy. People will sometimes turn away, preferring a plastic perfection to tattered reality.

This is why we can only choose authenticity if we are motivated by more than desire for influence or popularity. As with all aspects of apprenticeship, our authenticity springs from the vision Jesus revealed of His Father.

This is a God whose love rises not in response to our performance, but from His expansive heart. He operates an economy in which grace, not rank or merit, determines value. He tenderly restores the fallen and runs out to greet the prodigal returning home. He does not look at outward appearance but at the heart. In His kingdom outcomes depend not on straining labor but upon His multiplication of our modest offerings. He delights in humility. In Him our dignity is found not in status or accomplishment, but in being His beloved child.

Only in knowing this God are we freed to be truly authentic. Our confidence is in Him and His provision, not ourselves. So we can offer all that we are, and nothing we are not, to those around us.

In the end we will find that this was the only path to lasting connection and influence after all. For ultimately what does the person who shuns authenticity have to offer? What will be said of the one who parrots clichés and echoes conventional wisdom, skating safely on the surface of life and emotion, presenting a balanced and just-slightly-less-than-perfect personality, perhaps adding for sake of identity a bit of flair in clothing or a "passion" for chocolate, shopping, or a sports team?

Very likely, nothing.

The façade such communicators create is lackluster at best. It is as similar to thousands of others as one tract home to the next. Ironically, even while bearing an almost suspicious resemblance to those around them, they provide nothing that draws others to themselves or creates meaningful connection, nor do they inspire or leave lasting impact. They could hardly be said to exist. No wonder Ralph Waldo Emerson warned, "Imitation is suicide."[18]

In contrast, the way of Jesus delivers a presence and words that are utterly unique because they are utterly real. No other person has been formed quite like you or given gifts quite like yours. When you share these gifts with others, you give something no one else can give. It is *that*, and nothing else, that is ultimately God's unparalleled gift to the world through us.

LIFE THROUGH CONCRETENESS

Upend a Life of Abstract Ideas

Chapter 11

MAKING TRUTH TOUCHABLE

Dr. Tom Little and his wife first took residence in Afghanistan in 1977 to help run a Christian hostel serving world-traveling hippies. Within weeks Tom was volunteering at an eye hospital.

Over the decades that followed, the couple held fast through the Russian invasion, civil wars, Taliban rule, and the nation's tumultuous experiment with democracy. Afghans spoke of them as "the people who stayed." They raised their three daughters there in lives intertwined with their Afghan neighbors. When the eye hospital where Tom served was destroyed by rockets, he joined with others to open smaller house clinics on various sides of the war's shifting front lines. Later, when permission was granted, the eye care program extended beyond the front lines of fighting into remote areas.

In August 2010 Tom was invited to lead a small team to the remote province of Nuristan to provide eye care, maternal health care, and dentistry. It was his fifth trip to the area. To reach their destination, the team forged a sixteen-thousand-foot pass and rugged valleys. When snowfields made roads impassable, they lugged their gear and medical equipment for days with horses and on foot.

During such trips Tom was only able to place short calls via satellite phone. Though brief, the calls home confirmed that the team was well and provided colorful windows into the journey.

In one of the last conversations they would have, Tom recounted to his wife how the team had taken shelter at the end of a brutal day of hiking through freezing rain. Exhausted and shivering, the team of medical professionals peeled off their soaked boots and socks. The miles, moisture, and cold had left their mark. Angry blisters covered their feet. Seeing the open sores, the Afghan guide was deeply moved. Whatever else was true of these foreigners, he knew their wounds were made by love. "Beautiful feet," he marveled in his local dialect.

Tom reached his wife again later, shortly before a river crossing. "We'll call you from the other side. I love you," he said. It was the final time she would hear her husband's voice. Not long after the call, the medical team members were killed by unknown assailants. Their bodies were discovered by a shepherd boy, who brought the news to local authorities.

The medical organization with which Tom served consistently honored its commitment not to proselytize in the Muslim nation. But there's no doubt that countless Afghans *saw* and *felt* God's love in myriad tangible ways through all that Tom Little and his colleagues did to serve them. Beautiful feet indeed.[1]

Personal Notes: Erik

"Are you watching TV?"

Monica's call interrupted my morning at home where I was writing a speech before heading back to work near the US Capitol.

It was the morning of 9/11, and like so many, we watched silently as the world changed live on television. Like so many, it was impossible to believe our eyes.

Was this really happening?

Over the next few days, however, the reality of the attack became more and more concrete.

The pungent smell of smoke rising from the smoldering wing of the Pentagon as we drove into work.

The cries to "drop everything and run" when an imminent threat was believed to be headed toward our government offices, and we sprinted out of the building.

The friends on Capitol Hill forced to take Cipro pills due to possible exposure to anthrax as we wondered what would happen next.

What made 9/11 more real than any smoke or evacuations or white pills was what we encountered one day while serving first responders on the Pentagon grounds.

We didn't do much. Emptying trash cans and pouring water in the makeshift meal tents. We were asked to just be present, in case anyone wanted to talk. No one did.

The workers' despondent blank stares said enough: they were seeing things no man or woman should ever see. The automatic weapons attached to ATVs circling the Pentagon said it all: this was far from over.

News reports gave us the facts, the eyewitness accounts, the recurring images of falling towers, and pillars of smoke. But only when we went to the scene, stood a yard from hell, tasted the gritty smoke, and saw the faces of heroes did we fully grasp what happened and how we should respond.

GOD ISN'T ABSTRACT

One of the more curious accounts in the Gospels is Jesus's encounter with a deaf, mute man.[2] In many other recorded miracles, a simple verbal command from Jesus was all that was needed. "Peace, be still!"[3] "Lazarus, come out!"[4] But for the deaf mute, Jesus used not words but physical things. He spit on His hands, touched the man's tongue, and stuck His fingers in the man's ears.

These acts may seem primitive, even vulgar. But it seems Jesus felt these physical elements were somehow essential.

For a deaf mute living before modern sign language, words were a worthless currency. But both spit and touch were things that people in Jesus's day associated with healing. For a man who could not hear, these objects made Jesus's intent tangible: *I desire to heal your ears and your tongue.* Physical things—fingers in the ears, spittle, the touching of the tongue—conveyed meaning to the man in a way words never could.

It is not only the deaf who require language that can be seen. For every human, words alone often fail to communicate fully. Truth must somehow be embodied if it is to become real and lasting for us. Ideas that can be seen and touched, smelled and tasted tend to be understood more fully, impact more deeply, and be remembered much longer.

Remarkably, God never asks humans to *rise above* the physical beings He created us to be. Rather, God continually packages spiritual significance in physical objects.

"Take off your sandals," God directed as Moses approached the burning bush in the wilderness.[5] But why? Throughout most of Scripture, shoes have no bearing on communion with God.[6] Skin on dirt is no more sacred than wearing sandals. But God wanted to make the idea of holiness more tangible for Moses. He used words to explain that Moses stood on holy ground. But words alone may have left the concept hazy. So God gave Moses a physical sensation of holiness and reverence, helping him to *experience* a hard-to-grasp concept.

> It is in the scandal and the good news of the Christian faith that grace become concrete.[7]
> —GLENN HOBURG

This is God's way of communicating throughout the entire Bible. Yes, words play an indispensable role. Jews were known as *people of the Book.* But the Book itself is full of God's physical ways of communicating. Bitter herbs that stung the taste buds to remind of the bitterness of slavery. Feasts to commemorate and celebrate God's provision. Blood. Incense. Rainbows.

Stones piled to remind of past victories. Unleavened bread. A tabernacle with concentric rings that led to an inaccessible *holy of holies.*

Few, if any, of these objects were necessary in themselves. God could have simply explained in words and text. In fact, they all may strike the modern mind as archaic—like Jesus healing with spit-covered hands. We moderns may prefer the tidy Greek philosopher in his bleach-white toga, musing on abstract principle. But this is not the Creator's way of communicating. God consistently wraps the most lofty truths in the most tangible forms.

Even in its textual expression, God's Word is composed largely of stories. The Bible's image-saturated narratives make God's character and call tangible: a massive ark, slavery and liberation, a shepherd-king, a lion's den. Alongside these stories, countless word pictures turn ideas into vivid images: God's love...*a mother hen's wing enveloping her brood;*[8] spiritual revival...*bleached bones coming to life;*[9] longing for God...*a deer panting for water.*[10]

What makes this all the more astonishing is that the Bible unequivocally shows God to be utterly transcendent. He is holy, apart, above. He declares, "As the heavens are higher than the earth, so are my ways higher than your ways and my thoughts than your thoughts."[11]

Yet this transcendent God continually makes His truth touchable to humankind.

Even nature itself is described as a physical revealing of God's unseeable qualities. "The heavens declare the glory of God," writes the psalmist.[12] Paul describes, "For since the creation of the world God's invisible qualities—his eternal power and divine nature—have been clearly seen, being understood from what has been made."[13]

Personal Notes: Jedd

Rachel and I emerged from a breakfast diner with our four little ones in tow. A woman weaving her way toward us across the parking lot caught my eye. Even from a distance, her matted hair and sun-marred face spoke of homelessness. I started loading the kids into their car seats, my head down. I'll confess I hoped to avoid her. I wanted to dodge the inconvenience of trying to figure out what she really needed and, perhaps even more, of trying to provide it.

But Rachel greeted her, and the woman launched into the kind of story-leading-to-request that I'd anticipated. Rachel listened carefully, finally offering, "We don't give out money, but if you really need the food, I'd be glad to go with you to Save Mart." The woman accepted, and she and

Rachel went to the store while I sang "Itsy Bitsy Spider" with the kids in our minivan.

A few weeks later my daughter Siena and I were working on her weekly memory verse. "If anyone has material possessions and sees his brother in need but has no pity on him, how can the love of God be in him? Dear children, let us not love with words or tongue but with actions and it truth."[14]

"So what does that mean, Daddy?" she asked.

I offered a less-than-clarifying explanation, and Siena pondered it, her face still perplexed.

Suddenly Siena's eyes lit up. "That's like what Mommy did for that lady in the parking lot, right? I get it!"

She *did* get it. But not in the way any words I might have offered could have explained. She got it with the deeper, more vivid understanding that comes only by seeing an idea with skin on it.

George MacDonald wrote, "No thought, human or divine, can be conveyed from man to man except through the symbolism of the creation. The heavens and the earth are around us that it may be possible for us to speak of the unseen by the seen. . . . He is not a God that hides himself, but a God who made all that he might reveal himself."[15]

As we will soon see, this *making truth touchable* is the way of Jesus too.

Chapter 12

CONCRETE GRACE

Near the top of Jedd's list of living heroes are Salomon and Mery Hernandez. Even perched on a small stack of books, the aging Guatemalan couple would not reach most Americans' shoulders. Gray now streaks once-black hair, and wrinkles etch their faces. Their eyes, however, still cast sparks, glowing with vibrant life and unconditional welcome.

Salomon and Mery are *Ladinos*. Of the two distinct groups in Guatemalan society, the Ladinos have the upper hand—they're Spanish-speaking, lighter skinned, and generally more well-to-do. On the other side of a vast social chasm are the indigenous Guatemalans, the Mayans. These sharp-featured, dark-skinned people are set apart not only by their culture and native language but also by the poverty that dogs their existence.

Decades ago, when Salomon served as a pastor, the gaping divide between Ladinos and Mayans began to gnaw at the young couple. Here they were, seeking to lead people to be disciples of Jesus. Yet while the Master they claimed to follow consistently rejected such social divides, their own church embraced them.

Salomon and Mery didn't write a manifesto or craft a new sermon series on inclusiveness. Instead, they decided to learn *Quiché*, a Mayan dialect others referred to with derision as "the language of the poor." In fits and starts, their vocabulary grew. News began to spread among local Mayans of "the pastor who speaks *Quiché*." First one Mayan, then others, appeared at the church. Some understood little Spanish, grasping only bits of Salomon's sermons. Still, the fact that he knew *Quiché* drew them. "This man must care about us," they whispered to each other. "He is learning our language."

The Ladinos in the church were not nearly so impressed. Salomon and Mery could not help noticing the concerned glances cast at the newcomers. As time went on, the glances became glares of irritation and muttered complaints. Finally, a group broached the subject with Salomon directly.

They explained, "We're not sure it is best to have Mayans in our church. They have many diseases. It is not safe for our children. And their smell…"

Salomon gently reminded, "Jesus continually served people Jews hated, the Samaritans, and lepers, and tax collectors, even prostitutes."

That quieted the complaints, but it was not long before the group was back, this time larger. "We have decided we must build a second church building," an elder announced, "One for the Mayans, one for us."

Again Salomon resisted. "If we are going to follow Jesus, we need to grow *together*. We must learn to love and serve each other as a community," he urged.

Not many were convinced. The ultimatum came a short time later. "Salomon, we will let you make a choice," they offered, eyes cold. "You can either be our pastor, or you can serve the Mayans. Not both. The decision is up to you."

Painful as it was, the path was clear. Salomon and Mery had chosen their course long before. They would follow in the way of their Master, whatever the cost. Salomon would be the church's pastor no more.

Since that time Salomon and Mery have spent much of their lives working with the Mayan people. Some Ladinos still think they are fools to stoop so low. But many Mayans claim they have no better friends than Salomon and Mery Hernandez. And the giving has not been entirely one-sided. Mayan friends delight to invite Salomon and Mery into their homes and to their festivals, or to bring them corn from their fields or freshly harvested *malanga* root. And more than once during Guatemala's bloody civil war the couple was rescued from death at the hands of Mayan guerillas by friends they had served.

Years ago a man close to Salomon and Mery described to Jedd why the couple had influenced him so deeply. "They *are* thinkers with real theological depth," he explained. "And if you ask, both of them will share thoughts that will amaze you. But they never start there, with ideas. They start with doing something, acting on what they've come to believe. *Then* they talk about it. Not vice versa. Their actions lead their ideas. I *see* what they're talking about before they say it, so it sticks."

That is just what Jesus did on His final evening with His disciples. Without a word, He stood up from their shared meal. He stripped down to undergarments and wrapped a towel around His waist, then knelt with a bowl of water to scrub dirt from His disciples' feet. No doubt He could have simply explained the importance of humbly serving others. But He knew that wouldn't stick nearly as much as something they could see with their eyes and feel between their toes. Only when He had finished and redressed did He put the idea into words:

> "Do you understand what I have done for you?" he asked them. "You call me 'Teacher' and 'Lord,' and rightly so, for that is what I am. Now that I, your Lord and Teacher, have washed your feet, you also should wash one another's feet. I have set you an example that you should do as I have done for you."[1]

This is the most potent form of concreteness: example. Whenever possible, the apprentice to Jesus desiring to convey an idea will not start by reaching for words. She will ask herself, "Is there something I can *do* that will get this idea across?"

Joel Spolsky, now a respected software CEO, was serving in the Israeli army at age nineteen when he was assigned to work for a hard-driving sergeant major. The sergeant was the terror of the battalion, always dressed impeccably despite the alternating dust and mud of their outpost. He demanded a precision that matched his own well-starched dress uniform and precise manner.

On his first day Joel's worst fears seemed to be confirmed. The sergeant took him to the officer's bathroom and informed Joel it'd be his job to keep it clean. But then the sergeant did something entirely unexpected. "Here's how you clean a toilet," he said. Then, that fastidious military man, twice Joel's age and still dressed in his flawless dress uniform, got down on his knees before the porcelain bowl. He scrubbed it with his bare hands until it glistened.

Years later Joel described, "It completely reset my attitude. If he can clean a toilet, I can clean a toilet, I thought. There's nothing wrong with cleaning toilets. My loyalty and inspiration from that moment on were unflagging."[2]

Years later the lesson remained carved into Joel's mind as he established upscale new offices for his software firm in New York City. The coloring of the window blinds he'd just had installed looked filthy against newly painted walls. They needed to be replaced. A hired handyman could have done the fix-it job in a day. But Joel knew the power of giving a visible example of what he wanted leadership at his firm to look like. So he and his business partner spent two long afternoons hanging blinds in the offices of their junior staff.[3] Yes, that cost precious hours from two business owners who needed every second they could spare. But Joel understood it was investment well worth making. The sergeant major's vivid lesson had stuck and now was echoing across the years to people he'd never met.

MAKING IT TOUCHABLE

Even when we can't live out an idea we wish to convey, we can make it tangible. Thomas Clarkson did that as well as any. When Clarkson began his studies at Cambridge in 1779, slavery existed only in distant British territories. It remained largely out of sight and mind for most English people, Clarkson included. But when the tall, red-haired young man began to study the slave trade for a college essay contest, he was appalled at the brutality and ugliness he began to see.

Soon after writing the paper, Clarkson felt God calling him to give his life to ending the slave trade. But he and other abolitionists faced a major challenge. Because few people in England ever saw slavery firsthand, it rarely crossed their thoughts. The idea of a woman or man enslaved may have struck many as unfortunate, but the evil it represented remained distant and abstract. Clarkson knew he needed to change that if the abolition movement was to gain the broad support it needed to end the trade.

He began to secretly explore the ports of Liverpool and Bristol where slave ships docked. Talking with sailors and others involved in the trade, Clarkson learned specifics of what transpired on the long passage from Africa to the West Indies. He scrupulously recorded what he learned, capturing descriptions and vivid accounts.

Clarkson began to collect implements used in the slave trade—iron manacles, thumbscrews, leg shackles, branding irons, and horrible plierlike devices used to open slaves' jaws to enable force-feeding if they attempted to starve themselves. Alongside these vile tools, Clarkson also collected beautiful objects imported from Africa—from finely woven cloth and jewelry, to products such as palm oil and beeswax.[4] Their craftsmanship and beauty contrasted sharply with claims that Africans were just crude savages.

As he spoke throughout England, Clarkson exhibited a *box* he created containing many drawers filled with these items. They highlighted benefits of trading goods rather than slaves with Africa. They also made tangible the skill and creativity of African artisans—in essence, their humanity.

Clarkson also acquired a diagram of a slave ship, the *Brookes*. It revealed how 482 human beings could be crammed into the ship's hold. Posters that Clarkson made of the image became the emblem of the abolition movement.

All of these things—the gripping descriptions of slaving, the diagram of the *Brookes*, the brutal tools of the trade, and the quality goods crafted by African hands—made the reasons for abolition inescapably real.

The result was profound. As *The Economist* magazine declared in 2007, "If anyone was the founder of the modern human-rights movement, it was Clarkson."[5] The Abolition Project put it this way, "Before Clarkson joined the campaign, it had generated only limited interest amongst the public. Within a few years, Clarkson had turned abolition into the most prominent political issue of the day."[6]

In all of this Clarkson was simply following as an apprentice to his Lord. Jesus continually found ways to point to visible, touchable objects that embodied the ideas He sought to convey.

Personal Notes: Jedd

Some of my favorite moments working in the White House came outside of Washington, when I'd get to spend time with frontline nonprofits addressing key issues I was working on—from job training initiatives in the States to anti-malaria efforts abroad. During these visits local nonprofit leaders helped me understand their innovative models and how they could be replicated. I heard many unforgettable presentations, but one has stuck with me more than any other.

Typically an organization's presentation included a short speech or two followed by a facilities tour. But at one little Zambian ministry serving people with HIV/AIDS, they did something different. Just a few battered concrete buildings served as the hub for hundreds of volunteer caregivers. Not much to look at. But Lister Chingangu, the vibrant Zambian nurse who'd started the program with her husband, enabled us visitors to truly see and even feel their daily work.

Lister had set up six or seven stations where volunteer caregivers acted out what they did out in the field. At one station a small fire boiled a nutrient-rich mush created to help HIV patients regain strength. Each visitor shared in the bland but nourishing meal. At another station a volunteer modeled palliative care; she knelt over a woman on a bed mat, tenderly washing her neck and face with a cloth.

At another station a woman lay in a wheelbarrow. She showed how volunteers formerly transported patients too sick to walk to a clinic to get treatment, often several miles or more. Next to her a transport volunteer sat on the wheelbarrow's replacement: a new bicycle constructed with a flat "seat" in back to carry a patient. His smile gleamed as he motioned from the wheelbarrow to the bicycle. "You have made our job very easy for us," he declared.

Each of those scenes of grace and mercy remain etched in my mind. I can't imagine that words or PowerPoint alone could have even come close.

It is the climactic final day of the yearly Feast of Tabernacles. A great procession of priests and worshipers descend from the Temple Mount to the Pool of Siloam. From the pool, a priest fills a pitcher. Then the congregation again climbs the Temple Mount. There, amidst ceremony and singing, the high priest lifts the pitcher and pours its water over the altar.

The Feast of Tabernacles takes place toward the end of the Mediterranean's dry season, so the land is parched. The ceremony reminds poignantly of thirst—both of the land and its people—and also of God's gift of water to quench that thirst. It was here, standing alongside this tangible reminder of God's thirst-slaking provision, that Jesus proclaimed, "If anyone is thirsty, let him come to me and drink. Whoever believes in me, as the Scripture has said, streams of living water will flow from within him."[7]

Again and again Jesus did the same: connected abstract ideas to physical objects.

When Jesus's disciples began to squabble over status, He did not merely explain the significance of humility and service. Instead He asked a little child to stand beside Him. Then He expressed, "Whoever welcomes this little child in my name welcomes me; and whoever welcomes me welcomes the one who sent me. For he who is least among you all—he is the greatest."[8]

When challenged to either affirm or reject paying taxes to pagan Rome, Jesus held up a coin. Imprinted with the image of Caesar, the coin itself declared that it had been minted by an earthly king. God deserves our full allegiance, Jesus affirmed, but it was no affront to God to return to Caesar a portion of what Caesar had created.[9]

Seeking to explain that God valued the generosity of the poor as much as the generosity of the rich, Jesus pointed to a widow shuffling through the temple courts. She'd given an offering worth just a fraction of a penny. "I tell you the truth," said Jesus, "this poor widow has put more into the treasury than all the others. They all gave out of their wealth; but she, out of her poverty, put in everything—all she had to live on."[10]

Even Jesus's miracles often served a similar purpose. Yes, they were signs confirming Jesus's identity, bringing wondrous good to the people they affected. But also, Jesus's miracles consistently made visible the ideas He spoke of. Miraculous feedings made God's provision *tastable*. Water-turned-wine made the promise of a grand feast at the end of time drinkable. Healings made the coming restoration of all things tangible. As George MacDonald put it, through miracles Jesus put "into visible form that which before he had embodied in words. All shapes of argument must be employed to arouse the slumbering will of men."[11]

MAKING IT VISIBLE WITH WORDS

Personal Notes: Jedd

I love observing my friend Tom Davis communicate as he seeks to spur Christians to care for orphans. Sure, it's easy to get a person to nod in sympathy for destitute children. But Tom knows more is required to grow real conviction and lasting response.

Tom's first book was a straightforward presentation of global need and the Bible's explicit call to "defend the fatherless." Clear and concise, *Fields of the Fatherless* has led many a reader to fuller understanding and action.[12] But more recently Tom has been writing novels. In his compelling stories he takes readers deep into the struggles and hopes of children growing up without the love and protection of family. The gnawing of hunger. The terror of human trafficking. As a reader, your hopes rise and fall with the characters'; your pulse quickens in danger and distress.

In the 1850s, the novel *Uncle Tom's Cabin* helped Americans see and feel the realities of slavery. Today, Tom Davis's novels enable readers to see and feel the plight of orphans around the world, impacting more deeply than statistics or moral pleas alone ever could.

When Tom speaks, he makes things tangible as well. Gripping stories form the backbone of his remarks. And alongside the narratives, Tom incorporates physical objects as well. I still recall how two years ago, when he spoke about how an orphan girl had been forced into prostitution, Tom held up a hand towel taken from the very bathhouse where the girl had been compelled to work. The image, simple as it was, lingers with me still. It made the story more real and tangible for everyone who heard it and caused it to stick with us long and deep.

With stories and physical objects, Tom Davis brings distant need near. He makes hazy issues as real as a towel or a pounding heart.

It isn't always possible to make an idea visible via example or objects. But even when relying entirely upon words, Jesus took abstract concepts and made them powerfully concrete.

As we'll explore more in the next chapter, Jesus's favorite mode of communication was the story. Almost every page of the Gospels bears a parable Jesus told. These stories—of rebellious sons and tender fathers, callous clergymen and sprouting grain, lost coins and wandering sheep—all imbedded rich meaning within the vivid imagery of story.

Even when not using narrative, Jesus continually painted vivid word pictures. His disciples were not merely to be "a good influence" but to carry the savor and preservative influence of salt.[13] Jesus Himself was "the bread of life."[14] He offered "living water."[15] His kingdom carried the potential for explosive growth of a mustard seed,[16] the leavening of bread yeast,[17] and the immense but unrecognized value of hidden treasure.[18]

Charles Spurgeon, himself one of Christian history's greatest communicators, urged young pastors-to-be to follow Jesus's model in this. Using tangible language and illustrations is both a "duty and necessity," instructed Spurgeon, so "that they might be both interesting and instructive." Spurgeon concluded, "A sermon without illustrations is like a room without windows."[19]

CONCRETE GRACE

When we communicate like Jesus in this, whether via personal example, story, word picture, or physical object, we echo the incarnation. We bring the distant near and make abstract concrete. Ideas grow more real, sink deeper, last longer. Words become flesh.

In late 2010, just weeks after burying her husband, Dr. Tom Little's wife recounted the story that began the last chapter. Reflecting upon the legacy of Tom's life and death in Afghanistan, she concluded:

> In communities where power rules, strength prevails, where you work hard to attain honor and avoid shame, where you get what you deserve, an eye for an eye, a tooth for a tooth, this talk about God's grace, the vulnerability of God, and His loving-kindness is too foreign. It's too distasteful. It's almost repulsive. It needs to come in small doses over a long stretch of time…
>
> I think if Tom were here today, he would say that in these difficult places, grace, God's grace, is not something that you discuss. It's not something you debate. The idea of God taking on a form of weakness of a human being, coming in the body of Jesus, laying down His life, dying for us, has to be seen. It has to be experienced…[20]

Yes, experienced. *Seen. Tasted. Smelled. Felt.* And heard too in words that depict lofty truths in tangible ways. If our words are to be understood and sink deep, we must make them concrete. Always.

Section VII

LIFE THROUGH
STORYTELLING

Upend a Life of Facts Without Meaning

Chapter 13

THE MARVELOUS POWER OF STORY

If there is a truly global *lingua franca*—a universal currency welcomed across every country and culture, and every age of history as well—it is not English or French, the dollar or the euro, rare spices, oil, or gold. It is the story.

> There have been great societies that did not use the wheel, but there have been no societies that did not tell stories.
> —URSULA K. LEGUIN[1]

Soot-covered coal miners burrowed deep into the earth, barefoot shepherd girls guarding sun-drenched hillsides, pasty-faced bureaucrats holed up in dreary cubicles—all take pleasure in a tale well told. As communication professor Walter Fisher expressed, humankind could well be labeled *homo narrans*, the creature that loves narrative.[2] Even amid the blurring speed of modern life and technology, stories of all sorts remain as popular as ever, from *The Lord of the Rings* to the ballads of modern country music.

Jesus, however, did not tell stories merely as a garnish—to inject a bit of amusement, or as a transition to more weighty matters. Rather, stories stood as the very *centerpiece* of Jesus's communication.

Matthew, the taxman-turned-disciple, observed that Jesus expressed almost everything He wanted to convey through stories. Perhaps that was disconcerting for a man who'd spent much of his life measuring value with a balance sheet. Matthew's sweeping conclusion is remarkable: "He did not say *anything* to them without using a parable."[3]

These parables are yet one more reflection of the *incarnational* direction of all of Jesus's communication. They brought abstract ideas and hard-to-grasp truths into the gritty reality of ordinary life. His listeners—most of them, at least—loved it, paying rapt attention to the tales of lost coins and lost treasure, loving fathers and compassionless clergy, day laborers and homebuilders, wretched beggars and crafty businessmen.

Occasionally, usually with smaller groups, Jesus resorted to more direct, explicit means of conveying ideas. But, always, He would soon return to narrative—weaving in stories of seeds and sheep, pearls and pigs, kings and camels.

In the end, noted Bud Paxson, the founder of America's largest broadcast television station group, "He left us one sermon, and dozens of parables."[4]

> Nothing is more human than stories and storytelling.[5]
> —Os Guinness

Of course Jesus did not have to communicate this way. As screenwriter Dudley Nichols observed, Jesus "could have chosen simply to express Himself in moral precepts; but like a great poet He chose the form of the parable, wonderful short stories that entertained and clothed the moral precept in an eternal form."[6]

Madeline L'Engle, author of *A Wrinkle in Time* and other compelling tales, expressed her conclusion more succinctly in the words of one of her friends: "Jesus was not a theologian, but a God who told stories."[7]

Personal Notes: Erik

"What's that, Daddy?" Kolton, age six, asked as he drew close to where I was sitting.

"It's a preview of a movie," I responded, shielding the screen as I weighed whether he should see these images or not. "Oh, can I see?" he prodded. Movies are more irresistible than candy in our household.

I pushed play, and the trailer began. The images were vivid. A child his sister's age walking through an open sewer. The sullen eyes of a man drunk from African wine. A devastated building in Haiti. I began to interpret the story, unsure whether he needed it or not.

"These people don't have food or houses..." "This building fell during an earthquake..."

And then the image of a boy his age pounding rocks with a worn hammer, a slave to a debt created by his father forever trapped in an Indian quarry.

"This little boy hammers rocks all day. He has no toys, no school to go to..."

Kolton jumped up and ran toward his bedroom.

"I'm going to send him all my toys," he insisted in a panicked voice.

How do you tell a six-year-old that he can't without annihilating his grand hopes.

"Kolton, we can't do that, but Daddy can send money to help them," I attempted.

He ran back into his room and returned urgently, throwing his porcelain airplane bank on our bed.

"Give him all my money then," he pleaded.

Those are the moments that crush a parent—in a good way. I held him, my eyes tearing up, telling him what a special act of selflessness that was.

I know such instincts don't come from me—I certainly wasn't like that as a child. More and more I am convinced that the rising generations have two genetic mutations that are distinct from their parents: the ability to swipe, tap, and open apps on an iPhone by age two and the aspiration that no global problem is too big to fix.

A story—in this case, a true story—captured Kolton's heart and mind, and even more, his ambition. He didn't listen to what is practical or count his pennies or wonder if it was prudent. No, he heard and saw the story—felt it—and responded instantly.

Dropping nets. Leaving family. Abandoning jobs. Pouring perfumes. When we encounter the real, true Story, it results in holy spontaneity. I saw it in Kolton, and I yearn to see it in myself.

THE MARVELOUS POWER OF STORY

Watch those around you next time you are listening to a speech or sermon. What happens when the speaker ends a sentence that began something like, "It is therefore critical to recognize...," and launches into, "It was a stormy night in early winter..."?

Suddenly faces look up. Doodling pens pause. Even fidgeting kids sit still, at least for a moment. Thoughts of "When is this going to be over?" instantly become "What happens next?" The audience actually *wants* the speaker to go on.

Why? Because people love stories. We love sparking our imagination, our senses, our emotions, visiting new lands, distant frontiers, far-off ages. We love loving characters and despising them. We delight to find a person like us in a story, and to catch familiar glimpses of others we know. We want to find out how things are going to end up, where they will go, what will happen. Stories stir us—heart, mind, and soul.

Simply put, stories are the most enjoyed form of communication.

Stories keep people listening. In at least one remarkable instance, the eager crowds that had ventured to a distant lakeside to hear Jesus remained captivated by His stories for three days straight. Even after their satchels of bread, dried figs, fish, and other victuals ran out, the crowds remained, captured by His simple tales and the profound truth they contained. Jesus had to direct His disciples to find food for them to eat, or the people might well have listened until they were utterly famished.

It is almost as if stories contain a nourishment all their own. A good story "has the same effect on me that I suppose a good square drink of whiskey has on an old toper," stated President Abraham Lincoln. "It puts new life in me."[8]

The cold transfer of new information quickly grows wearisome to a listener. But well-told stories invigorate—quickening interest, stirring the imagination, and beckoning onward in exploration. Notes writer Art Kleiner, "You can't make someone listen; you can only entice, inspire, cajole, stimulate or fascinate. Stories do that."[9]

In short, stories cause people to listen.

An old Jewish parable describes Truth arriving in a village on a wind-swept night, shivering and bare. At every door she begs aloud to be let in, but not one is opened. Her nakedness and destitution cause all who see her to wince and turn away. When the old shepherd, Parable, finds her, Truth is huddled alone on the edge of town. Pitying her, Parable takes Truth in, tends her needs, and clothes her in story. So dressed, she returns to the homes in the village. Door after door is opened wide, and Truth, now garbed in story, is received with welcome and joy.

The stories Jesus told accomplished this well, opening doors for the truth He shared, even drawing people out from their homes to receive His teaching on mountainsides and lake shores.

And not only bookish students and scholars came. The gathered crowds spanned the entire spectrum of society. Stories dress concepts and ideas in a form capable of enchanting both large-eyed children and cynical old law-yers; they entertain illiterate laborers as well as intelligentsia; they grip the imagination of wiggly boys and distracted young mothers.

In fact, stories open the hearts of all types of audiences.

Jesus used stories as a way to deliver to each unique listener just what he or she was ready to receive. As a teacher, Jesus welcomed all comers. But He knew that while many sincerely longed for truth, some who joined the crowds had little interest in learning; they desired only to be entertained or perhaps to critique and condemn.

In Jesus's stories, each individual was given what he or she sought. The easily pleased novelty seekers and hard-hearted clerics found stimulation, but often remained "ever hearing, but never understanding...ever seeing but never perceiving."[10]

The earnest and humble, however, encountered profound wisdom in the simple, accessible form of stories. Each sincere learner, from the simpleton to the sage, was provided with just as much depth and complexity as he or she was willing to receive.

No communication better meets people where they are.

Personal Notes: Jedd

The room was nearly full, almost every seat taken by an ardent environmentalist. Only a handful knew me, but all were well aware that I served as chief of staff for a legislator who often crossed swords with groups like theirs. I could see people whispering and gesturing as I walked to the front. If we were to work together on legislation creating California's Sierra Nevada Conservancy as I hoped, we'd need to trust and respect one another. But I knew that wouldn't come easily.

"My father is a high school teacher in the town of Atwater," I began. "But when I was a boy, each June our family moved to the Sierra Nevada Mountains, where Dad worked as a horse patrol ranger in Yosemite..."

I recounted how our family lived all summer in a little tent cabin. The four boys spent our days rock climbing, fly fishing, and working in the campgrounds. It wasn't until I was twenty-one that I ventured elsewhere for the summer, to Moscow.

Living in Russia was fascinating, but I ached for California's mountains. So, to survive my first summer away from the Sierra, I pored over John Muir's book *My First Summer in the Sierra.* I envisioned the scenes he described and memorized passages. Even at the office my screen saver rolled continuously with Muir's words, "Nevermore, however weary, should one faint by the way who gains the blessings of one mountain day. Whatever his fate—long life, short life, stormy or calm—he is rich forever."[11] Muir got me through that summer, I explained, but I plan to never pass another without quality time in the wilderness.

The story was simple but heartfelt. And though the audience knew we'd have our differences along the way, they trusted that we cared deeply about many of the same things and could work together. If I'd tried to convey that fact directly, it likely would have drawn skepticism. The story, however, opened doors facts alone never could.

KNOCKING SOFTLY ON THE DOOR OF A HEART

The Middle Eastern monarch slouched, restless in his throne. He seemed to sense the rumors, buzzing like flies over dung in the spring air. It was whispered that the king, despite his reputation for justice and goodness, had taken the wife of a faithful soldier and then ordered the man murdered before he could discover the offense. Whether or not the courtiers believed it, not one would dare breathe the accusation in the king's presence.

The throne room fell silent as an old man with a ragged beard hobbled up its steps. It was the revered prophet Nathan. Normally welcoming, the king's eyes narrowed, and his jaw tightened. But as the wizened prophet transitioned from his respectful greeting into a simple narrative, relief washed over the room.

"There was peasant who owned a single ewe lamb," began Nathan. "This lamb was a pet to him and his children. It shared his food, drank from his cup, and even slept in his arms. He loved it like a daughter.

"Nearby lived a rich landholder, wealthy beyond measure. He owned vast lands pasturing countless sheep. But when a visitor arrived at his estate, the rich man did the unthinkable. Rather than use a sheep from his own fields, he directed his servants to go and steal the peasant's precious lamb, then prepare it for his guest."

The king rose from his chair, enraged. "How dare that wealthy man do such a thing. He deserves to die!"

The old prophet looked the king squarely in the eye, his voice firm. "*You are that man.*"[12]

The air quivered for a moment, tense as a straining bow. Then the king crumpled back into his throne and let out a long, weary breath. The message had struck its mark.

Every one of us harbors issues we would prefer not to confront. We each hold views and opinions we do not wish to have challenged. As anthropology professor Dr. Charles Kraft explained, "We ordinarily seek at all costs to maintain our present equilibrium, to protect ourselves from assimilating anything that will upset our psychological balance."[13]

As a result, communication that asks us to change is unwelcome. The trouble is, communication often involves just that—requesting change or expressing truths that can disturb comfortable habits and assumptions.

Stories are uniquely capable of knocking softly at the door of the heart. They arrive as welcome visitors, neither threatening nor combative. Once invited in and set down by the fireplace, a story can then deliver the truths that need to be heard.

Jesus's parable of the prodigal son did this brilliantly. Many in the audience, no doubt, identified from the start with the responsible older brother. Even as Jesus wove the tale, they felt a hint of disdain for the prodigal. *Asking for an inheritance before his father was dead? Blowing hard-earned assets on prostitutes? Unthinkable!* Perhaps they thought of people they knew who'd shown that same kind of recklessness.

But as the story winds to its close, Jesus adds an unexpected twist. The father approaches the returning son—not in angry censure but with delighted welcome! And though we may be surprised, even disturbed by it, a listener can't help but see the beauty of the father's lavish grace. Just as much, it is hard to avoid feeling the tragedy of the older brother's hard heart, still laboring in far-off fields with cold countenance even as the welcome home party has begun. If our heart is pliable even in the least, we know that that is not what we want for ourselves. And so we begin to consider: What might entering the Father's joy and extending His grace mean for me too?

"Advice is like snow," said Samuel Taylor Coleridge. "The softer it falls the longer it dwells upon, and the deeper it sinks into the mind."[14] In the right context, stories fall softer and sink deeper than any other form of persuasion.

Personal Notes: Erik

My niece, Abby, is a storyteller. She's only thirteen, and from her earliest years she's been surrounded by stories. When she was small, Abby and her grandfather would act out their "Dumbo Play Circus" for hours; these days she stars in the school play. Inevitably, when friends come over to hang, the day ends with a fully finished short film. She is the only teen I know writing a novel.

I work in Hollywood, the epicenter of storytelling. It's possible that the best storytellers in the world are typing scripts at a café in Santa Monica; we assume that is where real storytellers go to perfect their craft and to profit by it. But I doubt it.

I'd like to think that the best storytellers are found spinning tales at diners along Interstate 40 or by drama teachers at P.S. 87 or fifth-grade Sunday school classes in Jacksonville or at the bedside of three-year-olds..

As followers of the Master Storyteller, we should be good at telling stories—scratch that, we should be great at stories. Great at telling one and great at hearing one. "The Christian is the one whose imagination should fly beyond the stars," theologian Francis Schaeffer wrote.[15] Our story goes deeper and further and higher than most—we stand a yard from hell, as our story includes the cross, and rise beyond the cosmos, as our story includes the invisible realm, a dimension beyond this page.

And yet, imaginations are restrained. Storytellers corralled. Scripts shelved. Words hacked. Because we've been told that our stories must fit a certain type, have a certain ending, fall within a particular "rating" or genre. The effects have been astonishing: an entire generation that is like a junior high student at a school dance—not sure what to do and certain his parents are watching through a crack in the gym door.

It's changing though. Girls and boys like Abby are marinating a culture of stories—and the church seems ready to tell new ones, in new ways, with new mediums. I hope I am still in Hollywood when their scripts are ready. We need them.

LITTLE KEYS TO STORYTELLING

Each of our lives is a treasure trove of stories. We need not be a globe-trotter or celebrity. As expressed by Isak Dinesen, who wrote the epic *Out of Africa*, "To be a person is to have a story to tell."[16]

To begin, all we need to do is sink our hands into the soil at our feet: the delightful surprises, bruised expectations, moments of clarity, and hours of darkness that make up every human life. Others' lives too, both friends and those encountered in books and movies, provide a boundless supply as well.

And as we learn to be more present and attentive to others, we will be all the more likely to notice and remember. We would do well to write down at least brief notes on stories that particularly move us, so we can draw upon them later.

Of course like any art, the skill of storytelling invites a lifetime of learning and practice. A few key habits of great storytellers are worth keeping in mind no matter how long we've been doing it.

1. *Succinctness is a virtue.* Long, rambling stories quickly lose their appeal. The ideal length depends on the context, of course. But it's almost always best to err on the side of brevity. It's amazing to ponder how many unforgettable parables Jesus delivered in a paragraph or two.

2. *Despite the value of brevity, details bring stories to life.* Listeners enjoy stories far more when made to feel as if they are there. A good storyteller, like a cartoonist, needs only a line or two to sketch out a scene or character. A street "littered with glass and broken dreams"; a face "that protruded like a shark's"; a beggar "so destitute the dogs licked his sores."[17]

3. *Show, don't tell.* Never say, "It was hot." You want them to *see* hot: "Sweat trickled down my neck, and even the Golden Retriever lay sprawled in front of the fan." Don't merely tell, "She was happy to find her lost coin"; show that she "calls her friends and neighbors together and says, 'Rejoice with me.'"[18]

4. *Engage all the senses, not just the eyes.* Include smells, sounds, tastes, and touch sensations: the odor of hot tar on a blistering afternoon; the forlorn cry of a raven; the tangy

bitterness of a lemon wedge; the cold rubber of a corpse's skin.

5. *Your audience needs to wonder, "What happens next?"* Take a little extra time to build up the unsolved problem, the unexplained mystery, the inescapable dilemma. Suspense—even in very mild forms—keeps people listening.

6. *Use every tool at your disposal.* Aid your telling with your hands, arms, and body. Make faces. As Jesus did with a child, a coin, and a Roman centurion, reference objects nearby. Make sounds and mimic voices. Use props. Push your inhibitions a bit.

As with physical exercise, in learning to tell stories well, the most important rule is a simple one: just do it. The more tales you tell, the better you'll get.

Chapter 14

STORYTELLING FOR COMMUNITY, CAUSE, AND CONVICTION

Washington DC is famous for its partisan rancor and ideological divides. Moments that appear otherwise have usually been scripted. So what happened at a four-thousand-person leadership luncheon in 2007 took most everyone by surprise.

The diverse crowd was in town for the National Prayer Breakfast. Leaders of every political stripe filled the room. Alongside the safe politicians you might expect at such an event sat both dictators and dissidents, environmentalists and business titans, libertarians and socialists. As participants washed down their last bites of chicken breast, the lights dimmed, and a film began to play. It was a series of clips from the upcoming movie *Amazing Grace*, weaving together the story of eighteenth-century abolitionist William Wilberforce.

For many in the room, both conservative and liberal, Wilberforce had been a lifelong hero, a political patron saint. All hushed as the film's brief episodes pieced together a tale of uncommon courage, vision, and sacrifice. For many the story reminded why they'd gotten involved in politics in the first place.

As the lights came up, the event's organizers began moving toward the keynote speech. But there, in a town known for both discord and anything but spontaneous happenings, the four thousand lunch goers rose. Without prompting or planning, their voices joined in singing the great hymn "Amazing Grace," *a cappella*. For a moment, at least, a city divided had found community.

> I can only answer the question, "What am I to do?" if I can answer the prior question, "Of what story or stories do I find myself a part?"[1]
> —ALASDAIR MacINTYRE

Even amongst strangers, nothing grows community like story. Connection and common identity spring most of all from shared stories.

This is true at every level, even the most intimate. Psychologists observe that one key element in the growth of a romance comes as the couple forms and recounts their experiences together. It is their pulse-quickening first encounter, the misunderstanding that nearly ruined it all, and the revived passion at the end of a bitter fight that together begin to form *our story*. Two former strangers are knit ever closer as they shape and retell their story again and again.

Shared stories are vital for groups too. Consider the way a circle of friends, athletic team, or band of soldiers retell stories. They recount the most exhausting moments of their training, laugh again over comic blunders, or wistfully recall a member of the group lost to death. From the flippant to the sober, these shared narratives knit the group together. They not only tell history but also define and remind *who we are* and *what we're about*.

Personal Notes: Erik

Change is the only constant. At least that is how I explain myself to friends and family who ask, "Will you ever sit still?"

It's a fair question. Since 2004 Monica and I have had three kids, moved five times across country, and changed jobs three times. Our lives are like watching a tennis match.

Most recently, when we moved to Manhattan, the question was, "Why would you live in that tiny, overpriced New York City apartment with three small children and no car?" Another fair question.

My honest answer is this: I believe God is writing a story in our lives, as He did with every character of the Bible. New York is just another unexpected scene.

I'd vowed to never live in New York, but the story changed me. Here's what I mean: Years before, Monica and I felt called to be a part of a Washington, DC, church plant committed to being "In the city, for the city." Jedd and Rachel soon joined us and lived just down the street on Capitol Hill. It was there that we first felt the thrill of real community and a pastor who called us away from "safe and secure" to the big risks and dreams of God's upside-down kingdom.

Next, while in Los Angeles, we encountered Francis Chan. A three-minute video where Francis stands on a balance beam distills the big challenge we took from him. If you've seen it, you'll know what I mean. If not, google it. It became an idea that I couldn't shake: *Are we playing it too safe, especially with our kids?*

The story progressed. Monica and I were on the verge of moving to a big, comfy house when we were given the *Citywide Worship* CD from Trinity Grace Church in New York. I listened to it again and again. I could tell these gritty, hard-worn citified Christ-followers, locking arms together in Chelsea and Brooklyn and the Upper West Side, really believed what they were singing. There was no reason to go through the motions as halfhearted creatures. Either these words are true or everything is going to fall apart. When friends in New York invited us to join them there, we packed all of our belongings into an 8 by 8 by 16 POD and set off.

It's not always easy or fun. (Just ask me on a hot August day on the subway with the kids.) But it has been life giving. Sometimes a story changes your mind or haunts your heart. In this case, the story became my life. We tend to look outside ourselves for signs of God's hand, when most of the time He is scripting our hearts from within.

This uniting and defining power of story extends even to entire civilizations. Shared narratives—from *The Odyssey* to the Bible to Shakespeare— indelibly colored every aspect of the Western world. These defining stories gave Europeans and their offspring more than common cultural artifacts. They created a common understanding of the world and a sense of shared identity.

One glimpse of this came on Christmas Eve 1914, in the heart of World War I. Europe's nations were locked in brutal war, the very antithesis of community. But on that crisp winter day, soldiers from both sides of the war's Western Front spontaneously began to set down their guns and offer instead greetings and songs to the opposing lines. One by one, then in groups, men left their trenches and crossed the wasted "No Man's Land." Some even began to play soccer and sing carols together. Throughout the night, they exchanged food, drink, and gifts. War had gripped the continent with a violent evil. But to the chagrin of commanding officers, the story and meaning of Christmas still carried enough strength and shared identity among the warring soldiers to draw them together for one silent night.[2]

Jews of Jesus's day shared powerful stories as well. Despite fierce differences between various sects—from the Pharisees and Sadducees to revolutionary Zealots—all drew a distinctly Jewish identity from their communal stories. Regardless of whom He was addressing, Jesus often drew from this well of stories. Not only did they provide examples, but they also connected the audience in a shared sense of deep meaning and history, even those who opposed Him. "Just as Moses lifted up the snake in the desert, so the Son of Man must be lifted up."[3] "For as Jonah was three days and three nights in the belly of a huge fish…"[4] "Just as it was in the days of Noah…"[5]

To these ancient stories, Jesus added a host of new ones. There were His parables, of course, as well as the accounts of His life, death, and resurrection—rightly labeled, "the greatest story ever told." These narratives became a powerful uniting influence for the multiracial Christian communities that sprang up across the Roman empire and beyond. The early church soon added more stories. The accounts of martyrs and other faithful women and men were recounted over dinner tables and whispered by torchlight in Roman catacombs. Many were transcribed by church fathers. Some found their way into later works, such as *Foxe's Book of Martyrs*, which gave a sense of shared identity and historic continuity to persecuted Protestants during the Reformation. All of these stories not only conveyed Christianity's ideals. They also helped knit together Jew and Greek, Roman, African, and Asian into the most diverse community the world had ever seen.

Especially in an era when real community often feels painfully elusive, the storyteller can play a powerful role-knitting connection and common identity.

Personal Notes: Jedd

My great-grandfather was still a young farmer in Saskatchewan when a massive stroke struck him like a hailstone from clear skies. He died on a train en route to the hospital, somewhere along the Canadian prairie. Back at home, my great-grandmother surveyed the ripe wheat fields in despair. She had little money to hire help and no capacity to do it herself, not to mention five small children. She prayed fervently into the night.

A Native American man traveling through the nearest town the next day accepted the modest pay Great-Grandma offered to help her harvest. Day after day he worked from first light to darkness. At mealtime he'd accept only one cup of fresh milk, drink it under a tree, then return to work.

The grain all reached the barns before the rains. In gratitude Great-Grandma stood before the sunburnt man, her children gathered around her legs. She took the promised payment from her purse and held it forward.

Seven decades later, her daughter, my grandmother, could still recall vividly what happened next. The man shook his head. He motioned to the five small children, then pointed toward heaven. Then he walked away without a word.

They never saw him again, but the story continues to live in our family. To this day it invigorates our faith with a sense not just of God's provision but also of His provision *for us*. My Grandma told other stories too. About how she ventured to Chicago as a simple prairie girl, and then all the way to California on her own. How she turned down a marriage proposal from a wealthy suitor, assuming she may never get another, because she realized he wasn't committed to following Jesus. And many other simple, compelling tales of faith and faithfulness.

Stories like these told us not just who she was but what kind of people *we* were. We would trust God to provide. We would hold out for God's best. We would risk and anticipate good things. For my cousins and me, these

images of who we were formed who we became. Simple stories, yes, but
they help shape my sense of identity and of what matters to this day.

The stories parents tell their children cultivate a strong sense of identity,
belonging, and values. This can be especially true of stories drawn from
noble moments in family history. One catches a glimpse of this in the more-
than-just-a-cartoon movie *The Lion King*. In shame and insecurity, young
Simba has abandoned his role as king for a worry-free life in the jungle.
The ghost of his father appears to him, reminding of the many great kings
of Simba's line. Simba is of their blood, their heritage, his father reminds.
This identity means Simba is meant for more than just slurping grubs and
singing "*Hakuna Matata.*" He can, and must, return to fill a noble role for
the other lions and the entire community. And he does.

Parents can also help a child forge her identity by taking note of times
when she showed special kindness, courage, or perseverance. Writing these
down and retelling them from time to time enables the child to conclude,
"*That* is who I am."

Stories are just as important for businesses, churches, and other organizations. The book *Onward* by Starbucks's CEO Howard Schultz
models this brilliantly. With the ring of authenticity, he tells the story of
Starbucks's rise, near-fatal mistakes, and hard-fought turnaround. In doing
so, Schultz helped shift Starbucks's public image from "big corporation" to
"business with a heart."[6] But just as important, he gave tens of thousands
of Starbucks's employees a sense of their own story too, instilling values
Schultz hopes they'll reflect in every customer contact and espresso.

From a family to a business to a nation, stories are much more than history. They cultivate identity, belonging, and values in a way nothing else
can. In an age when all three of these are in short supply, the storyteller
may be the most significant communicator of all.

MAKING AN ARGUMENT WITHOUT ARGUING

Like the prophet Nathan, Anna Leonowens needed to deliver a difficult
message to an Eastern autocrat. Serving as a tutor within the palace of
King Mongkut, ruler of Siam, Anna desired to help the king grasp how
evil slavery really was. She knew, though, that a direct appeal would insult
his pride and make change impossible. Mongkut would never govern based
on demands from a foreigner, let alone a woman. He must come to the conclusion on his own.

In one portrayal of what transpired, Anna resorts to story. Using a play, she introduced the king to the rich narrative of *Uncle Tom's Cabin*. Rather than laying out the case against slavery, she would let the story reveal the humanity of the slaves and the despicable treatment they'd received from their master. She could not force her opinions. But the story, she knew, carried the potential to lead the king toward a *self-discovered* condemnation of slavery, just as it had for many Americans prior to the Civil War.

The exact details of Anna's efforts and their impact are debated by historians. We know, however, that Mongkut's son reversed centuries of Siamese tradition, allowing his slaves to go free.[7]

A theory is meant to help you know the world without changing the world yourself. A story is to help you deal with the world by changing it through changing yourself.[8]
—STANLEY HAUERWAS

The ancient Greeks referred to this approach to persuasion as *enthymeme*—essentially leaving out part of an argument so listeners can reach the final conclusion on their own.

Stories, particularly when their point isn't force-fed, become an invitation to this sort of personal discovery. They allow a listener space to reach conclusions on his or her own. As discussed in Section VIII on questions, self-discovered conclusions ultimately impact more deeply and permanently than those handed to us preprocessed.

Of course it requires self-restraint to leave it to the audience to notice what we want them to see. We must resist the fear that they may end up at a different conclusion than we intended.

This danger, however, is inherent to all forms of communication. It is delusion to assume we can somehow *insert* new ideas into another person's brain, whole and unprocessed as the blockbuster movie *Inception* portrays. In the final analysis, the power of persuasion resides in the mind of the listener, not the speaker. Whatever we wish to convey, it is the listeners who ultimately digest, establish meaning, and decide what role new ideas will have in their lives.

By embracing this reality, the communicator using stories actually has a greater hand in guiding the outcome. A mere fact-giver delivers new information but ultimately remains at the mercy of the receiver's processing. The storyteller not only provides new information but also offers a glimpse of how that information can be integrated into the listener's life. We see, right from the get-go, what the information looks like applied in real life.

As one scholar of biblical narrative describes, "The impact of the parables is directly tied to their…insistence that insight be embodied, incarnated…in human *lives*, not in the head alone but in and through the full scope and breadth of a human life."[9]

Stories lead, gently and effectively, to the most powerful form of learning: self-discovery. Truths embraced in this way are the most likely to take shape in action. And as they do, the actions are often guided by the story that started it all.

Here again we see that the way of the apprentice flows from our view of the Father. While the mysteries of Providence operate behind the scenes in ways we could never fathom, we see that God's way is persistently that of *invitation*. Continually He bids, "Come, all you who are thirsty, come to the waters…"[10] Even to the disobedient He holds out His hands "all day long."[11] He woos like a lover, waits patiently like the father of the prodigal son, knocks gently at the door of the heart. From the insight of the Proverbs to the testimony of creation, God continually offers wise argument without arguing.[12]

This was the quiet power of Jesus's storytelling too: wooing, waiting, knocking, inviting. Offering wisdom without arguing.

MAKING THE TRUE INTO THE REAL

Gary Haugen, now the president of the International Justice Mission, directed the United Nations' investigation of the genocide in Rwanda. Prior to arriving in the African nation, he had read the reports, reviewed the statistics, studied the history. But it was not until he encountered Rwanda firsthand that the tragedy became real for him. Looking back, he wrote, "It seemed *true*, but not real—not to me. I did not dispute the accuracy of the reports, but they might as well have been pictures from Sojourner on Mars or reports about people who lived in ancient Rome…all true enough, but not real."[13]

We all have limited capacity to see and feel beyond our immediate experience. Stories are uniquely equipped to help with this dilemma. They can give those who receive them eyes to see what would otherwise have remained fuzzy and far off.

These story-given eyes can see things both too terrible and, sometimes, too wonderful to believe without seeing. As Gary Haugen encountered the scenes and personal stories of Rwanda's anguish—as well as tales of glimmered hope—it all became real for him. We often cannot travel as he did to experience global realities firsthand. But stories can play a powerful role in helping us enter realities that previously felt true but not real. Knowing this, Haugen himself has become a master storyteller, viewing this as a vital part of his role as an advocate for justice. His well-told accounts help Americans who've tasted little of real injustice to *see* and to *feel* what it would be like to be a father whose entire family is trapped in servitude at a brick factory in India, or a thirteen-year- old girl trafficked into slavery in a Cambodian brothel.

> That's how we absorb the weight of each other's pain, through story. And once we do that, we each carry some of each other's burdens.[14]
> —FILMMAKER JONATHAN OLINGER

Storytellers like Elie Wiesel and Aleksandr Solzhenitsyn have been awarded the Nobel Peace Prize for this very reason. Their stories have given an incredulous world eyes to see the depths of human suffering and evil, calling us to stand boldly against it.

This is true for each new-fledged evil the world must confront. A fascinating article by columnist Nicholas Kristof explores the factors that can get busy people to pay attention to serious problems in the world and act in response. Effective storytelling, Kristof concludes, is right at the heart of the answer. He explains of the once-ignored genocide in Darfur:

> Ultimately, Darfur did catch the public's attention and rise to a place on the global agenda, partly because organizations got better at telling stories of individual Darfuris. Hundreds of thousands of American students and church and temple members joined the Save Darfur movement, protesting, fasting, or otherwise supporting a people halfway around the world who mostly didn't look like them, who belonged to a different religion, and whom they'd never heard of a few years earlier. For me, it was a reminder that emotional connections are possible even with the most remote suffering.[15]

Stories can bring distant anguish near. But just as important, Kristof reminds, stories can help us see the potential for good too. Summarizing several recent psychological studies, Kristof reports, "We intervene not because of stories of desperate circumstances but when we can be cheered up with positive stories of success and transformation."[16]

Stories can make not only evil vivid but also good. They can make hopes of renewal as real as the ugliness that surrounds us. They sing of far-off beauty and convince us that it is, after all, *possible*.

Jesus's stories did this. Not only did they *explain* truth, but they also helped people *see* and *feel* what it looked like. A housewife throwing a party to celebrate the discovery of a valuable coin she'd lost. A father lifting his robe above his knees to run along a dusty road to his bedraggled son, finally returned home. For the guilt-ridden man who could hardly lift his head, for the woman who'd never felt valued by others or by God, stories like these helped make the improbably distant feel possible. Lavish forgiveness. Profound value. Eternal hope. In a dawning understanding that goes deeper than words, Jesus's stories made the true into the real. They still do so today.

The same can be said of well-told stories of deep goodness in every realm. It can take a story like that of the priest in *Les Miserables*—who rescued Jean Valjean from returning to prison despite Valjean's attempt to rob him—to enable us to grasp the profound power of grace.

It frequently takes narratives such as those of Abraham Lincoln's many lost elections, Helen Keller's painful struggle to learn to speak, or Albert Einstein's struggles in high school math to enable us to see the value of perseverance and hope.

It takes an account such as Frederick Douglass's rise from slavery to prominent statesman to make believable the promise and possibility our world contains alongside all of its suffering.

This is why Jesus explained the kingdom of God not mainly with statements or formulas but with stories. He knew the things He wished to portray would be novel and beyond His listeners' typical experiences. So He told tales of hidden treasure, gleaming pearls, and an enemy sowing seeds in a farmer's field. Each story gave its hearers an *experience*—partial but poignant—of the future reality He wanted them to make the very foundation of their existence.

Stories help communicators to turn the *true* into the *real*, whether the darkest edges of human experience or its highest potential.

A UNIVERSE WOVEN OF STORIES

In the disturbing film *Memento*, viewers enter the experience of a man who knows facts and nothing more. Severe head trauma has left Leonard Shelby incapable of making new memories. If he is to recall anything later, he must create mementos by scratching quick notes on scraps of paper, taking Polaroid photos, and even inscribing messages on his body via tattoo. The recorded details accumulate: *He is staying at the Discount Inn; Teddy cannot be trusted; Natalie has lost someone she loves; the person who killed his wife was a white male with access to drugs.* Over time Shelby's world overflows with facts. And yet it remains clear that he is utterly lost, for Shelby has no story.

 All life is an allegory. We can understand it only in parables.[17]
—G. K. CHESTERTON

It is sobering to realize how little facts mean without story. Essentially, nothing. Facts alone convey no more meaning than do strands of thread piled in haphazard tangles on the floor. Stories alone weave these threads into tapestries, creating context, value, and significance.

For Jesus, reality itself was woven of story.

The heartbeat of Jewish faith, as Jesus presented it, had little to do with dusty theories about God or requirements of legalistic virtue. It was the expansive story of a God whose creatures rebelled against Him, and of His tender pursuit to draw those wayward children home. Narrative was not merely a means of telling *about* deeper reality; this Narrative *was* deeper reality.

Embroidered throughout this grand epic were countless smaller narrative accounts as well. Each story throughout the Bible revealed unique truths about the character of this God and His quest to rescue self-willed humankind: a couple's tragic encounter with a devious serpent; a young farmer driven by envy to slay his brother; a flood sent to purge the earth of evil; a slave elevated to Pharaoh's right hand; a stuttering shepherd who became an agent of deliverance; the list could go on for pages.

Of course this story-based reality spills out far beyond the pages of Jewish Scripture. It is indelibly stamped upon all of human experience. As C. S. Lewis put it, "All history in the last resort must be held by Christians to be a story with a divine plot."[18]

Living in such a universe, the advice offered by storyteller Annette Simmons merits pondering. "Your listeners *have* enough information. They have all the facts and statistics they could ever want. In fact, they are drowning in information. Depression is at epidemic levels because all of this information simply leaves us feeling incompetent and lost. We don't need more information. We need to know what it means. We need a story that explains what it means and makes us feel like we fit in there somewhere."[19]

 The universe is made of stories, not of atoms.[20]
—MURIEL RUKEYSER, AMERICAN POET

That is just what Jesus's stories did. Our stories can do so as well.

LIFE THROUGH QUESTIONS

Upend a Life of Giving the Answers

Chapter 15

HOW TO START A REVOLUTION

How do revolutions begin?

Certainly times of social tumult and radical change are frequently birthed with fiery rhetoric and booming calls to arms. In these often-bloody hours every leader's sentence ends with an exclamation point.

> Once the question mark has arisen in the human brain the answer must be found, if it takes a hundred years. A thousand years.[1]
>
> —JULES VERNE

But look back a bit further to what really started the revolution, and we will almost always find something else. It's something gentler and less emphatic, a symbol shaped as though it were bent over in humility: the question mark.

Wise leaders understand that well-formed questions can become a battle horn. They begin soft and low, slowly growing as they echo from one individual to another, then another. They become an invitation, drawing people to weigh possibilities never before considered.

Revolutions—whether of a nation or a single human heart—begin when someone asks a question.

AGENTS OF TRANSFORMATION

A stumpy, toga-draped figure with a homely face is counted among the most influential individuals of all time.

Unlike the other great characters of ancient Athens, he chose to steer clear of politics and climbing the civic ladder. And unlike other popular philosophers of his era, he wrote no books, established no school, and did not even offer any formal classes.

Yet this man has stood at the heart of Western philosophy for twenty-four hundred years. And his influence grew almost entirely from conversations built upon a single tool: the question.

Day in and day out, Socrates shaped the thoughts and perspectives of the students and others who gathered around him. He drew them with his questions toward new insights and perspectives:

→ "If a speech is to be good, must not the mind of the speaker know the truth about the matters of which he speaks?"[2]

→ "But is it not better to be ridiculous than to be clever and an enemy?"[3]

→ "He who has learned what is just is just?"[4]

The leading Athenians of Socrates's day had their faults, but they cannot be accused of being unperceptive. They knew that Socrates's unassuming dialogues and probing questions—what is today called the *Socratic Method*—presented more of a threat to Athens's status quo than even the enemy armies of mighty Sparta.

Despite his sincere piety and patriotism, Socrates was put on trial for subversion. He was charged with corrupting the youth and undermining religious practices. A small majority of the jury voted to convict.

Rejecting their offer of life in exile, Socrates submitted to the jury's final sentence: death by suicide. He spent his final hours with students and family members. As the sun drew low, the aging teacher raised a cup of hemlock to his lips. He walked around the cell, allowing the poison to move into his bloodstream. Then, as those gathered around him wept, he lay down, never to rise again.

His question-centered communication, however, continues to reverberate. Athens, and with it the entire Western world, has never been the same.

Consider other great transformations in society: The fight for American independence. The invention of human flight. The struggle for civil rights and women's suffrage. The fall of the iron curtain or the end of apartheid in South Africa.

All these *tipping points* in history started with questions—inquiries, second-guesses, an "is this the way things have to be?" that set in motion fundamental change.

Patrick Henry's patriotic challenge—"Is life so dear, or peace so sweet, as to be purchased at the price of chains and slavery?"[5]—drew blacksmiths and bankers alike to risk all in a David-versus-Goliath battle for American liberty.

The suffragettes doggedly questioned why, if women were truly of the same value as men, they should not be allowed to vote. Ultimately, age-old conventions crumbled.

Martin Luther King Jr.'s revolution was heavy with questions as well. If indeed "all men are created equal," why then should some be treated as more equal than others? Of those who wished to join him, Dr. King asked, "Are you able to accept blows without retaliating?" And of those who criticized him as extreme, King demanded, "The question is not whether we will be extremists, but what kind of extremist we will be. Will we be extremists for hate or for love?"[6]

Indeed, whatever the status quo may be, and no matter how smug, stifling, or self-satisfied it has become, it has no greater enemy than the question. Writing from behind the iron curtain in Soviet-dominated Czechoslovakia, Milan Kundera expressed, "The true opponent of totalitarian kitsch [valueless culture] is the person who asks questions. A question is like a knife that slices through the stage backdrop and gives us a look at what lies hidden behind it."[7]

Revolutionaries—those initiators of transformation in human lives—are men and women who understand the power of a question.

TOE-TO-TOE WITH THE ESTABLISHMENT

Asking questions may not seem revolutionary at first glance.

In fact, it often seems the opposite. To many, asking a question suggests lack of knowledge, uncertainty, even confusion. We assume powerful communicators deliver statements, assertions, and well-worded claims. They are continually declaring, alleging, pronouncing, affirming…*anything* but asking.

And no wonder. *Questions release control.* They seem to place the listener in the driver's seat. And that, we often assume, is the death knell of effective communications.

Or is it?

Admittedly, modern communication is driven by assertions. Go there. Believe this. Buy those. Do that. Each day brings a fresh whirlwind of messages, each demanding that we alter yet another aspect of our beliefs and behaviors. These declarations are *answers*, bold and emphatic.

Executive boardrooms and the corridors of Capitol Hill rarely hear three simple words: *I don't know.* We are a culture ruled by answers and assertions. Deliberation is distrusted. Doubts are to be erased. Inquiry is suspicious.

But something remarkable happened to people when Jesus—the self-proclaimed answer—began asking questions.

Personal Notes: Jedd

My friend Matt is the kind of winsome guy you can sense really cares about you, even after just five minutes of conversation. He's been out of college only a few years and now does campus ministry at Cal State University–San Francisco with his wife, Leah. They work together to nurture the young faith of Christian students. They also desire to dig into spiritual issues with other students too, many of whom start with a negative view of Christianity.

When I asked Matt how he gets students thinking about spiritual matters, he answered simply: "Good questions." Matt shared that he used to feel awkward bringing up spiritual topics with students he didn't know well, like he was forcing it. He confessed, "Truth is, I often saw 'ministry' as just trying to get as many words out as I could to help people understand the gospel." But recently Matt has been amazed at how sincerely asked questions lead to meaningful conversation.

"Sometimes I'll just share that I serve with a Christian organization on campus and that I'd like to ask their opinion on spiritual matters," explained Matt. "If they're up for it, I ask. And then I listen. Honestly, I learn a ton. And most of the time I sense that it really gets their wheels turning. The questions open the door to a place in their heart they may not have visited before, at least not recently. Frequently they'll ask my thoughts as well, which makes for a great opportunity to share my heart for Jesus."

Matt expressed that, ironically, it's often the students who start with the most negative views of Christianity who express the most gratitude for the questions. "It's as if just asking questions and listening is healing for them. They'll say, 'This is really a different Christianity than I've experienced before. It's always seemed to be just about loud opinions, preachy. But you're asking questions and getting me thinking. I really appreciate that.'"

Matt has plenty of insightful things to share too, and often he does. But with his thoughtful questions and sincere listening, he's a great contrast to "talkative Christianity"...and ultimately points to Jesus Himself.

A QUESTION WITH AN ANSWER IN IT

The eyes of the religious rulers narrowed as they surveyed the scene before them. What gall for this Jesus to venture into *their* territory, the temple courts, teaching the gullible masses as if He had something the priests and theologians could not provide.

Clearly, the people were being mesmerized by the charlatan. The name of Jesus was on everyone's lips, from shopkeeper to centurion. There was danger of riots, even open revolt. It was all a little too much for those who valued status and stability. For months the chief priests and elders had been watching and waiting, plotting, and biding their time.

Now here was the opportunity they'd been waiting for, a chance to force Jesus's hand. They paraded onto the scene, robes flowing out behind them, faces flushed with anger. How dare this troublemaker come here! They demanded an answer, once and for all.

A leading elder raised his voice, forcefully inquiring, "By what authority are you doing these things? And who gave you authority to do this?"

The rulers must have pursed their lips in satisfaction and rubbed their hands in delight. At last, this magician, this revolutionary, this fraud would be exposed here—in the house of God—before hundreds of His followers and witnesses.

It was a good question. A mind game. A trap. Just who had given Him the right to make the bold claims He made? Jesus's answer would certainly expose Him as a liar, or worse, a blasphemer—claiming to be the Son of God, an answer that would certainly incite the people against Him.

Jesus knew He was being set up. He looked soberly around at the crowds hushed with anticipation, and nodded at the craftiness of the question. The rulers likely had spent many hours forming it.

"I will ask you one question," Jesus began. "Answer me, and I will tell you by what authority I am doing these things." The crowd gasped. The rulers' eyes narrowed, and their jaws clenched. Jesus continued. "John's baptism—was it from heaven or from men?"

The aged, bearded men turned to one another. Whispers circulated the temple. Jesus had turned the tables. Instead of falling into the trap, He asked a question.

The rulers weighed their response, huddled together, gesturing, arguing in hushed tones. Answering that John the Baptizer had been nothing special would anger the crowd since the people viewed him as a prophet, but if the leaders affirmed John, they would implicate themselves for refusing to believe him, just as they were now doing with Jesus. Frustrated and entangled in their own snare, they responded, "We don't know."

Jesus nodded. "Then neither will I tell you by what authority I am doing these things."

A murmur of delight rippled through the crowd. This carpenter had stymied the bluebloods again. And that question He'd asked—it seemed to have an answer imbedded in it as well. After all, John *was* a prophet anointed by heaven, the people knew that much for certain. And John *had* declared emphatically that Jesus was even greater than himself, the very "lamb of God who takes away the sin of the world." Could it be...?[8]

THE ANSWER WHO ASKED QUESTIONS

The Gospels, which record only a fraction of all Jesus said and did, contain more than one hundred fifty questions asked by Jesus. That's not exactly what you would expect from someone who claimed to be "the way and the truth and the life"[9]—the very answer to all of life's deepest questions.

The eighth chapter of Mark alone contains sixteen questions, each unique and piercing. They test faith, gently rebuke, explore the disciples' understanding of Jesus, and invite them to examine what they truly value.

Of course Jesus was not one to shrink from controversial statements and bold assertions. But He also understood the profound power of the question.

Statements alone can be rigid, easily picked apart, and then disregarded in a debate over details. They tend to make demands of the audience rather than requests. They often give little space for the listener's own thought process, but instead try to orchestrate that process for him.

Jesus's questions, in contrast, invited others to participate in the activity of discovery, to take hold of truth for themselves. He understood that when an idea is *imposed*, however reasonable it might be, it is rarely held for long.

Consider some of Jesus's questions:

- → "Who do you say I am?"[10]
- → "What do you want me to do for you?"[11]
- → "Why do you call me good?"[12]
- → "What were you arguing about on the road?"[13]
- → "How many loaves do you have?"[14]

These are straightforward questions. Each one, however, goes deeper than might appear at first glance. It delves into murky corners where unspoken reservations and self-protection dwell. It exposes dark corners to the light of honest reflection, inviting to self-examination and self-discovery.

Abraham Lincoln expressed well what we all intuitively know. If we seek to motivate others by attempting to "dictate to his judgment, or to command his action," we will almost certainly meet with failure. "He will retreat within himself, close all the avenues to his head and his heart; and tho' your cause be naked truth itself…you shall no more be able to [reach] him, than to penetrate the hard shell of a tortoise with a rye straw."[15]

Jesus's way stood in sharp contrast to a dictate-and-dominate approach. Instead His questions invited sincere listeners to embark on a search. The question sent them off, candle in hand, in search of answers.

Jesus knew that in the process of honest searching, aided by God's Spirit, the person would often encounter the very instruction he or she needed most. It might be remembrance of a truth known in childhood long buried. Or finally confronting a gap between his beliefs and actions. Or recognition of a harmful attitude carelessly embraced. Within the ample space for reflection that questions allow, the searcher could ponder his or her discovery. In such a place, false assumptions and thoughtless habits could be exposed and found wanting.

Many of us are tempted to try to illuminate the way for others with a floodlight powered by our own blazing assertions. We want so badly to lead quickly and unambiguously to the answers we wish to provide. But *our* solution to the dimness might well have left those listeners blinded and recoiling, their eyes shut tight against light for years. The candle, though perhaps through a slow and stumbling process, often achieves far more.

It is impossible to force people to think or act or believe a certain way. Present all the right facts, have all the right answers, say all the right things, but they still might choose another path, buy the other product, or vote for the other candidate.

What we can do is *prepare* them. Communication that is rich with thoughtful questions erects signposts and hands them gentle illumination for the journey. The expedition from thought to action, from ear to hand, from listening to responding is theirs. Our job is just to help them along the way and leave the rest to God.

Chapter 16

CHANGE DEEPER THAN
FORCE COULD BRING

Nico Smith, like most Afrikaners of his era in South Africa, grew up drinking a doctrine of white superiority with his mother's milk. When the 1948 elections brought the Afrikaner Nationalists to power, nineteen-year-old Nico took to the streets to celebrate the arrival of government-sponsored apartheid.

In his thirties, as an influential figure within the Dutch Reformed Church, Nico was recruited to join the elite fraternity known as the Broederbond. This group connected many of the most powerful members of society in a secretive brotherhood, working behind the scenes to advance the Afrikaner political and ideological agenda. These connections soon propelled Nico into a respected professorial position at Stellenbosch University.

But on a visit to Switzerland in 1963 Nico met the great theologian Karl Barth. Near the end of his visit Dr. Barth approached Nico and inquired politely, "May I ask you a personal question?" Nico nodded. He viewed conversing with the famed Christian thinker as a high privilege.

"Are you free to preach the gospel in South Africa?" asked Barth.

"Yes, of course I am." Nico replied pleasantly. "Freedom of religion."

Barth shook his head. "That's not the kind of freedom I am asking about. Are you free in yourself? If you come across things in the Bible that are contrary to what your family and friends believe, will you preach it?"

Nico shrugged. "I've never come across something like that."

The elderly theologian would not be dissuaded. "Are you so free that even if you come across things in the Bible which are contrary to what your government is doing—that you will preach it?"

A crimson blotch rose on Nico's cheek, and he looked away. It was an awkward question, and he did not feel he had an adequate answer.

Nico was soon safely back in South Africa, but Barth's questions had somehow managed to travel with him. They lodged in his thoughts and stuck, like seed-carrying burrs caught in one's sock—not growing, but certainly not comfortable either.

It was a full ten years later at a meeting of the Broederbond that the revolution Barth had gently seeded finally took root. As Nico pondered the attitudes and actions of his associates, the answer to Barth's question sprang into his mind: *I'm not free!* He stood and walked out of the meeting.

Nico knew that quitting the Broederbond was social suicide. At best he could hope to step away without drawing much notice. He would live quietly, keeping a healthy separation between his newfound Christian convictions and political issues. For several years he did. But the questions would not be so easily satisfied.

When the government bulldozed a group of black squatter homes on the outskirts of town, some of Nico's students asked him what the Christian response should be. More questions. As he pondered the answer, he realized he could remain silent no longer. Nico drafted an official criticism of the government action and offered it for publication. There was now no going back.

A political firestorm began to envelope Nico. With little else to do, Nico sought guidance in prayer. As if in answer, the next Monday morning a telegram arrived from the black township of Mamelodi. The residents were asking that Nico become their pastor.

"God, no, I didn't ask for this," lamented Nico. Emotion surged over him, and he began to cry right in front of the postman. As he waited for his wife's return, Nico began to hope that she would reject the idea, giving him an easy out with God.

Ellen, however, provided him no excuses. "Nico, you realize that we'll have to go," she said after reading the telegram. The decision was made.

In the face of staggering social and even physical risks, Nico and Ellen left the university at Stellenbosch and filled the pastorship of the Mamelodi parish. Initially they lived in a white suburb within driving distance of the township and commuted to the church. In time, however, they realized they could not truly minister to the people of Mamelodi without drawing nearer. A short while later Nico and Ellen became the first whites under apartheid to receive official permission to live in a black area—the only white residents in a township of three hundred thousand.

Nico and Ellen Smith's labors continue to bring healing to a torn nation. The seeds of their transformation were little more than a few simple questions.

THE CHARACTER OF JESUS'S QUESTIONS

There are many kinds of questions. Leading questions. Rhetorical questions. Condescending questions. Combative questions. Questions that are intended to obscure or instruct, insult or enlighten.

And while each distinct communication goal calls for its own unique questions, the best questions share a number of characteristics.

The questions Jesus asked were first of all sincere.

A question holds sincerity when the asker really cares what the listeners' response will be. That does not mean Jesus never knew what reply He would be given or never sought to guide discussion toward particular conclusions. It is just that what His listeners' thought and felt really mattered to Him—and that is why He asked, not to confuse them or make a point or demonstrate His own cleverness.

Personal Notes: Jedd

It's struck me in recent years that I almost always feel most connected and close to people who are good question askers. When a friend or even an acquaintance puts a little effort into thoughtful questions and listening, I feel respected, valued, loved.

The opposite is also true. I recall a favorite college professor sharing with me that he'd visited a number of friends in the course of a recent cross-country trip. He observed that very, very few of his hosts had seemed interested in asking questions beyond the basics. "They were all friendly and welcoming," he recalled. "But when it came to conversation, it seemed they mainly just wanted to talk about themselves. I know they didn't mean any harm by it, but honestly, it kind of hurt."

In contrast I think of friends like Danny and Emily. Whether over a shared meal or just a quick phone call, they have a way of making clear that they really want to know what's on your mind. Their questions aren't intrusive, just inviting. If you're not careful, you realize at the end that you've done all the talking. It's remarkable how cared for I always feel being with them. And often the questions gently nudge me to ponder things of real significance as well.

As I've sought to become more like that, I've realized that good questions don't always just pop into your head. So often, before friends come over for dinner, Rachel and I will think about our guests and choose a few questions likely to invite meaningful conversation. We'll pray together that we'll be a source of God's blessing to them. And sometimes, I'll take notes afterward, so I can remember to follow up on things they've shared. As we've done this, we've seen that putting just a little thought into preparing for time with others can do a lot to make it more rich and meaningful. It's a practical way to show interest and love and to grow as an apprentice to Jesus in daily interactions.

Jesus's questions were always attuned to the uniqueness of each situation.

Effective question asking requires a sensitivity to what is occurring at the moment and also to the readiness of others to receive the questions. As discussed in Section III, genuine attentiveness to others is a critical part of honing effective, fitting inquiries.

Jesus consistently did this. His questions mixed naturally with the discussion at hand, frequently flowing out of the events unfolding at the time: a dispute among His disciples, a hungry crowd, or a verbal attack from the religious authorities. Quite often His questions were directed at subtle attitudes or subplots that most busy people would not have even noticed. Questions are always most fruitful when well matched with the moment at hand.

Jesus's questions were fit to the audience.

Each one of Jesus's questions showed a deep awareness and thorough consideration of the audience's beliefs and biases, background and assumptions, fears and priorities.

Take, for instance, the story of "the good Samaritan," a phrase Jesus's audience would have considered an oxymoron. From the Jewish perspective this parable painted a shocking image. Jesus presented a despised, half-breed heretic whose active concern for a crime victim surpassed that of two Jewish holy men. If Jesus had force-fed His conclusion, it may have been too much for the audience. So rather than conclude with a mandate, Jesus used a question, "Which of the three was the true neighbor?"[1]

No doubt many in the audience writhed internally at the notion that a filthy Samaritan was portrayed as the protagonist. Yet still, the prickly truth could hardly be avoided. We all sense deep down that true love of neighbor is not based on race or group identity but upon a decision to serve. Jesus's question served as a crowbar, perfectly fitted to the task of breaking apart ancient prejudices and assumptions about the limits of loving one's neighbor.

Jesus's questions were also decisively clarifying.

They penetrated to the heart of the matter. They peeled back layer after layer of what appeared to be the real issue in order to address what actually was the real issue. Often they helped the listener see the crossroads that stood before them.

"What good is it for a man to gain the whole world and lose his soul?"[2] posed Jesus. "Which of you by worrying can add a single hour to his life?"[3] "Is not life more important than food and the body than clothes?"[4] Questions such as these spark self-scrutiny, a rethinking of priorities, and ultimately, critical decision. Will temporary, external things such as possessions and status continue to dominate life? Or will there be a reorientation of energies toward matters of eternal significance—seeking God and serving neighbors?

Finally, Jesus's questions provided space for the listener to decide.

Despite His passion for truth, Jesus's communication was not manipulative or coercive. He never pushed for the hard sell.

Whether using questions or not, Jesus consistently left room for His listeners' decision-making process. Nearing his death in prison, John the Baptist sent to ask one last time, just to be sure, if Jesus was indeed the Messiah. Jesus did not respond with a criticism of doubt, nor did He provide an exclamation point affirmation. He simply instructed the messenger to describe to John what he could observe for himself—lame beggars leaping for joy, a once-sightless man tracing clouds with his fingertip, a deaf little girl tapping her feet to a tune. The conclusion John would have to draw for himself.

This noncoercive, put-the-ball-in-their-court approach flies in the face of a *close the deal ASAP* mentality. It places itself at the mercy of the listener, and her unpredictable and slower-than-ideal processing. When a quick sell is your only measure of success, you won't likely choose the way of Jesus. But whenever long-term buy-in or enduring life change is the goal, there is simply no substitute for questions.

LAUNCHERS

As told in chapter 12, the way Thomas Clarkson made the evil of slavery concrete played a watershed role in the British abolition movement. But there's more to the story. What was it that first roused Clarkson himself to the fight against slavery?

The first seed wasn't a well-crafted book or impassioned speech. It was a question: *Anne liceat invitos in servitutem dare?* Prior to encountering this query, Clarkson had given little thought to the issue of slavery. But the vice chancellor of Cambridge, Peter Peckard, was a respected theologian of abolitionist conviction. It was he that made the topic for the 1785 Cambridge essay contest a probing question: *Is it lawful to enslave the unconsenting?*

Clarkson took up the challenge, reading all that he could find on the subject. He even interviewed people who had personal experience with slavery. Clarkson's essay won first prize. But he'd been cut to the heart by what he discovered and would never be the same. The question had set his life on a new course. As Clarkson later described, "If the contents of the Essay were true, it was time some person should see these calamities to their end."[5] Not long thereafter he felt God calling him to devote his life to this work. The next year Clarkson's essay was published widely, fanning the flames of the growing abolition movement and launching his lifelong role at its center.[6]

But the significance of question asking to the abolition movement did not stop there. Clarkson met William Wilberforce in 1786, and the two cofounded the Committee for the Suppression of the Slave Trade in 1787.[7]

Wilberforce too felt a clear sense of God's calling to this work. In what has become a frequently told story, he'd initially considered abandoning his position in Parliament for the pulpit. But former slave trader John Newton urged him not to leave his post but instead to offer God his political talents. Soon after Wilberforce penned in his journal, "God Almighty has set before me two great objects, the suppression of the slave trade and the reformation of manners [i.e., the moral character of the country]."[8]

Wilberforce knew such changes would not come easily. They represented deeply embedded aspects of British law, behavior, and character. A revolution was required, no doubt. But ending slavery and re-creating the nation's moral compass would be far harder than dethroning a king, which can be done easily enough with strong men and guns. This would be a struggle to win hearts, change assumptions, and significantly alter conduct.

Armed with a squeaky voice, a slight build, and a loyal band of friends such as Clarkson, Wilberforce spent the next forty years pouring himself into these two goals. He introduced resolutions in Parliament, gathered like-minded leaders, drafted pamphlets, and winsomely urged others to reconsider their assumptions. Alongside small victories came harassment, hardship, and even violence.

Among Wilberforce's key tools, often overlooked, was his use of questions, or "launchers," as he called them.

As a political leader, he interacted daily with the trendsetters and opinion leaders of Britain. Before arriving at a social event or dinner party, he always spent at least a few moments thinking about the hosts and guests. He wrote down questions that might direct conversations toward higher purposes and deeper thinking. He sought to develop the kind of questions that would *launch* conversations into areas of morality, faith, and cultural values—everything from marital fidelity to the scourge of slavery.

Personal Notes: Jedd

My dad often takes students from the local university into the Yosemite wilderness. He normally loves the students and exploring together. But this trip—a week backpacking with a dozen incoming freshman—showed warning signs from the start.

As they readied their packs at the trailhead, complaints and sniping from the students overshadowed the enthusiasm my dad usually felt. The F-bomb served as universal noun, verb, and adjective for several young men. The group's dominant flavor was cocky and jaded.

But something big changed along the way. "It was one of the best trips ever," my dad told me afterward. "We all had a great time, and the group ended up as close as any I've seen."

When I asked what turned it around, he reminded with a smile, "A week out in God's creation can do wonders for just about anyone." He went on, "But I think the *questions* were really the catalyst this time. They made the trip unforgettable."

Each day Dad had planned a few questions to ask around that evening's campfire. At first they were mostly just fun. Best ice cream? Favorite cartoon as a kid? If money were no issue, where on earth would you visit? Happiest childhood memory?

But as the days went by and the group got more comfortable, some of the questions went deeper. On Tuesday night Dad asked, "Who is the one person who's influenced your life the most, and how have they changed your life?"

On Wednesday night Dad decided to risk any even tougher one: "What's the hardest thing you've been through?"

The first to answer that night, a burly football player, kept to the surface. He told how he'd once hurt his back and missed part of a season.

The next to speak, however, opened up. She shared how she'd been wronged profoundly by a mentor figure. A second student followed, describing what it had been like to grow up with a substance-addicted mom.

Still another described the struggle of living with a severely depressed dad who'd attempted to take his own life many times and the great insecurity it'd brought her. By the time each student had spoken, no one had a dry face, including my dad.

Last of all, the football player spoke up again, "OK, so hurting my back wasn't *really* my hardest thing..." He began to recount how a beloved family friend had been murdered by her jealous boyfriend. But part way through the story, the young man dissolved into weeping. His tears were received tenderly, with comforting touch and words that drew the group even closer.

When school started two weeks later, many of the students stopped by Dad's office on campus. One girl—who'd acknowledged around the campfire that she could not bear to hug a man because of wrongs that'd been done to her—greeted my dad with a warm embrace. She expressed what many other students said as well: the backpacking trip, especially the sharing invited by the questions around the campfire, had been one of the most meaningful and healing experiences of her life. Best of all, she'd found a sense of belonging she'd not felt in a very long time.

Wilberforce's questions steered hearts and minds toward truths that many people normally avoided. Through the conversations that flowed from these relevant and personal questions, a great many leaders were challenged to rethink long-held assumptions about slavery and the social order of the day.

It was not until Wilberforce lay stretched on his deathbed that the joyous news was delivered: Parliament had voted to abolish slavery in the empire. Meanwhile, his steady efforts to elevate the nation's character are believed by many historians to have nurtured an era of fresh moral clarity and newfound concern for the downtrodden. Wilberforce never raised a sword, but the effects of the revolution he helped lead remain to this day.

QUESTIONS THAT SERVE AND TRANSFORM

For the apprentice to Jesus, communication is always about the audience, whether a single friend or crowded room. We sometimes forget that. Questions are one sure means of turning the focus back where it belongs— on the person before us.

By asking questions, we *honor* the listener, conveying a respect for her autonomy and a trust in her ability to choose. When the question is asked and the communicator pauses, suddenly the listener is once again the focal point. A faint spark of pleasure passes through her as she realizes her thoughts matter and her opinion is valued.

In this way question asking is an inherently subversive activity.

Our culture consistently declares that what *I* want and what *I* think is supreme. We know we ought to care about others too, of course, but always for ourselves first. The word *me* stands at the middle of every equation. Even those of us who imagine ourselves good listeners, if the truth be told, spend the bulk of every conversation thinking—if not speaking—about our own interests and concerns. Question asking slashes against this status quo. It places *the other* at the center point, undermining the corrosive institution of self-centeredness.

So it is that we must draw from more than just Jesus's example if we are to follow Him in this. Like all aspects of apprenticeship to Jesus, asking thoughtful questions is ultimately a way of serving others well. Each turning of focus from ourselves to others is a small but real death to self.

For this we must draw not only a model but also motivation and life itself from Jesus. Anyone can ask questions here and there merely to add to their own appeal and influence. But for our minds to consistently consider and form the kind of questions that encourage, engage, and spur others onward requires more. It places others at the center and us to the side.

This self-losing habit can grow only if we have come to "love because he first loved us"[9]—and in similar fashion. We pursue others because God pursued us first. And we wait patiently for response, knowing how long God often waits for ours.

Admittedly, honoring listeners with questions carries hazards. We may lose an element of control as they become involved in the learning process. But the truth is that we never really had control in the first place. In the final analysis, even our best attempts to impact and influence must end with the listeners deciding for themselves.

Questions simply lead toward those crucial decisions, inviting others to places where answers can be found.

This kind of learning impacts us more potently than other forms of influence. Ideas pushed on us from the outside tend to remain on the surface of our lives, beaded up like water droplets on a sealed deck. But answers we arrive at *on our own* sink in. We start to *own* and *apply* a new perspective even in the process of answering the question for ourselves.

That is why self-discovered truths are always far more powerful and enduring than those that are imposed or spoon-fed. They inevitably penetrate deeper, reside longer, and influence more thoroughly. Often they will continue to impact for a lifetime.

If we want to make a statement, ask questions.

If we want to point others to new outlook, ask questions.

If we want to honor our listeners, ask questions.

If we want to change hearts and minds for the long haul, ask questions.

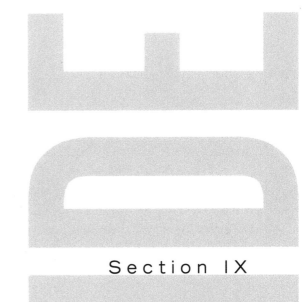

LIFE THROUGH TIME
AWAY FROM THE CROWD

Upend a Life of Frenetic Activity and Visionless Words

Chapter 17

WE CANNOT GIVE WHAT
WE DO NOT HAVE

Those who consume communication today—and that includes all of us—hunger for more than we are getting.

That is not to say that we cannot be pacified, often quite easily, by cardboard amusements. The most outlandish daytime TV and abrasive talk shows never lack for large audiences. Even many of our more thoughtful forums, from blogs to political debates, often deliver little more than stimulating distraction. From the Internet to iTunes, we're dished up a steady diet of infotainment that "serves to kill time, to lull the faculties, and to banish reflection."[1]

However, just beneath these surface impulses, a yearning for real substance simmers.

Instinctively we long for words that call to us above trivial pursuits, noise, and technologies. We want to be wooed toward something deeper, fuller, higher. We ache for a calling deserving of our sacrifice, for pursuits worthy of passion.

In a word, we hunger for vision.

Yet few people today can offer such vision. Simply put, as communicators we can do no more than *echo* the garbled static around us if we never take time to escape it ourselves. It is a law as fixed as gravity.

> Prophets, apostles, preachers, martyrs, pioneers of knowledge, inspired artists in every art, ordinary men and the Man-God, all pay tribute to loneliness, to the life of silence, to the night.[2]
> —A. G. SERTILLANGES, FRENCH DOMINICAN SCHOLAR

Expressing a conclusion reached by many wise women and men throughout history, Mother Teresa of Calcutta observed, "You cannot give what you do not have."[3]

For this reason Mother Teresa consistently urged volunteers, novices, and fellow Missionaries of Charity at her homes for the sick and dying to spend time in both silent reflection and shared prayer every morning before beginning a day of service.

This time of quietness, of course, could have been employed to lift more sore-covered bodies from Calcutta's gutters and into the sisters' homes. Countless needs went unmet every day. Mother Teresa had devoted her life to meeting these needs, but she knew that a mere shell of a smiling face could communicate little of the compassion, wisdom, and love the destitute most lacked.

That sort of message had to come from deeper. Without daily time in solitude, prayer, and reflection, the sisters would ultimately run dry. But as they drew near to God each morning, they could give anew the very things they'd received from Him—complete presence, deep attentiveness, incarnational nearness, and much more.

THE PLACE OF STRENGTH AND STRENGTHENING

The previous night had been a late one at the home of Simon Peter's mother-in-law in the lakeside town of Capernaum. With the sun finally dipping into the horizon, townspeople began arriving at the door, one by one and in small groups. It was not long before it seemed the entire town was trying to jam its way into the home. They jostled each other, pressing nearer and nearer to Jesus. Many with serious afflictions sought His healing. No doubt, as described in other Gospel passages, He felt power going out from Him as He brought them health. All evening they listened, questioned, reached for His touch, and strained to hear His voice.

The lamps were guttering, nearly out of oil, when the last visitor exited. A time for long-awaited rest had finally come. Jesus knew the next day—only hours away—would bring more of the same.

Despite the brief sleep, He roused Himself early. Moving quietly, Jesus slipped out the front door, careful not to wake the others. Silence hung over the empty streets. Dawn had not yet broken, and stars still reflected from the glassy waters of the Sea of Galilee. Jesus strode briskly to a place where He would not likely be disturbed, perhaps outside of town along the water's edge. He sat alone, thinking, pondering, praying, "My Father..."

As is often the case for great communicators, Jesus's moments in precious solitude would be brief. The eager townspeople were knocking at Peter's mother-in-law's door soon after sunrise. Peter and some others set out to find Jesus, apparently oblivious to how much He valued the time alone. When Peter found Him, he fixed Jesus with a where-have-you-been stare and exclaimed, "*Everyone* is looking for you!"[4]

> In repentance and rest is your salvation, in quietness and trust is your strength.
>
> —ISAIAH 30:15

Jesus, of course, was well aware His presence and words were in demand. That is precisely why He traded an hour or two of sleep for time alone. For Jesus, solitude and quiet, reflection and prayer, were lifeblood.

This was not an isolated incident. It was the rule. Noted the physician Luke, "Jesus often withdrew to lonely places and prayed."[5]

As Dallas Willard observed, these times of chosen solitude, deprived of noise and activity and friendly interaction, were not enfeebling, dull, or even lonely for Jesus. They were "the primary place of *strength*..."[6] From these moments flowed the very content and character of Jesus's communication. In those quiet hours He cultivated the insight and wisdom that could disrobe convention and strip false assumptions naked. Piercing insight. Rock-solid wisdom. Real vision.

No wonder everyone was looking for Him.

A WORLD DESIGNED TO KEEP US FROM STILLNESS

It almost seems that modern life is *designed* to prevent meaningful time alone in quietness, reflection, and prayer.

On some level it actually is. Providers of goods and services make their profits when you are interacting with their products, not off in quiet reflection. Moviemakers do all they can to get us to watch; restaurateurs urge us to dine; store owners push us to shop. Our bosses could use more hours at work, and the church looks for our attendance and aid. Family and friends too want more of our time. Most of these engagements are legitimate, even desirable. But the net result is that virtually every influence in our lives is working to see that we do not spend moments alone in quiet solitude— at least, not if that choice would take time away that we currently give to them.

And we go along with it, daily, led like lumbering bulls back into the mad arena. It escapes our notice that the ring in our nose pulling us forward is forged of almost nonsensical assumptions from our culture: *busyness equals importance; continuous activity is the key to meaningful existence; you must be going somewhere if you are always moving.*

If we ever do pause to think about it, we discover with some concern that we often feel hardly capable of more than merely plodding forward for another day. We've grown numb, weary, and as uninspiring to others as we are uninspired.

Where can we look to replenish vitality and vision?

Amidst the wearying pattern of activity, our moments of escape often include little more than passive consumption of media. The day starts with the gibbering of morning DJs, and ends with a lullaby from the eleven o'clock news or a final e-mail check. Almost every moment that *could* be quiet is filled. As Italian film director Federico Fellini describes, this "has mutilated our capacity for solitude. It has violated our most intimate, private, and secret dimension."[7]

At times it all seems suspiciously similar to Aldous Huxley's *Brave New World*, where residents of the future resort continually to the drug *soma* for stimulation, relaxation, and comfort. Our ubiquitous drug of choice is not *soma* but media: movies, music, magazines, TV, and Internet.

Although we might like to think otherwise, most of this media was not *really* created to educate, motivate, or even provide rest. It was designed in light of one central, driving necessity: to keep us watching. After all, advertisers pay for viewers and listeners, not meaningful content. Just like the Ivory-selling soap operas of old, most programs and websites today rise or fall based on their ability to hawk products to a rapt audience. Audiences are less captive now than ever, so they must be captivated; they must be *entertained*.

> What prevents [us] from becoming dull, sullen, lukewarm bureaucrats, people who have many projects, plans, and appointments, but who have lost their heart somewhere in the midst of their activities?[8]
> —Henri Nouwen, in *The Living Reminder*

In some cases the entertainment takes the form of tawdry daytime talk shows or reality TV. For more *sophisticated* consumers, it is delivered via political talk shows, documentaries, and the evening news. The format is a secondary concern. What matters is the ability to sell products—whether soap or cars, fast food or chewing gum.

The consequences of this entertain-or-become-irrelevant ethic are detailed in Neil Postman's piercing book *Amusing Ourselves to Death*. He quotes Robert MacNeil of the *MacNeil/Lehrer NewsHour* to describe the rules guiding the creation of the media we consume daily. The only essential, MacNeil says, "is to keep everything brief, not to strain the attention of anyone but instead to provide constant stimulation through variety, novelty, action, and movement."[9]

With rare exceptions, watchers and web surfers receive little more than info bits, sound bites, and salacious stories in the process. So after yet another day of media consumption, we find ourselves neither greatly refreshed nor newly inspired; only entertained.

Ultimately the communication we deliver will resemble the communication we have consumed. We can give only what we have. In a tragic cycle, *our* audiences will find themselves neither greatly refreshed nor newly inspired by our words; only entertained.

Of course there is certainly a legitimate place for entertainment, just as there are times for intense labor. But if our words are to offer more than *just* these things, if we wish to call to others and stir their deeper parts, we must nourish ourselves with something more.

A DANGER GREATER THAN HAVING NOTHING TO SAY

It is critical we realize that the greatest danger for the communicator is not merely finding ourselves with nothing to say. That is the least of our worries.

Personal Notes: Erik

Our family lives one hundred steps, fifty skips, and twenty-five jumps from the west edge of Central Park, or so that is the challenge I give our kids on our way home from the 68th Street playground or Sheep's Meadow.

I couldn't live in New York City without Central Park; I doubt anyone could. The park is oxygen to the intensity and density of the city. It's quiet amid the sirens and construction sites, subways and midtown, midday crowds. It's space (and therefore grace) for recreation and re-creation. A year would not be enough time to explore the thousands of trails and rocks and corners of the park; it may be hard to believe, but you can get *lost* in Central Park, and thankfully, many do.

Cities need margins; Central Park is certainly designed to be one in Gotham. People need margins; we overbook, run late, make excuses, push people off, prioritize competing demands, and set iPhone reminders—but what about the unexpected conversation with a stranger or the unexpected run-in with an old friend; is there time for that? Finances need margins; how can we be generous if we don't? Art needs margins—space for the audience to encounter, to take in, and to interpret what is seen or heard.

I think God works most in the margins of our life, of our cities, of our art, of our finances—when there is much to offer, to experience, to take in, to be interrupted. The extra money to be generous to a friend in need. The allowance of time for a slower walk along a longer path. Or a little more time to teach your child to tie his or her own shoes.

Far more disturbing is the prospect that we might continue communicating despite having little worth saying. In such cases we are no longer driven by a desire to move our listeners toward something better and higher. We are in love with the *words* themselves, the *image* we present, and the personal *impression* we leave behind.

In a book that recounts his own decision to pursue regular times of solitude, writer Henri Nouwen confessed, "Words, my own included, have lost their creative power. Their limitless multiplication has made us lose confidence in words and caused us to think, more often than not, 'They are just words.'" When this is the case, Nouwen warned, "The word no longer communicates, no longer fosters communion, no longer creates community, therefore no longer gives life."[10]

This is a danger we all face, from speechwriter to homemaker.

If we ignore this hazard and simply slog forward, hoping that our techniques and persona alone will cover for the lack of substance, we may very well wake one day to the same recognition as the professor in Milan Kundera's *The Unbearable Lightness of Being*: "And suddenly he realized that all his life he had done nothing but talk, write, lecture, concoct sentences, search for formulations and amend them, so in the end no words were precise, their meanings were obliterated, their content lost, they turned into trash, chaff, dust, sand…"[11]

BOTH REFRESHMENT AND FURNACE

Expeditions into solitude can take many forms and serve many purposes, especially for the communicator.

Jesus valued *daily* moments of solitude…a single hour, perhaps just ten minutes, on a rooftop, walking a hillside, sitting at the water's edge.

But there were also less frequent periods of *extended* aloneness. At least once Jesus spent forty days straight, unaccompanied, among the jagged rocks and dusty stream beds of the Judean wilderness. Another powerful communicator, the apostle Paul, also spent a lengthy period of time alone in the desert—as did Moses, King David, and many others in history's pantheon of great leaders.

So few of us have tasted such experiences that the benefits of extended solitude remain largely a mystery, even to our leaders. Solitude is, as William Penn described it, "A school few care to learn in, tho' none instructs us better."[12]

Those who embark upon extended times alone report back to us that the experience can be at least as significant today as it was for the greats of the past.

First, this time alone—both in short and longer doses—allows for refreshment.

Such experiences offer a deep, soul-rinsing rest not accessible among crowds or supplied by the buzz of entertainment. In these times we reset our focus and renew our strength for the daunting tasks of serving others through our communication.

Jesus sought this renewal not only for Himself but also for His disciples. Observing the constant swirl of noise and crowds, questions and dust, He urged, "Come with me by yourselves to a quiet place and get some rest."[13] This invitation still stands today.

Personal Notes: Jedd

Solitude and quiet do not always feel inspiring or even refreshing to me. Taking time alone, there are occasions when I start to feel antsy or bored, or as if I'm waiting for something that never arrives. Contrary to what I sometimes wish for, specific directions for life rarely fall from the sky.

As I do make a practice of time away from the crowd, though, I rarely come away empty.

I recall the summer after my freshman year in college. The previous semester had been rich and full, almost dizzying. It had also been thick with questions and doubts, particularly in my faith. I spent many hours that summer alone in the Sierra Nevada Mountains, sometimes hiking or fly fishing, but just as often reading, writing in my journal, praying, and reflecting on life and creation. I do not regret those hours. Even to this day I see that summer as a turning point in my life, a time of renewed faith, purpose, and clarity.

The mountains remain my favorite place for time alone, although I find extended solitude in other settings as well, sometimes even at home when alone for a day. On a daily basis too I seek to quiet myself to pray, listen, read, and reflect.

Often, if I enter solitude expecting particular questions or issues to be tidily resolve, I do not find what I sought. Questions often remain unanswered. If willing to wait, though, my spinning world begins to slow. What matters most appears more distinct; my body and mind feel refreshed; gratitude and nearness to God rise where none had appeared for months. And I wonder, "Why did I wait so long to return?"

Second, meaningful time alone provides opportunity for focused prayer.

Solitude is not isolation. Far from it. For Jesus, time spent in prayer was nothing less than intimate conversation with God. This is why Lord Byron could write, "In solitude, where we are least alone."[14]

In authentic prayer our own rough-edged language pours out thankfulness, bleeds pain and doubt, and begs guidance and strength. We may choose also to draw upon written prayers that help guide our thoughts and put words to hard-to-express feelings. There are many rich sources, from the Psalms to the *Book of Common Prayer* to more recent classics such as *A Diary of Private Prayer*. These scripture-saturated prayers draw us not only to God but also into the fellowship of saints from ages past.

Prayer is listening too. We open ears and heart to receive from God's still, small voice what we could not hear amid the roar of ordinary life. Over time we will find that this listening learned in quiet places enables us to hear God in other times as well. This attentiveness to the influence of the Holy Spirit ultimately becomes the apprentice's secret well, an ever-fresh source of wisdom, guidance, and true vision.

Third, solitude provides opportunity for focused thought and learning.

The wise and great women and men of history wait patiently in the ink of countless books, eager to share observations and truths garnered over lifetimes. Surely many of them offer us much more than we can pick up via today's outdated-within-the-hour headlines and infotainment.

During such times of reflection and study, we also experience our richest, most formative interaction with God's revealed truth. His eternal wisdom—what the Bible calls "the *logos* of God"[15]—is declared in the wonder of creation, written upon our hearts, and articulated in Scripture. This message is often drowned out by the noise that pervades our work and leisure. But in calm and quiet, this living Word begins to penetrate, instruct, and inspire. As it does, we will increasingly see our own words doing the same in the lives of others.

Finally, as Henri Nouwen described, "Solitude is the furnace of transformation."[16]

The dizzying pace of our lives is itself a sort of anesthetic. Nonstop doses of activity, interaction, and stimulation serve to numb and blur our senses. We can hardly feel pain, let alone discern what habits and choices might be causing it.

The great mathematician and philosopher Blaise Pascal wrote extensively about the consequence of distraction. He concluded, "I have discovered that all the unhappiness of men arises from one single fact, that they are unable to stay quietly in their own room."[17]

That may sound overblown. But Pascal knew what he was talking about. Though the means of distraction may have been less sophisticated in the mid-1600s, human nature was no different. Then, as now, people craved diversion and novelty not just to be entertained but also to drown out life's most important questions. *What are you on earth for? Does what you're seeking really matter? If there were a God, what would He want for you?* Noise and activity keep those questions at bay. But solitude stops the drip of the anesthetic, forcing us to face ourselves and the world in their stark, sometimes troubling, reality.

In the silence, alone, we can no longer ignore the gnawing sense that all is not as it should be. As the opiate wears off, discomfort may increase, but so will clarity. We begin to see things for what they are. The world's gilded promises and our own self-deception lose their beguiling power. Aspects of our lives that carry little value or purpose are laid bare: thoughtless patterns of behavior, parroted clichés, and unquestioned assumptions. As we see the vanity in many things we'd foolishly valued, their hold on us loosens. We can lay them down before God. Then we turn to Him, hands empty, to receive the gifts of solitude.

THE FOUNTAIN OF THE LIFE OF AN APPRENTICE

The refreshment, communion with God, learning, and transformation found in solitude become the fountainhead for a life of apprenticeship to Jesus. These gifts are the deep-down source of the apprentice's words, wisdom, and character.

Solitude shapes both *what* and *how* we communicate. Absent solitude, we will have little to offer worth receiving. Our words will carry little more than repackaged observations picked up from the chatter around us. Our actions will reflect little more than the self-absorbed thoughts within.

This is why Dietrich Bonhoeffer could write so starkly, "Only in aloneness do we learn to live rightly in fellowship....One who wants fellowship without solitude plunges into the void of words and feelings....Right speech comes out of silence."[18]

All of the other elements of apprenticeship to Jesus in communication are nurtured by this one. In fact, many are impossible without it. Without practices of solitude, our ability to be present to others will be disjointed at best. Our attentiveness will be partial. Our questions will lack incisiveness. Our speeches and stories and observations will rarely provide compelling vision.

But supplied by God through solitude and silence, we increasingly have much to provide. We grow in both the personal qualities and the wisdom that underlie every aspect of apprenticeship. We are readied to love well and to serve others through our speech.

This is perhaps especially true of attentiveness. For the practice of solitude, silence, and listening prayer grows in us an attentiveness that goes beyond merely noticing details. It cultivates a perceptivity to the deeper, often-hidden realities of our friends, children, audiences, and even life itself. The result, as Don Postema observed, is often "a deep insight into reality, a capacity to see beneath the surface of nature and people, an awareness that uncovers for us a spiritual vitality in our world, in ourselves—and points us toward God."[19]

Here we see the ultimate gift of solitude. Beside it all other gifts pale: a growing nearness to God Himself. He is the first and the final good. And to know Him, not merely theories about Him, is the one true wellspring from which every aspect of apprenticeship flows. Our choices to be fully present, attentive, incarnational, authentic, concrete...all spring from what we come to know of God's heart toward us.

This is why Dallas Willard urges, "The first objective is to bring apprentices to the point where they dearly love and constantly delight in that 'heavenly Father' made real to earth in Jesus and are quite certain that there is no 'catch,' no limit, to the goodness of his intentions or the power to carry them out."[20]

Certainly, life in Christian community plays a vital role in nurturing this vision of the Father too. But if we are intent on seeking Him for ourselves, time alone with Him cannot be replaced. Only then will we quest for it as Jesus did. We will begin to understand what the psalmist felt when he penned, "My soul thirsts for God, for the living God. When can I go and meet with God?"[21] For though His gifts are wondrous, His presence outshines them all.

Yes, this too ties back to our apprenticeship as communicators. For as seen many times already, our ability to make the choices of an apprentice springs foremost from our view of Jesus's Father. We give the gift of presence to others lavishly, because presence is His most precious gift to us. We are freed to share ourselves with authenticity because His grace embraces us in all our beauty and brokenness. We quest to incarnate our words and very selves to others because He drew near to us. Over and over again, in expression after expression, we love because He first loved us.

Chapter 18

ONE UNCROWDED DAY EACH WEEK

Solitude is not the only way to choose time away from the crowd. Christians throughout history have practiced other ways to diminish noise and activity and to nourish soul-deep creativity and vision. God's grace flows through these practices in ways that can give our words and presence new weight and wisdom. Perhaps the most significant of these is receiving the gift of Sabbath.

Like solitude, Sabbath begins with saying no. For one day in seven we turn away from the distractions and activities that fill the other six. We decline the world's demands and even most of what we typically demand of ourselves. We set our to-do list aside, along with anything else we'd consider work. Sabbath becomes a carved out space where we don't feel guilty for not doing things, because we decided ahead of time that they're off limits.

> Blessed be God for this day of rest and religious occupation, wherein earthly things assume their true size.[1]
> —WILLIAM WILBERFORCE, PENNED IN HIS JOURNAL

But far more important is the yes that Sabbath carries. It is a booming affirmation of rest, refreshment and worship. As Jesus made clear, God came up with the idea of Sabbath *for us*.[2] It's a gift. We're not under Law and don't have to receive the gift. But as we come to understand a full sense of Sabbath, mostly by experience, we begin to feel we'd be foolish to miss out.

In a recent interview Eugene Peterson described how forty years ago, amidst the busy life of a young pastor, he and his wife chose to make a regular practice of Sabbath. Since he preached on Sundays, Monday became their "day of unplugging." They'd often pack a lunch and spend the day exploring the woods. He explains, "We'd hike for three or four hours in silence. Then we prayed, had lunch, talked, and worked our way back home....We played and we prayed and didn't do anything that wasn't necessary. Unplugged everything, basically."[3]

Looking back, Peterson concludes that this practice was among the most significant choices he's ever made. By unplugging from everything else, he plugged into a God-breathed renewal and creativity. The legacy of Peterson's teaching and writings, amazing in their consistent depth and freshness, undoubtedly springs in part from this regular practice. As he describes:

> It transformed our lives, our family life, our personal lives, and our congregational life....I've been doing this for at least 40 years consistently, and I've had dozens of students and parishioners who have also adopted this practice. Most of us find it's the most radical thing we've ever done—and the most creative.[4]

As is clear from Peterson's description, Sabbath isn't meant to be cold and sterile. It's celebratory, like a feast. Refreshing, like an afternoon nap. It's invigorating, like sunrise on a mountaintop. Often it's all three. Far from the "boring day" we might have envisioned, or even experienced, Sabbath can be the best day of the week.

Like solitude, practicing Sabbath isn't easy. We already feel overwhelmed trying to get everything done in seven days. How could we possibly do it all in six? Indeed, for busy people, Sabbath can be a sacrifice, in the old-fashioned sense of the word. We lay a day of productivity before God on the altar. We do so trusting we'll be able to accomplish everything that really needs doing in the six that remain.

Even more, our decision to rest acknowledges that our straining labor isn't the ultimate source of great outcomes. Rather, what brings through us the good the world most needs is always a *gift*—the grace of Sabbath, the grace of God's labor in and around us.

> Unless the LORD builds the house,
>   its builders labor in vain.
> Unless the LORD watches over the city,
>   the watchmen stand guard in vain.
> In vain you rise early
>   and stay up late,
> toiling for food to eat—
>   for he grants sleep to those he loves.[5]

Here, once again, we see that decisions to apprentice to Jesus ultimately flow from our view of His Father. If God is for us, working even when we rest, we can release our white-knuckled grip on our list of all that needs to get done. If He is as attentive to our praying and eager for us to approach Him as Jesus portrayed, then our time could have no better use than doing so. If He sees and rewards what is done in secret, then what we do alone can be just as important as what we do before a multitude.

And we will quickly find that what we gain in embracing Sabbath far outweighs the sacrifice. One uncrowded day each week becomes a much-anticipated experience, enriching the other six days too. It makes us more the kind of person others might just *want* to listen to, and grows in us the kind of words they have good reason to hear.

Personal Notes: Jedd

A few years ago my wife, Rachel, was asked to write about our family's experience with Sabbath. Her short article described it honestly and well:

Sunday morning starts the most anticipated day of the week in our house. Peeking into my daughters' room, you'll see their favorite dresses set out, the girls bounding from bed to the once-a-week "Sunday Drawer" that holds their most enjoyed toys and books. Sure, the girls still have their arguments, teeth must be brushed, and plates loaded into the dishwasher. But they would also tell you with grins how they look forward to a special visit to the bagel shop for breakfast before church, a leisurely afternoon with grandparents or close friends, or a picnic dinner.

It wasn't always this way. Five years ago, with our oldest moving beyond infancy and our second on the way, my husband and I began to think seriously about what a true Sabbath might look like for our family. Until then, Sunday meant little more than a morning at church. Meanwhile, the idea of "Sabbath-keeping" carried images of serious people in hard chairs, clean as a whistle but bored stiff and waiting for Monday. Avoiding these cold legalisms, we and our friends had opted for a Seventh Day that looked much the same as the other six.

Yet we wondered if we might be missing out. Amidst the dizzying pace of our life, Isaiah's description of how the Sabbath could be a wellspring of enjoyment and renewal sounded downright alluring (Isa. 58:13–14). So my husband and I set out to discover what this Day of Rest, practiced by God Himself, held for our family.

Sabbath now begins with boundaries that set it apart. We start by lighting a candle at sundown on Saturday. This simple act invites us to move from constant bustle to calm. We turn off our computer. The Sabbath will be a day to draw us inward toward each other, not outward to the demands of our inbox. The door to the laundry room is shut. Sunday will carry as little housekeeping as possible. We eat out, share a meal with friends, or rely on simple foods to minimize cooking.

Knowing that our task list is off limits frees us to do things we feel we "just don't have time for" other days. The quiet of early afternoon is often spent napping, curled up with a book and coffee, enjoying extended reflection and prayer, or lingering over a meal in conversation. Picnics, parks, hikes, and relishing all things created typically fill the rest of our daylight hours.

Sticking with this habit has required determination. It's tough to set aside the unending cycle of jobs that wait upon us. But the rewards—physical and spiritual renewal, recollection of our Father's kindness, sweet hours with our children, and a tradition they can carry on—have convinced us of Jesus's words: the Sabbath was truly made for us as one of God's greatest gifts (Mark 2:27).[6]

THE CLAW THAT FREES

In the Narnia series' *The Voyage of the Dawn Treader*, the peevish Eustace Clarence Scrubb falls asleep on a mound of hoarded wealth. When he awakes, he finds himself wrapped in sinewy flesh and glistening scales. The boy has turned into a dragon.

Initially Eustace exults in the dominance dragonhood will give him over the other children. It is not long, however, before his new identity ceases to be fun. Loneliness becomes misery. The contempt for others that defines his character is slowly replaced by a sense of the value of friendship, and he even begins to feel affection toward individuals he once scorned.

But thick dragon flesh still shrouds the boy deep inside. Instructed by the Great Lion, Aslan, the boy-turned-dragon uses his claws to begin peeling off his own skin. His progress is so limited, however, that he finally accepts Aslan's offer to take over the job, knowing it will be painful. Layer by layer, the lion strips back the skin. His claws sink deep, shredding through the scales and tough outer fibers into softer, more sensitive realms. It burns sharply, tearing deeper and deeper. The smarting sting, however, finally achieves its end. The scales and knobby skin are peeled away, and Eustace becomes a boy once more.

Times of solitude, silence, and Sabbath can be uncomfortable, perhaps as much so as the peeling back of dragon skin, layer by layer. Having become accustomed to a cocoon of activity and noise, even brief moments in quiet and rest feel prickly and unnatural. Extended solitude can be downright painful.

We are conditioned to consistently high doses of stimulation—news bits, incoming messages, and background noise. A single day without it, even a half-hour, and we begin to experience withdrawals. *Something* we crave is missing, and—like any addict—we feel compelled to grasp for the substance we desire heedless of consequences. We can hardly stand it!

But we *can* stand it.

And we must. Time away from the crowd is not superfluous. At least, not if we desire the character and, ultimately, the *communication* that offer more than the colorful monotony found everywhere else. The benefits found in solitude and Sabbath—refreshment and strengthening, focused prayer, insight and wisdom, and soul-deep refining—are the wellspring of truly great communication.

Together these gifts produce the quality that is much sought but rarely found in communicators today: *vision*. It is wisdom that stands like a stone monument amidst ever-shifting trends, opinions, and convention. Truth that will outlast the earth. Insight. Depth. The kind of knowledge people perish without.

This process, difficult as it can be, enriches not only our communication but also all of life besides. Thomas Merton relates, "We do not live more fully merely by doing more, seeing more, tasting more, and experiencing more than we ever have before. On the contrary, some of us need to discover that we will not begin to live more fully until we have the courage to do and see and taste and experience much less than usual."[7]

The results will not be instant. Even after we have stepped from the merry-go-round, the dizziness fades slowly. It may take hours, even days, for our thoughts to stop spinning and allow us to enter fully the experience of solitude.

Everything in our life will conspire against it. Urgent projects will appear from nowhere. Invitations and requests will pound at the door. Endless to-do lists will cry for attention. Our appetite for stimulation will growl to be fed.

Yet in the midst of all this, the decision to take time away from the crowd remains ours—as difficult, and as simple, as *choosing* to do so. Today.[8]

Personal Notes: Erik

In 1942 C. S. Lewis wrote *The Screwtape Letters*, an ironic book of letters between a senior devil (Screwtape) and his undisciplined pupil (Wormwood) on the techniques and tactics for pestering the Enemy (God) and beguiling His followers. Reflecting upon modern times of media and motion, I wrote my own "Screwtape Letter." I hope CS would be pleased.

My Dear Despicable Wormwood,

Good news! The latest commendations have arrived from the Council of the Pit. You impress the lower-downs, my zealous Wormwood. They have heard of your schemes on the Noise Proliferation Committee (NPC). Indeed, places of solitude and moments of silence grow ever more scarce in the Enemy's vast and vulgar dominion. Oh, what euphoria to see his insufferable creatures rush to fill the dead air with a cacophony of cell phones and music, leaf blowers and manipulated car exhaust pipes, twenty-four-hour news and iPhones. Those nauseating humans cannot escape their self-made dungeon of din!

My pride bubbles like brimstone, Wormwood. It is down-wrong delicious that you are able to entice your assignments into believing that quiet and solitude are a waste of time, even harmful to their pursuits. We must be the demon in the whirlwind, invading their private space, cluttering their innermost being with commotion.

Make them feel empty without a Blackberry on their hip or a television blaring in the background. Tune their alarm clock to a raucous station with bombastic DJs. Call their cell phone on their way to work or during a meal. Put TV screens in banks and hotel lobbies, gas stations and airplanes—anywhere humans might have time to reflect. Offer deals to Walt Disney World and casinos, and make a weekend in the Catskills appear unexciting or inconvenient. Over time the humans will grow unaware of the high-pitched ringing in their ears.

But oh, how dreadful it is if they do notice and, worse yet, begin to reject the delightful opiates we offer. An hour's walk or an evening alone can be hazardous. Even a drive with a broken radio carries risk. Peace and quietude, after all, are the Enemy's handiwork. He waits patiently for them in the stillness, whispering for them to rest or ponder or, dare I say that repulsive word, meditate.

I trust you understand what is at stake. If allowed to contemplate the empty pursuits and hollow activity that often fill their days, there is no telling what horrific changes they may make in their lives. As long as the volume is high and the lights are flashing, there is little danger of this. But when allowed to face things as they really are, stripped of the comfort provided by our dizzying distractions, our subjects often choose against our ways.

This kind of activity, or rather inactivity, is a breeding ground for all manner of destructive outcomes. Rest gives them refreshed bodies and clear minds. Clarity draws them to that which we most hate: truth. In such moments their vision grows strong and purpose is rekindled. For hell's sake, do not let this happen!

Some devils say it is of lesser importance, but I would advise you to keep all thoughts of old friendships, childhood dreams, or yearnings for simple delights far from them. These are the noxious things of the kingdom of peace; we are the kingdom of noise.

So hurry! Cue the fire engine, the beeping pager, the woman calling for a cab. Cause the head to turn, the eyes to wander, and the mind to work overtime. Even in times of silence, cause their minds to fill and spin like a tornado. If necessary, you may even need to bring forward some of the Enemy's tools to achieve our ends. Use a good cause to keep the schedule jam-packed.

Beautiful music, grating as it is to our ears, chases the silence away same as any other sound.

Given the stakes, you must do whatever it takes to keep quietude at bay. Remember, do not grow weary in doing bad.

Your affectionate uncle,
Screwtape

Section X

WHERE IT HAPPENS

Chapter 19

WHEN WE GET OUR WISH

Kurt Cobain was born in 1967 in Aberdeen, Washington, the first child to a secretary and a mechanic. His adolescent years were rough, leaving enough hurt and loneliness to fuel both Kurt's art and his anger for the rest of his life.

His escape was music. His mother recalls him as a little boy singing even to strangers at downtown stores. And unlike most pimply, frustrated teens, Kurt's garage band didn't stay in the garage. Party gigs in a nearby college town grew to larger audiences, then real stages with screaming fans, then record deals.

Cobain never claimed to have answers or special insight. But willingly or not, the raw poetry of his lyrics and potency of the sound made him a spokesman for his generation. As a communicator through music, he ranks with the greats—Dylan, Zeppelin, Cash, U2, and the Stones. To date, his band, Nirvana, has sold more than fifty million copies worldwide—and climbing. *Rolling Stone* heralded the runaway album *Nevermind* as seventeenth of its five hundred all-time greatest albums list.[1]

With the world at his feet, cheering at sold-out shows and clamoring for more, Cobain saw nothing to satisfy his restless soul. Nor could the drugs and alcohol sufficiently distract or numb it. At twenty-seven he overdosed on tranquilizers in an apparent failed suicide attempt. A few months later, in a cottage overlooking Lake Washington, he aimed a shotgun at himself and pulled the trigger.

Cobain left behind "a legion of stunned fans, and a small body of music that changed the course of rock history."[2] Even a decade after Cobain's death, MSNBC's Eric Olsen could write of "a small, frail but handsome man" who became a "Generation X icon, viewed by many as the 'last real rock star'...a messiah and martyr whose every utterance has been plundered and parsed..."[3]

THE TASTE OF SUCCESS

History's pantheon of powerful communicators have disagreed on what success looks like: *Crowds waiting on your words…a reputation for eloquence…articles written, books published…respect-filled glances from people around you…admirers drawn near for sexual intimacy…artistic honors and professional recognition…promotions and raises…invitations to the right homes, the right parties.*

Most people never reach the final pinnacle of such success. Rather, we spend a lifetime pursuing it—like a donkey lumbering after a carrot hung just a few feet beyond his face. With the carrot always just out of reach, we never discover if it will really satisfy after all. Instead, we tell ourselves day after day, "If only I reach this milestone, that achievement, *then* life will be all that I hope."

C. S. Lewis called it the "inner ring." His brilliant essay under that title describes how most all of us feel the yearning "to be inside the local Ring and the terror of being left outside."[4] We all know the feeling—the party we weren't invited to, the teammate who gets the big-time scholarship, the staffer who must stand outside the closed door meeting, the student who is rejected by the sorority.

But though we may never reach the innermost ring, we can learn a lot from those who have.

Ernest Hemingway, among the greatest writers of the English language, won the Pulitzer Prize in fiction and the Nobel Prize in literature. He was a war veteran and world traveler, bullfighter, and big-game hunter. He lived for adventure, pleasure, and glory, and he grasped all three in spades.

Actress Norma Jeane Mortenson stands as arguably the single-most recognized icon of the silver screen. Living under the name Marilyn Monroe, she became the object of men's desire and women's admiration. She married baseball's immortal Joe DiMaggio, then later playwright Arthur Miller. Even today her image personifies beauty and sexuality.

Painter Mark Rothko is recognized among the titans of twentieth-century art. His paintings set selling price records for post–World World II works, including his canvas *White Center* that went for $72.8 million in 2007.[5] Even while he lived, his works were sought by the world's finest collectors and took center stage at institutions from Harvard to the Guggenheim.

Each of these individuals reached the pinnacle. *Admired. Wealthy.*

Influential. Sought after. Measured as successful communicators in the world's eyes, few have surpassed them.

Yet after having grasped what they most desired, each ended in the same way: a tragic admission that all was not as it seems, that everything amounted to nothing. They chose "not to be," committing that ultimate admission of emptiness: suicide. In their calculation, death and the uncertainty beyond were preferable to living even one more day haunted by the success they'd attained.

The suicide note that Kurt Cobain left behind may have rambled, but it described well the place to which his success had led. No doubt it spoke for many of us, as well—no matter where we are in the arc of success: "I haven't felt the excitement of listening to as well as creating music along with reading and writing for too many years…" he wrote. "I've tried everything within my power to appreciate it (and I do, God, believe me I do, but it's not enough)."[6]

Success. *How do we define it?* The answer may reveal more about us than any single thing. It whispers of what we most desire and colors indelibly our sense of what matters and what doesn't.

Ask friends or strangers the question: *What would you rather have—fame, influence, wealth?*

Very likely only a handful will respond with "none of the above."

There are few examples of parents refusing to upgrade as paychecks grow or pastors purposefully downsizing their churches. It's hard to find businesses that give more away as profits soar or politicians who say "Not now" when crowds urge them to run for higher office.

But there are some. Francis Chan is a *celebrity* pastor and speaker, although he would shudder at that description. Not long ago he told his congregation in Simi Valley, "If you are here for *me*, you are here for the wrong reasons." Soon after, he announced that he'd be stepping down from his place at the helm of a booming megachurch. There had been no scandal; he simply viewed success differently than most, even many, pastors. He described, "I started to just feel too much like this earth was my home in some ways—you know you get your roots in and get comfortable. And then I started feeling this call…"[7]

A decision like that is a subversive blow to the world's trajectory toward *more*. The bottom line is that Chan defined success differently. As he put it, "Our greatest fear as individuals and as the church should not be of failure, but of succeeding at things in life that don't really matter."[8]

VIEW FROM THE TOP

Simone de Beauvoir, one of the most recognized writers and thinkers of the twentieth century, spoke with similar honesty. This brilliant woman, unbound by convention, accomplished everything she'd set out to do as a girl. Yet a 1965 profile in *Time Magazine* describes the outcome in haunting detail:

> The smile is unreal, put on, perhaps, for the photographer; she cannot accept or endure the fact that she is now 57. Her mortality has obsessed her for a generation. "Since 1944, the most important, the most irreparable thing that has happened to me is that I have grown old. How is it that time, which has no form or substance, can crush me with so huge a weight that I can no longer breathe?"
>
> Simone de Beauvoir attained everything that she ever aspired to as a girl: celebrity as a writer, the full exercise of her rebel spirit. Nevertheless, at 57, she finds herself "hostile to the society to which I belonged, banished by my age from the future, stripped fiber by fiber from my past.... The promises have all been kept. And yet, turning an incredulous gaze toward that young and credulous girl, I realize with stupor how much I was gypped."[9]

De Beauvoir's words parallel those of one of Rome's great emperors, Septimus. He'd risen from humble beginnings to the highest power in the land. But as described in the ancient *Historia Augusta*, "Even after fortune had led him step by step through the pursuits of study and of warfare even to the throne, he used to say: 'Everything have I been, and nothing have I gained.'"[10]

These reports—coming back to us from the summit that most people expend their lives hungrily climbing—should give us pause. From emperors to intellectuals to artists, they echo the words of Ecclesiastes, written nearly three thousand years ago: "Yet when I surveyed all that my hands had done and what I had toiled to achieve, everything was meaningless, a chasing after the wind; nothing was gained under the sun."[11]

In many ways it's far easier to go through life plodding after objects desired but never attained. For then we at least have something to pursue, false though it may be. The walls may not come crumbling down until we grasp the object, sought so long, and find it to be made of cardboard. An incisive column by writer Cynthia Heimel depicts the effect of this realization with brutal honesty. Remembering friends who acquired the fame they sought, Heimel describes:

> It's not what they had in mind. . . .
>
> The night each of them became famous they wanted to shriek with relief. Finally!Now they were adored! Invincible! Magic!
>
> The morning after the night each of them became famous, they wanted to take an overdose of barbiturates.
>
> All their fantasies had been realized, yet the reality was still the same. If they were miserable before, they were twice as miserable now, because that giant thing they were striving for, that fame thing that was going to make everything okay, that was going to make their lives bearable, that was going to provide them with personal fulfillment and (ha ha) happiness, had happened.
>
> And nothing changed. They were still them. The disillusionment turned them howling and insufferable.[12]

What does all of this tell us? If nothing else, it is that what most people view as the *big* things will not deliver. If misdefined at the start, success itself fails to satisfy. And the higher the success, the deeper the anguish at the discovery of its emptiness. In such a place self-destruction, even death, seems a better option.

Jesus's words could not be more descriptive: "Whoever finds his life will lose it."[13]

FIND IT AFTER ALL

Thankfully, Jesus doesn't stop there. The emptiness found in status and beauty, riches and access alone is just part of the picture. He describes a second truth also. Like the first, it is as binding as any law of physics:

> Whoever loses his life for my sake will find it.[14]

These are daunting and daring words. They echo the strange, deathward call heard throughout Scripture. "Offer your bodies as living sacrifices"[15]; "take up [your] cross"[16]; "lay down [your] life]."[17]

Really now. Would any sane person enter a room with words like those printed above the doorway? They whisper of loss, sacrifice, even death.

Who among us makes our lifelong goal to be the usher, not the guest? The second chair, not the solo? The understudy, not the lead? The backup quarterback, not the star?

Is that what God is asking? *What does it mean to* lose *our life for His sake?*

We miss the point if we imagine this is a call to a single grand sacrifice. It is death, no doubt. But literal martyrdom is asked of only a few. Nor will it require a revolutionary's banner and raised fist. The road is subtler, less imposing…and often much more difficult. It calls to a small kind of radical.

As we'll explore in the final chapter and conclusion ahead, losing our life is most of all about little, daily decisions to apprentice to Jesus.

It's giving the gift of full presence to a lonely friend when our worries and task list pull in every other direction. Sharing transparently from our own weakness. Leading others gently to self-discovery with stories and questions rather than driving hard toward our own conclusions. Taking Sabbath rest to honor and draw fresh life from God instead of pressing on with urgent work. And myriad other often-unnoticed decisions that turn us from self to others and from building our own kingdom to seeking God's.

Small choice by small choice, they add up to the loss of the life the world prizes. Small choice by small choice, they add up to finding the unparalleled life Jesus gives.

Chapter 20

THE BIGGEST DECISIONS
WE'LL EVER MAKE

*G*et the big things right, conventional wisdom urges, *and everything else will follow.* Correctly understood, that's great advice. But often we assume that "big" means only what job to take, whom to marry, and where to live. These things *are* big, and they'll shape our lives profoundly. But what we might miss is that such life-altering decisions—and virtually everything else we view as "big"—are mainly the *fruit* of other things that come before and beneath them.

 How we live our days is how we live our lives.[1]
—FRANCIS CHAN IN *CRAZY LOVE*

A farmer would affirm, "Produce a great apple crop, and everything else will follow." But watch him for a week. You'll quickly see that his daily life has very little to do with large, luscious apples. It's comprised of things such as pruning, fertilizing, and irrigating. It's spreading cow manure and checking drip lines. If you want mouth-watering apples, *these* are the big things.

That's why Jesus got so excited about little things: a widow plinking her last pennies into the offering plate; a foreign soldier who just assumed Jesus could heal as easily from a distance as He could up close; prayer alone in a closet; a desperate Gentile woman begging Him to cure her child.

These things could easily have been overlooked. But Jesus saw in them seeds likely to grow into the fruit He most desired.

This was always Jesus's way. He seized the small and overlooked and declared it of great significance. *He began in a backwater place like rural Palestine. Chose blue-collar workers for leadership roles. Welcomed foreigners and children and outcasts to the inner circle. Made a Samaritan woman the first missionary and a former prostitute the first witness to His resurrection.* Little people. Matters easily ignored. Yet for Jesus, these were seeds that grace could grow into a whole orchard of succulent apples.

Admittedly, Jesus's call carries a certain grandeur. He speaks of kingdoms and feasts and thrones. And yet the places this grand vision must be lived out today are often downright pedestrian. As Jesus put it, if we wish to be great, we must become the servant of all. This, if nothing else, should clue us in. Whether we are a senator or a fast-food worker, our apprenticeship to Him will be most often lived out in servant's work—unheralded choices and menial tasks.

This may be especially true in our communication. The decisions that matter most are the small, often unnoticed ones. Listening attentively to the intern. Making ideas concrete for others in example and word pictures. Asking children good questions and telling them stories of consequence. Taking regular time in solitude and prayer. And a thousand other easily overlooked ways to serve others well through our communication.

Why are such small things the focus of the apprentice? Five factors play a key role:

1. MAJOR EVENTS DON'T ALTER LIFE AS WE'D EXPECT

There's an ongoing riddle in the field of SWB, or *subjective well-being,* research. It's the simple fact that major life events, the kind we imagine will change *everything,* actually make surprisingly little difference in the long run.

Life's most desired outcomes—as diverse as landing a plum job, winning the lottery, or getting married—may supercharge our sense of well-being for a while. But after even a short period of time our happiness tends to return to where it was before the event.

Perhaps even more mysterious, the same can be said even of tragic events. A 2005 study found that although satisfaction falls sharply after the onset of a moderate disability, within just two years it's at the same levels as before the disability. This trend proves largely true even of severe medical issues such as chronic kidney failure or paraplegia.[2]

These findings have prompted Jonathan Haidt, a psychologist at the University of Virginia, to reach a startling conclusion. Whether you lose the use of your legs in a car accident or reap millions in SuperLotto, your feelings about the world will soon be about the same as they are now. Says Haidt, "Within a year, lottery winners and paraplegics have both (on average) returned most of the way to their baseline levels of happiness." Reviewing the data, Haidt concludes, "In the long run, it doesn't much matter what happens to you."[3]

Of course, Haidt or anyone else would choose a lottery win over paralysis if given the choice. But the sobering reality is that many of life's biggest happenings—including those we most yearn for—will likely have far less impact upon our experience of the world than we expect. Quite possibly, none at all.

The simple truth is, that *big thing* we've been waiting for probably won't make us happy after all. At least not for long.

That's a sobering fact. Few people would classify themselves as pie-in-the-sky dreamers. But don't most of us secretly harbor a short list of things that we imagine will, if finally reached, yield that elusive well-being we've been waiting for?

But pause for a moment. Hasn't that short list been there for as long as we can remember? The hoped-for items have changed, but not the expectation of satisfaction when we attain them. Haven't most of us gone through life imaging that that next threshold will leave us feeling that we've finally arrived—content, complete, able to enjoy? *When I get to high school. When I get my driver's license. When I'm a senior. When I get a boyfriend/girlfriend. College. A job. A well-paying job. Marriage. Kids. Kids able to pick up after themselves. Kids out of the house. Retirement. Grandkids.*

Personal Notes: Jedd

I was deeply moved when I first heard of Salomon and Mery Hernandez's decision to give up Salomon's job as a pastor rather than condone racial divisions in their church. (See chapter 12.) They abandoned a good job and security to live without compromise for Christ. Long before I met the couple, that story defined them in my mind.

But spending time with Salomon and Mery in Guatemala, I came to see things differently. Yes, that decision did reveal their remarkable character in a special way. And it set them on a new vocational track too. But looking deeper, it was clear that the beauty and profound impact of their lives lay elsewhere. The depth of Salomon and Mery's relationships, the love neighbors harbor for them, the influence they carry with those who know them—flow not from that one decision but from myriad others they make daily.

I saw it in Salomon rising to open the door at 2:00 a.m. when a stranger needed medicine. The gentleness of Mery's voice as she spoke with the woman whom the Hernandezes took in after her husband left her. The couple driving twenty minutes out of the way to give a ride home to a man walking with a heavy load of firewood. The way even tollbooth workers and street sweepers light up at Salomon's ebullient greeting, *"Como esta, joven?"*

Not long ago at the Westmont Bethel Hospital that Salomon and Mery helped create, a patient recovering from surgery spotted a woman walking past his room. Taking her for a nurse, he called out for help. She stopped and cheerfully obliged, ultimately providing a sponge bath as well. "Can you clean my feet too?" the man asked. The woman washed his feet and even combed his hair.

Later, when his regular nurse checked in on him, the man reported that another nurse had taken care of everything. "That was not a nurse," she corrected. The man was shocked to discover that the woman who'd so graciously tended his needs was Shelly Hernandez, the hospital's COO. Had the man known Shelly's parents, he would have better understood how she came to be the woman she is.[4]

But the SWB studies tell us what we should have learned from experience. Though we all imagine that major events determine the quality of our lives, this rarely proves true in the real world.

2. THE SMALLEST THINGS ARE WHAT MOST SHAPE US

It could be said the smallest and least visible things on the planet are our thoughts. Dozens can rise and vanish in any mind by the minute, billions worldwide. Thoughts cannot be weighed, smelled, or touched. Most are forgotten as quickly as they are formed.

Yet Jesus placed supreme importance on our thoughts. The desires, resentments, and hopes that we silently visit and revisit ultimately color the deepest parts of who we are. As Marcus Aurelius observed, "The soul is dyed by the thoughts."[5]

> The battle is lost or won in the secret places of the will before God, never first in the external world.[6]
> —OSWALD CHAMBERS

From these deep-down places flow the words and deeds that make our life what it is. As Jesus described, "A good man brings good things out of the good stored up in his heart, and an evil man brings evil things out of the evil stored up in his heart. For the mouth speaks what the heart is full of."[7]

Jesus flips our sense of what is big by continually stressing these root-level things. He puts more emphasis on anger than murder, on a lustful glance than an extramarital affair. It's not that murder and adultery aren't of huge consequence. It's just that anger and lust are at the root; they're the source from which visible actions rise.

When the small, invisible, deep-down things are healthy, all that flows out from us will be nourishing and good. "Make a tree good and its fruit will be good," says Jesus. The opposite is true too. "Make a tree bad and its fruit will be bad."[8]

As Dallas Willard incisively points out, "The ultimate freedom we have as human beings is the power to select what we will allow our mind to dwell on."[9] This smallest of all choices is also the biggest. The little things—from the pattern of our thoughts, to subtle habits of attentiveness to others—are what most form us. Then they ripple outward from there.

3. WE CAN NEVER KNOW WHAT WILL RESULT FROM DECISIONS, SMALL OR LARGE

The time-bending movie *The Curious Case of Benjamin Button* offers a single scene twice in a row. The dancing career of Benjamin's true love, Daisy, is blossoming in Paris. But as she exits the Opera House after a rehearsal, she is struck by a taxi. Her leg is shattered, along with her dreams of becoming a great dancer. In anguish and shame at her condition, she spurns Benjamin's compassion and drives him away.

The differences in the alternative version of the scene at first appear trivial. While Daisy is finishing her rehearsal, a random woman on the other side of town returns to her flat to fetch a forgotten coat. The woman's forgetfulness sets in motion a series of equally insignificant events that cause the taxi to drive by the Opera House just a moment earlier. So instead of striking Daisy, it narrowly misses her. Daisy's leg is spared, her career as a dancer blooms, and an entirely different panorama of life spreads out before her.

Realizing how much can pivot upon even the most trivial things can be dizzying. *A forgotten coat. Failure to wrap a package. A stopped delivery truck.* With a feeling like vertigo, we realize that we can never search out what will result from each choice or happening. This may drive some to a sense of futility or fatalism. For the apprentice to Jesus, it is the opposite. Not even a sparrow will fall to the ground apart from the loving presence of God. Our days too are in His hands. And He has invited us to participate with Him in the grand work of restoration, renewal, and reconciliation.

The fact that we'll never be able to know how our actions—large or small—will eventually play into outcomes give us a freeing humility. We still labor with diligence, desiring to someday hear from God, "Well done." But in the meantime, we can find a certain humor in the way the "best laid schemes of mice and men" so often come undone. The foolishness of self-centered striving grows more obvious.[10] We still seek results but prize relationships even more. The significance of prayer looms larger.

> Sometimes when I consider what tremendous consequences come from little things, I am tempted to think there are no little things.[11]
>
> —BRUCE BARTON

Perhaps most importantly we can find significance even in mundane tasks and unseen acts of love. For we know that things we have imagined to be of great importance may soon prove to be of no consequence. And in God's kingdom small actions can shake the foundations of the world.

4. THE BIG DECISIONS ARE MADE BY THE TIME WE GET THERE

Dietrich Bonhoeffer's willingness to risk—and ultimately lose—his life to aid a plot to assassinate Hitler is viewed as the defining decision of his life. It stands even today as a vivid emblem of Bonhoeffer's integrity, and it sealed in blood the significance of his work as a theologian. But as inspiring as that story is, there's something decidedly *un*exceptional about the decision as well.

Bonhoeffer did struggle with whether to join the conspiracy against Hitler. He had no desire to die. He knew the heartache it could bring to his family and to his fiancée, Maria. As a pastor committed to non-violence, he also wrestled with the ethics of killing as means to protect others.

Yet it could also be said that Bonhoeffer's deeper, gut-level decision had been made long before. He grappled mightily over the particulars of *how* to stand for justice and defend life. But that he *would* stand, boldly and sacrificially, was certain. Like a gully carved over decades by countless raindrops, the pathway was deep and clear.

Years prior Bonhoeffer had concluded, "When Christ calls a man, he bids him come and die."[12] He modeled this losing-life-to-gain-it daily, from habits of regular time alone with God to the way he served his seminary students. In choice after choice, he carved a pathway of faithfulness to Christ as deep as any ravine.

One such decision came in 1939 on the eve of World War II. Bonhoeffer was safe in New York with a coveted post at Union Theological Seminary. Yet seeing the need for bold witness in Germany, Bonhoeffer determined he must return. Friends urged against it, warning that his well-known opposition to the Nazis would put his life at risk. But Bonhoeffer felt he could best serve God's purposes in his homeland.[13] He returned to Germany on the last scheduled steamer across the Atlantic.[14] It was but one more droplet, carving deeper the Christward course of his character.

Upon his return Bonhoeffer's work in Germany during the war consistently flowed in the same direction. He trained underground seminarians; aided the escape of Jewish Germans; sought God's heart in disciplines of prayer and study. Was his much-remembered choice to risk life to help bring an end to Hitler's evil actually Bonhoeffer's biggest decision? Or were the countless preceding choices bigger because they made that final choice instinctive, even inevitable? That is impossible to say. What we can affirm, though, in the words of Oxford professor Iris Murdoch, is this: "At crucial moments of choice most of the business of choosing is already over."[15]

> His master replied, "Well done, good and faithful servant! You have been faithful with a few things; I will put you in charge of many things. Come and share your master's happiness!"
> —MATTHEW 25:23

5. CHANGE HAPPENS BY SMALL MEANS

A good thunderstorm can be unforgettable. Lightning rips the darkness apart and thunder rattles even the trees. But when the storm subsides, the nerve-jangling sounds have altered nothing. Rather, it is droplets of water, falling one by one, that ultimately will shape the landscape. Over time they massage sharp peaks into rolling hillsides. They etch out canyons and valleys, all the while grinding boulders into a fine topsoil that can nourish forest and meadow.

WATER, NOT THUNDER

Strange allure calls from the martyr's dread load,
That winks and woos as if it were the easier road.
Don't misunderstand; I know my strength might buckle
    before I reach the bier.
But my little false self wants a simple once-for-all:
    Apostatize or go into the fire.

One epic sacrifice seems of less daunting weight
Than bearing up mercy's daily freight.
But those who know whisper that St. Stephen's door
Is not opened with one final dying, but in the thousand
    before.

Deepest good isn't born with a boomed, *"Here I stand!"*
Ever so much as by patient voice and an oft' offered hand.
No roar can smooth stones, just waves beyond number.
Earth's carved by water, never by thunder. [16]

Those who grasp this truth have special ability to influence change because they understand where it begins.

When Rudy Giuliani became mayor of New York City, the Big Apple had come to be viewed as rotten, defined more by its grime and crime than gleaming skyscrapers. Giuliani wanted to turn this reality upside down. But he avoided the politician's temptation to aim for sweeping change all at once through a grandiose "master plan" or huge spending program. Instead he placed special focus on small things, such as enforcing long-ignored laws against drinking in public and dispatching rapid response teams that removed graffiti within hours of it appearing.

What is now considered one of Giuliani's most significant changes seems downright trivial in light of the fact that New York was viewed as a hotbed of murder and violent crime. For years when cars stopped in New York traffic, aggressive "squeegee men" would begin scrubbing their windshields whether needed or not, then demanded payment for their service. It was intimidating and unpleasant, but residents had come to live with it. Giuliani made a priority of ending the practice. Since windshield washing wasn't technically illegal, he had the police arrest for jaywalking those who persisted. Soon, squeegee-ing was a thing of the past.

It was a small thing. But many New Yorkers now see it as a turning point in their city's history. For both visitors and residents, it altered New York's feel, its *ethos*. Over the decade that followed, the bigger things changed too. Crime dropped dramatically, with murder rates hitting their lowest since 1963, when reliable statistics first were kept.[17] Were squeegees the only catalyst of change? Certainly not. But what *New York Times*' columnist John Tierney dubbed the "Squeegee Watershed"[18] played a far larger role than most anyone could have imagined when it started.

> We hear much about moments of decision, but often you don't know they have happened until later and there you stand in your cooling skin.[19]
> —LEIF ENGER, *SO YOUNG, BRAVE, AND HANDSOME*

This, most often, is how change happens. Take any story of great transformation highlighted in this book, from the end of the British slave trade to the civil rights revolution. Consider less visible changes too, such as the slow recovery of an addict or new direction of an ex-con. Admittedly, the study of history highlights the milestones and zenith moments. But in almost every single case, from the global to the personal, change comes not in a single majestic victory but via myriad small choices, actions, and sacrifices.

We see this in every facet of life. A child says "thank you" to the waitress. But how many times did his parents have to remind him prior to that moment? A jaded college professor returns to the faith of her childhood. But how many times had a committed friend shown true attentiveness to her before she came to believe there may be more in faith than "poor little talkative Christianity"?

"If you're in this business because you want to change the world, get another day job," renowned journalist Izzy Stone warned fellow writers. "If you are able to make a difference, it will come incrementally, and you might not even know about it."[20] The same could be said to parents and politicians, teachers and social workers. This is how change happens, if at all.

LIFE BY A THOUSAND CUTS

The remarkable short story *The Man Who Planted Trees* begins in 1913 as a young backpacker crosses the low Alps of eastern France. The region once hosted thriving villages. But centuries of drought, wind, and charcoal-seeking peasants have scoured it. The expanse now stretches barren and colorless, devoid of human habitation and even foliage, a wasteland of wild lavender and coarse grass.

Seeking water, the backpacker unexpectedly encounters a quiet but hospitable shepherd named Elzéard Bouffier. After a good night's sleep in Bouffier's simple home, the backpacker observes a silent morning ritual. The shepherd fetches a sack and pours a pile of acorns on the table. With great concentration, he separates the good from the bad, then carefully selects one hundred to take with him.

Once he's taken his sheep to pasture, Bouffier climbs a nearby hillside. With the thick iron rod he uses as a walking stick, the shepherd begins thrusting holes into the earth. He then plants each with an acorn. When asked, Bouffier answers that he does not own the land or know if anyone does. For three years he's planted one hundred per day. That's more than one hundred thousand total. He believes that about one of every ten will survive.

The backpacker departs, and the Great War soon engulfs Europe. He all but forgets Bouffier and his trees. But returning after the war, he marvels at a gray carpet now covering expansive stretches of hillside: oak trees. The earliest planted reach taller than a man. Their presence is clearly affecting other things too. Spreading branches now shelter snow far into the spring, and spreading roots retain moisture in the soil. As a result, water again runs in streams long dry, which in turn nourish willows and rushes and blooming meadows. Bouffier is still planting too.

It is decades later, in 1945, that the backpacker goes to visit the aged shepherd one last time. At first the visitor imagines he has come to the wrong place. Everything is different. Even the wind is gentler, filtered by forests rich with scents. Abandoned ruins have become villages, bustling with young families and surrounded by gardens and planted fields. The backpacker marvels at how, seed by seed, "that old and unlearned peasant...was able to complete a work worthy of God."[1]

Jesus harnessed a similar metaphor to explain the kingdom of God. "It is like a mustard seed, which is the smallest seed you plant in the ground. Yet when planted, it grows and becomes the largest of all garden plants, with such big branches that the birds of the air can perch in its shade."[2]

Personal Notes: Jedd

As a student pondering life beyond college, two opposing examples loomed large before me.

My parents embodied one route. It was rooted, local, steady. They'd raised my three brothers and me in the same community where Dad grew up. He taught at the local high school. Mom taught in public schools too when not raising us four boys.

Aunt Marlene and Uncle Gary modeled the other path. They lived all over the world, going wherever they felt God could use them most. Bolivia and Peru, Hawaii and North Carolina—in roles ranging from missionary and pastor to college professor.

These two paths seemed polar opposites to me, two contrary options. I found the adventure and variety of Marlene and Gary's journey deeply compelling. But my parents had something special too in their lifelong friendships and rooted sense of place. "Which approach to life," I wondered, "would lead me to the richest experiences and kingdom impact?"

But as the years have passed, I've observed something unexpected. Despite the notable differences in the paths they've walked, both couples' lives are defined by remarkably similar outcomes. They've both nourished and inspired countless others. They've remained fresh and creative while others their age become stagnant. And I've seen them grow more thankful, winsome, and Christlike with each year that passes. In short, both couples model the kind of vibrant fruitfulness I pray will define my own life.

The simple truth is that for both my parents and my aunt and uncle, it was not chiefly the big decisions that led to this. Certainly, choices of vocation and location played a part. But what made the biggest difference, I see now, were their small, daily choices to reflect Jesus. It came from the way Dad allowed students to keep him late after school to talk over their struggles; how I never once heard Mom pass on hurtful gossip; the way Marlene and Gary expressed gratefulness in both plenty and in want. These and countless other things shaped the people they've become and the impact they're leaving. I'm confident now that following a similar route will yield a road well worth traveling, wherever it leads.

Jesus speaks of this smallest-of-seeds elsewhere too. Even if our faith is miniscule as the mustard seed, He taught, its latent power is sufficient to uproot the Rockies.[3]

At the heart of both of these metaphors is a simple truth: wee things the world overlooks carry great effect in the kingdom of God. Explore a bit further, and we see more too.

For starters, a seed *grows* from insignificant to magnificent. It's no more than a speck in your hand at the beginning. But through small, incremental, mostly invisible expansion, the seed rises into a living tower. It becomes an entire city, complete with xylem water systems, phloem food elevators, and energy generators more complex than any power station.

But just as important, the metaphor also hints that the operative power isn't in the seed itself. It contains the mere *potential* of life. Factors beyond its control or ability to supply will prove decisive to its future. Without water, soil, and sunlight, the kernel will achieve nothing. Yet nourished by these gifts, it can give shade to generations of children. In a word, *grace* received from beyond itself enables the seed to become a source of grace to others.

This is the way of life in the kingdom of God. Little things easily overlooked become things of great consequence. Small choices. Daily decisions. Bite-size bits of faith. Nourished by grace, what appears little more than a speck in the hand can grow into a towering presence that refreshes and protects all who encounter it.

HUNGER FOR THE GRAND

Over dinner at a friend's house, Jedd met Fayed.* Fayed came from a Muslim family in the Middle East. When he first decided to follow Jesus at age seventeen, his friends and relatives rejected him. Pressure and risks mounted as he held fast to his faith. Later, when Fayed joined a ministry to the persecuted church worldwide, the costs of discipleship became even more vivid as he traveled and served. Many whom he came to know suffered profoundly for Christ, including imprisonment, torture, and even death.

But as those around the table marveled at this courage, Fayed grew stern. "I am often troubled by the way many Western Christians see our persecutions," he expressed. "There is fascination with dramatic stories—fingers chopped off, people burned alive for refusing to recant. Yes, that happens sometimes. But focusing on those sensational stories lets you off the hook."

---

* Name changed to protect identity.

The room was silent as Fayed continued. "I see people thinking of underground Christians in the Middle East or elsewhere, 'Oh, those are the super Christians.' And you wonder what you would do if you had a sword at your throat. But that's not the important question. You can never know the answer to it, anyway. What matters is whether or not you will follow Jesus today in every choice you make."

Heads nodded, but no one spoke. Fayed's dark eyes flashed, but the hint of smile played on his lips. He wanted to inspire, not condemn. "The obvious costs of following Jesus may be harder in some places than others. But the daily choices are the same. Will you serve your neighbor? Will you be thankful in disappointments? Will you remain faithful to Him? Are your wants the final priority or His? Whether you're in America or Saudi Arabia or North Korea, *these* are the choices, over and over again."

Fayed nailed it. Everyone listening knew it. Something in all of us is drawn, almost irresistibly, to contemplate and praise the grand sacrifices. We relish the big and bold and once-for-all. Decisions that feel commonplace slip to the background.

There's nothing inherently wrong in this. It's mostly just the natural intrigue of the sensational. But it carries real hazard. As Fayed explained, focus on the large and grand can divert our focus from the one place where we truly can serve God and others: the small choices and actions of everyday life.

In Dostoyevsky's *The Brothers Karamazov*, a medical doctor describes the irony of his zeal for humanity. "I love mankind," the doctor explained to the wise elder Zosima, "but I find to my amazement that the more I love mankind as a whole, the less I love individual people." He continued:

> I often visualize ecstatically the sacrifices I could make for mankind and, indeed, I might even accept martyrdom for my fellow men if circumstances suddenly demanded it of me. In actual fact, however, I cannot bear to spend two days in the same room with another person.... Whenever someone is too close to me, I feel my personal dignity and freedom are being infringed upon. Within twenty-four hours I can come to hate the best of men, perhaps because he eats too slowly or because he has a cold and keeps blowing his nose. I become a man's enemy...as soon as he touches me. But to make up for it, the more I hate individual people, the more ardent is my general love for mankind.[4]

As Dostoyevsky reminds, loving the masses is not at all the same as loving the one. In fact, it can often be the opposite. A sweeping love for humanity may actually subtly draw us away from the small, humble, difficult acts that love requires.

This is true of all virtues, not just love. Influential cities such as Washington DC are full of individuals yearning to "do good" for the world. Yet it's easy to speak and even work to exhaustion on issues of justice and compassion—while rarely connecting these concepts to small choices made each day. As George Elliot describes, "People glorify all sorts of bravery except the bravery they might show on behalf of their nearest neighbors."[5]

Why? In short, because focus on grand ideals and distant aspirations let us off the hook. Paying attention mainly to the "big" things can turn us from the more costly daily choices that constitute real love, real courage, real justice, and real compassion. Only in choosing to show love, courage, justice, and compassion in the small things can we truly live them at all.

It's like a husband who often harkens back to wedding day vows or speaks of "forever" but never holds his wife's hand or praises her before others. Yes, life's valleys and mountaintops reveal a great deal about us. But love and leadership are most of all worked out on the wind-swept plains that stretch as far as the eye can see.

Personal Notes: Erik

Last week a dear friend died. A young man, taken without warning.

Do you think I've thought much in the past week about the title he'd held or his résumé or achievements? Not a whit. It's been all about the little things.

Every Sunday our kids would run down 73st Street toward him. He stood outside the church, waiting to greet them. We could see his smile like a lighthouse a block away. He reminded that God was welcoming us too—waiting, smiling, cheering us into His kingdom. When the kids would get close, he'd bend down to embrace them. Just as God does.

Our friend's last tweet before he died was one word: FAITHFUL.

That final word wasn't about the meal he was eating or thoughts on fashion. It was a simple, matter-of-face statement: FAITHFUL. And for those who knew him, loved him, that one word told so much. His life was propelled by adoration of Christ, and daily the heartbeat—even at its last beat—was for the Savior who was making all things—especially him—new.

Our kids wept when they heard the news, their little minds and hearts remembering nothing more than a friend who loved them through a smile on a busy street. In the end that was more than enough. No titles. No status. No college degree. Just faithful.

SMALL CHOICE OF OLYMPIC PROPORTIONS

Issues of race and politics buzzed just beneath the surface at the 1936 Olympic Games in Berlin. Hitler stood at Germany's helm and desired to harness the games to showcase a resurgent nation under the Third Reich. His disdain for blacks and Jews was well known.

The long-jump became a microstage for this clash of civilizations. The local favorite was Germany's Luz Long, holder of the European record. Going toe-to-toe with him was a black American, Jesse Owens, who held the current world record. Luz Long wowed the home crowd by setting an Olympic record during the qualifying round. Meanwhile Owens fouled on his first attempt, then on his second. If Owens fouled again or failed to reach 7.15 meters on his third attempt, he would be disqualified from the finals. Owens sat down on the field in gloom. Luz Long would likely have set an Olympic record and walked away with gold had he waited for Owens to foul a third time. But he didn't. Instead Long went to the American and encouraged him to try a different tactic. Owens could easily clear 7.15 meters, Luz pointed out, so why not jump from a mark several inches behind the take-off board? Even if Owens lost a few inches, ensuring he didn't foul again, he should have no troubling earning a spot in the finals.

Long's advice was spot on. Owens cleared the qualifying distance with room to spare. The finals later that day were astounding, with the jumpers besting the prior Olympic record five times. Owens ultimately took the gold. Long won the silver and was the first to congratulate Owens on his victory. They posed together for photos and walked arm in arm to the dressing room.[6]

The small choice that Long made to give his opponent a piece of helpful advice could easily have gone entirely unnoticed. In some ways it was just a kind but trivial expression of the sportsmanship that Long modeled throughout his career. But small as it was, it came to define his life and his legacy—perhaps more than any gold medal would have. Jesse Owens never forgot it either. As Owens expressed later, "You can melt down all the medals and cups I have, and they wouldn't be a plating on the twenty-four karat friendship that I felt for Luz Long at that moment."[7]

Long's small choice played a turning-point role in helping Owens set an Olympic record that stood unmatched for nearly fifty years. Further, by winning four gold medals in Berlin, Owens humiliated the Nazis' theories of racial superiority. Decades later President G. H. W. Bush posthumously honored Owens with the Congressional Medal of Honor, describing what he achieved in Berlin as "an unrivaled athletic triumph, but more than that, a triumph for all humanity."[8]

It's worth noting too that even for Owens himself, Olympic success was the product of innumerable small choices. We all join in celebrating such great victories. But we must also know the legacy of a life is not forged in such moments; it is merely unveiled. Countless little decisions prior to that day in Berlin formed the men that August 4, 1936, revealed Owens and Long to be. For Owens, that included endless hours of training, practice, and self-denial. Likewise, Long's willingness to aid Owens came as the natural expression of a character formed in him over decades. By the time they reached the long-jump pit, all they could do was draw upon the reservoirs they already possessed.

CHOOSING UGANDA, DAILY

Katie Davis was hardly out of high school when she made the decision. She would give up an enviable existence in the United States to serve the orphans of Uganda. Permanently. She left behind what many would say is the best life has to offer: loving family and a yellow convertible, cheerleader popularity and a wide circle of friends, a great boyfriend, and boundless options. In exchange Katie has become both servant and beloved friend to an entire community in Uganda. She's also now mother to a beautiful brood of adopted daughters.

Katie's remarkable blog and book by the same name, *Kisses From Katie*, confound a typical American sense of what's important. Yet the more a reader gets to know Katie, the harder it is not to agree with her claim that she has the better end of the bargain. She has traded comfortable living for deep purpose; security and convenience for vibrant faith; a well-paved future for the unparalleled adventure of costly love. For the first time she felt, "I knew it was what I was created for."[9] At first glance it is easy to conclude that the doorway to Katie's new world was her once-for-all decision to abandon everything for Uganda. In a sense, that is true. Had she swerved from that choice at the last moment, she likely would be in grad school now or starting a family in a suburban Nashville neighborhood.

Personal Notes: Jedd

When I was five, my mom bought me a batch of Valentine's cards to give to my friends at kindergarten. One had a cartoon lion with the message, "For the King of my Heart!" I immediately concluded that that card couldn't go to a friend. God alone deserved it. My mom even let me convince her to offer the card as a "burnt offering" in the family fireplace. I especially liked the fire part. But I meant it: I wanted God to be first.

That's been my desire since before my earliest memories. But alongside it, I've also struggled at times with deep doubts, especially during college and the decade after. I can recall trying to pray, then stopping with an icy whisper: "Do I *really* believe Anyone is listening?"

Over the years some of the questions have been answered. Some haven't. They've lingered like loose threads on a sweater, threatening to unravel the whole thing.

Yet I can honestly say that my faith today is more like that five-year-old's than it has been for years.

Why? I think it comes down to two things. First, I've realized that *every* idea or philosophy requires some measure of faith. Even physics. Logic itself. At some point along any chain of ideas, the "How do you know it's true?" question can't be answered with certainly. So you have to weigh evidence and arguments and then decide. No wise person waits to act until he knows beyond any doubt. By that standard, none of us would ever get married or even get out of bed. Good decisions are based on *reasonable confidence*, not total certainty. When I grasped that, I realized I wasn't required by intellectual honesty to sit on the sidelines until I had everything figured out.

Logic, though, can only get you so far. Jesus pointed to something even more significant in what He said to people who were uncertain about Him: "If anyone chooses to *do* God's will, he will find out whether my teaching comes from God..."[10]

I used to think I had to know before I could fully act. But Jesus urged something different: I need to act before I can fully know.

I've taken that to heart. And as I've acted upon mustard seeds of confidence I've had, making small choices to obey Jesus and grow as His apprentice, I've seen His words and ways prove true again and again.

"Obedience is the soul of knowledge," explained George MacDonald.[11] "Do the truth and you will love the truth. For by doing it you will see it as it is..."[12]

That, I've come to believe, is the essence of faith. It's the decision to respond to God's invitations despite not having answers to every question. My intellect will always be an important part of my faith too. But only in the *doing* of faith can my *knowing* become clearer and richer. As I've followed hard after Jesus, I can say without doubt that it has.

And yet, consider another scenario. Katie could also be living in Uganda in a very different way than she is now. After all, people can live self-centered, miserly lives in Africa too—even as missionaries. The real legacy of Katie's life is being shaped, even today, by a hundred daily choices: pausing to help a little boy huddled in the rain; listening attentively to a lonely blind woman; stopping amidst myriad tasks to kneel before God; cooking beans and *posho* over an open fire in the backyard to share with neighborhood kids; answering an unexpected knock even though she's just sat down to a meal.

Ultimately, if she is to live as an apprentice to Jesus, Katie must choose Uganda every day.

Writer Beth Clark expresses so well in the foreword to Katie's book:

> I've noticed something about people who make a difference in the world: They hold the unshakable conviction that individuals are extremely important, that every life matters. They get excited over one smile. They are willing to feed one stomach, educate one mind, and treat one wound. They aren't determined to revolutionize the world all at once; they're satisfied with small changes. Over time, though, the small changes add up. Sometimes they even transform cities and nations, and yes, the world.[13]

DEATH AT THE BEGINNING

Apprentices to Jesus who serve the most destitute seem to understand the significance of small things with special clarity. Perhaps that is because they see daily how vast and complex our world's hurt really is. As Katie Davis describes of her work in Uganda, it can feel like "emptying the ocean with an eyedropper."[14]

Yet Davis is not crushed by this finding. Rather, she is nourished by an even deeper truth. "We aren't really called to save the world, not even to save one person; Jesus does that," she explains. "We are just called to love with abandon."[15]

> The kingdom of God is built with small, beautiful, true encounters.[16]
>
> —JON TYSON

Another woman who also loved Jesus and the destitute with abandon, Mother Teresa of Calcutta, used similar words. "We can do no great things, only *small things* with *great love*."[17]

Yes, to love with abandon. Small things with great love. Not in a once-for-all decision, for it can't be done that way. Rather God's grace flows through us to others in choices made and remade nearly as often as we breathe. It is silencing the buzz of our self-concerned thoughts so as to be wholly present to the student who came in after class. Helping a lonely woman feel the weight of her worth with our focused attention. Making a great truth concrete for a child by using a simple object or vivid word picture. Revealing both the beauty and brokenness of our own lives with a humble admission before close friends. Jotting down a few questions before the dinner guests arrive to provoke discussion of more than trivial matters. Forming habits of solitude and prayer, that we may know God's heart more deeply and share more of it with others. These are the choices that make an admirer of Jesus into a true apprentice.

And in them we find answer to the questions that began this book. For in these mostly unheralded moments, eternal truth intersects daily life. Here, apprenticeship to Jesus forges something truly extraordinary from ordinary interactions. Here, our influence quietly begins to reach farther, deeper. The relationships and authentic community we yearn for take root and flourish. As we learn to serve others well through our communication, our presence grows into an outpost of grace. Amidst a shadowy world, the kingdom of God beckons with warmth and light.

If such success seems too costly, or perhaps just too small, we would do well to listen one last time to those who reached the pinnacle along other routes. Cobain. Hemingway. Monroe. Rothko. Simone de Beauvoir. Septimus. The writer of Ecclesiastes. Perhaps as much as any who've walked the earth, they grasped the grand successes they wished for. Yet in so many ways, each found only death. In gaining their life they lost it.

With Jesus, the decision to embrace death comes not at the end, but at the beginning. "Whoever loses his life for my sake will find it."[18] There may be no more disturbing but exhilarating invitation in all of history. And then, in a twist as beautiful as it is startling, Jesus pairs His sweeping decree with the simplest of instructions. "If anyone gives even a cup of cold water to one of these little ones…he will certainly not lose his reward."[19]

This is where apprenticeship to Jesus is lived out, if at all. Small acts of great love. Daily choices that mirror the heart of the Master. Taken together, these form the person we are becoming and the legacy we will leave behind.

Day by day. Choice by choice. Seed by seed. Word by word.

NOTES

INTRODUCTION

1. Dictionary.com, http://dictionary.reference.com/browse/upend, s.v. "upend."
2. As often as it may be blithely used by Christians, what's meant by the term *radical*—getting to the real root of things—is indeed what we need. David Platt's book *Radical* (Sisters, OR: Multnomah, 2010) presents a potent vision for what this really means.
3. In humility and contrition, Jason made a decisive turn back toward Christ and his family that has affected every facet of his life. He's an utterly different man today. Far more joyful and purposeful, and—although not in Hollywood—making a significant impact for the kingdom, using his filmmaking skills for redemptive ends. He's an inspiration to both of us.
4. Peter Hutchison, "Facebook 'Friends' Mock 'Suicide' of Woman Who Posted Goodbye Message," *The Telegraph*, January 6, 2011, http://www.telegraph.co.uk/technology/facebook/8241015/Facebook-friends-mock-suicide-of-woman-who-posted-goodbye-message.html (accessed February 28, 2012).
5. 1 John 2:6.
6. We'd never be able to list the countless women and men who've helped to inspire and guide these thoughts, from contemporary teachers and friends to great saints of ages past. Many of these individuals are quoted and referenced in various ways in this book, although certainly not all. While we certainly won't be able to affirm all of these significant influences, especially when it comes to the theme of apprenticeship, we'd be remiss in not acknowledging the linchpin role that Dallas Willard has played. Although he's quoted numerous times throughout the book, his wise perspective informs far more in this book than could be directly attributed.

CHAPTER 1—ETERNAL TRUTH AND THE DAILY GRIND

1. The 2010 Cape Town Congress video of Antoine Rutayisire speaking may be accessed at: http://conversation.lausanne.org/en/conversations/detail/11416 (accessed January 10, 2012).
2. Ibid.
3. Paul's remarks in Romans and elsewhere about the "flesh" being opposed to the spirit are sometimes taken to affirm a division between a lower physical realm with a higher spiritual realm. But by "flesh" (*sarx*) Paul means not our physical bodies or other aspects of the tangible world, but rather the fallen human nature. The contrast he paints is not "spiritual against physical." Rather, what makes anything "fleshly" is its corruption by sin—including the body, mind, and soul. (We would do well to remember that spiritual beings too can be either good or evil.) Paul makes clear that the redemption God intends for His children includes not only their mind and soul but also their mortal body. He expresses in Romans 8:11, "And if the Spirit of him who raised Jesus from the dead is living in you, he who raised Christ from the dead will also give life to your mortal bodies through his Spirit, who lives in you."
4. Genesis 1:31.
5. 1 Timothy 4:4.

6. Remarkably, even Jesus's resurrected body could be touched, break bread, and eat fish. The spiritual is not totally distinct from the physical. Rather, the two are always intertwined. The spiritual impacts the physical and vice versa.

7. Expressed to Jedd in a personal conversation over breakfast. Quoted with permission. Learn more about Celestin Musekura's work leading African Leadership and Reconciliation Ministries (ALARM) at www.alarm-inc.org.

8. As noted early in this chapter, the most important aspects of apprenticeship happen below the surface. Others have written more effectively than we could on the ways in which a Christian can choose to participate in God's reshaping of our deepest parts, even our emotions and desires. This process of *spiritual formation* happens especially through the spiritual disciplines. From fasting and solitude to prayer and memorization, the disciplines have been practiced by all of history's great apprentices to Jesus and, in fact, by Jesus Himself. This book touches on some of these practices, but its primary focus is on mirroring the choices and disciplines Jesus modeled that relate directly to the way we communicate. We strongly recommend other excellent books that focus on the full range of spiritual disciplines. These books include Dallas Willard's *The Spirit of the Disciplines*, *Renovation of the Heart*, and *The Divine Conspiracy*, each of which has had a profound influence upon our perspective on apprenticeship. Other excellent books on the disciplines include *The Way of the Heart* by Henri Nouwen, *Celebration of Discipline* by Richard Foster, and *Invitation to Solitude and Silence* by Ruth Haley Barton.

9. See Matthew 18:23–27. The debt Jesus described was of ten thousand talents. One talent equaled roughly twenty years of a day laborer's wages. See: http://www .biblegateway.com/passage/?search=Matthew+18&version=NIV (accessed January 9, 2012).

10. Dallas Willard, *The Great Omission* (New York: HarperCollins, 2006), 81.

11. Matthew 7:24–26, emphasis added.

12. John 13:14–15, emphasis added.

13. 1 Corinthians 4:7.

14. Philippians 3:12–14.

15. 1 Timothy 1:15.

16. Philippians 4:9.

17. 1 Corinthians 11:1.

18. 2 Corinthians 3:18.

CHAPTER 2—THE KINGDOM VISION

1. Philip Hallie, *Lest Innocent Blood Be Shed* (New York: Harper Perennial, 1994).

2. Ibid.

3. Although many brilliant Christian thinkers have helped us see the meaning of the kingdom of God more clearly, we are especially indebted for the thoughts shared here to Dallas Willard, especially his book *The Divine Conspiracy* (New York: HarperCollins, 1998).

4. Psalm 103:19 expresses this reality, which is reflected throughout Scripture.

5. Psalm 8:5–8 describes this truth with special clarity.

6. Matthew 6:10.

7. See Psalm 85:10.

8. Isaiah 11:6–9.

9. See Matthew 12:28.

10. We first encountered this description—"loving others through speech"—from Dr. Greg Spencer, whose "Theories of Rhetoric" class is unequalled in compelling vision and insight. Many other ideas from Dr. Spencer have shaped this book, both overtly and also (we are certain) in ways we don't even explicitly remember.

11. Mark 10:42–44.

12. Matthew 6:30.
13. Matthew 5:44–45.
14. Luke 12:32–33.
15. 1 John 4:19.
16. Ephesians 3:18–19.

CHAPTER 3—THE GIFT OF PRESENCE

1. Mark 5:33. Read the entire story in Mark 5:21–35.
2. Quoted by C. S. Lewis in *George MacDonald: An Anthology* (New York: Simon & Schuster, 1996), XXVIII.
3. Anne's name was changed to avoid family embarrassment.
4. Maggie Jackson, *Distracted* (Amhurst, NY: Prometheus Books, 2009), 13.
5. The term *continuous partial attention* (CPA) was coined by Linda Stone in 1998. See http://lindastone.net.
6. Noted in interview with Maggie Jackson on *Mars Hill Audio Journal* 94, Nov/Dec 2008, http://www.marshillaudio.org/Resources/Issue.aspx?id=94 (accessed February 15, 2012).
7. Randall Bush, "Not Global Villagers, but Global Voyeurs," *The Christian Century*, September 9–16, 1992, 809–811.2.
8. Clive Thompson, "Brave New World of Digital Intimacy," *New York Times Magazine*, September 5, 2008, http://www.nytimes.com/2008/09/07/magazine/07awareness-t .html?pagewanted=all (accessed January 10, 2012).
9. Ibid.
10. Matthew 19:14.
11. See Matthew 9:36; 14:14; 15:32; 20:34.
12. See John 11:35.
13. Luke 23:42–43.
14. This story is recounted in various sources, each sharing the same core details and all consistent with the grace and compassion that mark Sir William Osler's personal and professional life. This version is drawn from Gordon MacDonald, *Restoring Your Spiritual Passion* (Nashville, TN: Oliver-Nelson, 1986), 137–138.
15. Quoted in Norman MacAfee, *The Gospel According to RFK* (Boulder, CO: Westview Press, 2004), 83–88. Andrew Young quotes drawn from Arthur Schlesinger Jr., *Robert Kennedy and His Times* (New York: Balantine, 1978), 852.

CHAPTER 4—ALL THERE

1. Mitch Albom, *Tuesdays With Morrie* (New York: Doubleday, 1997), 135–136.
2. Noted in interview with Maggie Jackson on *Mars Hill Audio Journal* 94, Nov/Dec 2008, http://www.marshillaudio.org/Resources/Issue.aspx?id=94 (accessed February 15, 2012).
3. Eyal Ophir, Clifford Nass, and Anthony D. Wagner, "Cognitive Control in Media Multitaskers," *Proceedings of the National Academy of Sciences* (August 24, 2009): http:// www.pnas.org/content/106/37/15583.full (accessed January 10, 20112).
4. Mark Bauerlein, author of the provocative book *The Dumbest Generation*, helps explain the Stanford finding, "When people spend months and years trying to multitask, their mental habits follow. Most important, their capacity to filter out distractions and irrelevant items deteriorates. As one of the researchers put it, 'They're suckers for irrelevancy.'" (Mark Bauerlein, "Multitasking Is Dangerous to Your Health," *The Chronicle of Higher Education*, September 30, 2009, http://chronicle.com/blogs/brainstorm/multitasking-is-dangerous -to-your-health/8278 [accessed January 10, 2012]).
5. Annie Dillard, *The Pilgrim at Tinker Creek* (New York: Harper Perennial, a division of Harper Collins Publishers, 1974), 34–35.
6. Dietrich Bonhoeffer, *Life Together* (New York: HarperSanFrancisco, 1954), 79.
7. Matthew 6:28–32.

8. Romans 12:15.
9. Psalm 19:1.
10. Psalm 34:8.
11. Gerard Manley Hopkins, *Letters to Robert Bridges and Correspondence With Richard Watson Dixon* (Oxford: Oxford University Press, 1955). Elizabeth Barrett Browning (1806–1861), "Aurora Leigh" (London: J. Miller, 1864; Reprint: Chicago: Academy, Chicago Printers, Cassandra Editions, 1979).
12. Elizabeth Elliot, ed., *The Journals of Jim Elliot* (Grand Rapids, MI: Revell, 2002), 278.

CHAPTER 5—OUR CULTURE'S RAREST COMMODITY

1. Terry Felber, *Am I Making Myself Clear? Secrets of the World's Greatest Communicators* (Nashville, TN: Thomas Nelson, 2002).
2. Studs Terkel, *Working* (New York: Pantheon Books, 1974).
3. Interview in *Rolling Stone* magazine, December 29, 1994, 68.
4. Taylor Caldwell, *The Listener* (New York: Doubleday & Company, 1960). Caldwell's presentation of Christ is, of course, her own creation. Yet while perhaps it could be critiqued for elevating the listening of Jesus to the loss of His potent words, it is hard to deny that the way the novel conveys the presence, attentiveness, and truly transformative grace of Jesus certainly mirrors all that we see in the Gospels. One rating by a reader on Amazon.com reads, "If you read this book you will become mesmerized by Christ's power and love." Another describes, "This book made me—a firm atheist—a believer in the existence of God." Caldwell's own biography includes both a wandering from and return to rooted Christian faith.
5. Ibid.
6. Mother Teresa, *In My Own Words* (Ligouri, MO: Liguori Publications, 1997), 91.
7. See Luke 19:8.
8. We see the same pattern poignantly in Jesus's encounter with another social outcast, the woman at the well. (See John 4:1–42.) Just to be seen talking with a woman could provoke scandal for a respectable rabbi. Worse yet, this one was an adulteress and—most troubling of all—a Samaritan, loathed by the Jews. The woman came to the well to draw cool water from deep below. It was Jesus, however, who drew up even deeper waters, lifting up the story of her past and her hopes of future redemption.
9. Guinness made this remark in a small group discussion with Jedd and others in November 2008.
10. William Easterly, *The White Man's Burden: Why the West's Efforts to Aid the Rest Have Done So Much Ill and So Little Good* (New York: The Penguin Press, 2006), There is plenty in *The White Man's Burden* for both the political Left and political Right to be peeved about, and we'd share some of these critiques. Certainly—as Easterly himself clearly affirms—certain forms of foreign aid can make a real difference. But it is hard to refute the central claim of the book that the current way of "doing aid" in the developing world often achieves little good and, sometimes, great unintended harm. Foreign aid "planners" produce endless conferences, road maps, and sweeping programs—yet almost never come close to realizing the grandiose dreams they promise. Meanwhile, the humble work of the people Easterly calls "searchers" often produces modest but meaningful improvements. Perhaps all of this argues for what we could call "Incarnational Aid." Under such a vision, most all efforts to "change people" and improve their lot from a distance with one-size-fits-all schemes should be exchanged. Instead, the focus of both government and individuals would be supporting efforts that emphasize presence and attentiveness, coming near with a humble heart and listening ear so as to know, love, and then serve alongside local residents.
11. This quote by Liberia's president, Ellen Johnson Sirleaf, came from a speech she gave in 2008, hosted by USAID.
12. Easterly, *The White Man's Burden*, 16.

13. Mother Teresa, *In My Own Words*, 23.
14. Ibid., 192–194.
15. E. M. Forster, *A Passage to India* (New York: Harcourt, Brace & World, 1952).

CHAPTER 6—THE MINISTRY OF LISTENING

1. Bonhoeffer, *Life Together*, 97.
2. Ibid.
3. See Luke 18:10–14.
4. 1 Peter 5:7.
5. See Luke 15:11–31.
6. Timothy Keller, *The Reason for God* (New York: Riverhead Trade, 2009).
7. Dillard, *The Pilgrim at Tinker Creek*.
8. Philippians 2:4.
9. William Law, *A Serious Call to a Devout and Holy Life* (New York: HarperSanFrancisco, 2005), 90, 92.
10. See John 17:20.
11. Rudyard Kipling, "I Keep Six Honest…," http://www.kipling.org.uk/poems_serving.htm (accessed January 10, 2012).
12. See 1 John 4:20.
13. Don Postema, *Space for God: Study and Practice of Spirituality and Prayer* (Grand Rapids, MI: CRC Publications, 1983), 16.

CHAPTER 7—DRAWING NEAR

1. Robert Byrne, *The 2,458 Best Things Anybody Ever Said* (New York: Fireside, 2002), 570.
2. John 1:14, NKJV.
3. G. K. Chesterton, *Gloria in Profundis* (London: Faber & Faber Ltd., 1927).
4. See Matthew 4:23; 9:10; 8:3, 14–15; 9:23, 35; 12:1; Mark 1:16; Matthew 13:54.
5. Stephen B. Oates, *Woman of Valor: Clara Barton and the Civil War* (New York: Free Press, 1995); National Park Service, U.S. Department of the Interior, "Clara Barton at Antietam," http://www.nps.gov/anti/historyculture/clarabarton.htm (accessed January 10, 2012).
6. Quoted in Annette Simmons, *The Story Factor* (Cambridge, MA: Perseus Book Group, 2001), 27.
7. C. S. Lewis was a master at this as well, translating lofty ideas into expressions and stories that even children could grasp. He put it well: "Any fool can write learned language. The vernacular is the real test. If you can't turn your faith into it, then either you don't understand it or you don't believe it." (C. S. Lewis quoted in *The Christian Century* [December 31, 1958]: 1006–1007.).
8. Simple does not always mean unambiguous. As Dr. Greg Spencer describes, Jesus sometimes spoke with an *intentional ambiguity* that invited listeners toward further exploration if they truly desired to do so. For example, when Jesus told Nicodemus he would need to be "born again" to enter the kingdom of God, the scholar was puzzled. Jesus's vivid metaphor had been *simple*—even a child could grasp the basic concept—yet the full meaning was not entirely obvious. Jesus was essentially asking Nicodemus if he wanted to dig deeper. Nicodemus responded as Jesus intended, probing further.

CHAPTER 8—TAKING ON FLESH

1. Frederick Buechner, *Listening to Your Life*, quoted in Leland Ryken, ed., *The Christian Imagination* (Colorado Springs, CO: Shaw Books, 2002), 56.
2. Dr. Gary Chapman, *The Five Love Languages: How to Express Heartfelt Commitment to Your Mate* (Chicago: Northfield Publishing, 1995).

3. John Sowers, "Reflections From Q Chicago," http://fatherlessgeneration.com/news/tmp-at-q-conference-in-chicago/ (accessed January 10, 2012).

4. Philippians 2:5–9.

5. See Hebrews 2:10.

6. Hebrews 4:15.

7. Esther Havens made this remark at the orphan-issues Idea Camp in 2011.

8. See Esther's compelling images at www.estherhavens.com.

9. Richard Selzer, *Mortal Lessons: Notes on the Art of Surgery* (New York: Harcourt Inc., 1996).

CHAPTER 9—A DROUGHT OF THE REAL

1. Quotes drawn from Stephanie Rosenbloom, "Authentic? Get Real," *New York Times*, September 9, 2011, http://www.nytimes.com/2011/09/11/fashion/for-only-the-authentic-cultural-studies.html?pagewanted=all (accessed January 11, 2012).

2. See Luke 18:9–14.

3. Paul W. Swets, *The Art of Talking So That People Will Listen* (New York: Fireside, 1992).

4. John Eldredge, *Wild at Heart* (Nashville, TN: Thomas Nelson Publishers, 2001), 52.

5. See Luke 10:21.

6. See Mark 3:1–5.

7. John 6:67.

8. See Luke 19:41.

9. For examples, see Matthew 9:36; 14:14; 15:32.

10. Matthew 26:38.

11. See Matthew 23:23–36.

12. Mark 3:14, emphasis added.

13. Robert Coleman, *The Master Plan of Evangelism* (Grand Rapids, MI: Fleming H. Revell, a Division of Baker Publishing Group, 1993), 41–42.

14. Samuel Coleridge, "The Rime of the Ancient Mariner," The Literature Network, http://www.online-literature.com/coleridge/646/ (accessed January 11, 2012).

15. *New York Times*/CBS Poll taken July 17–19, 1999; NYT Poll # 99007B.

16. Read Mercer Schuchardt, "A Tribute to Neil Postman," *The New Pantagruel*, Issue 1.1, 2004.

17. Trey Sklar, Jedd Medefind, Mike Peterson, and Matt Kronberg, *Four Souls* (Nashville, TN: Thomas Nelson, 2001).

18. Sheldon Vanauken, *A Severe Mercy* (San Francisco: HarperSanFrancisco, 1987), 238.

CHAPTER 10—A DRAUGHT OF THE REAL

1. Adam Young, "My Hope Is Found," *Owl City* (blog), October 25, 2010, http://owlcityblog.com/2010/10/25/my-hope-is-found/ (accessed January 11, 2012).

2. See 2 Corinthians 3:18.

3. Quoted by Dr. Greg Spencer in his article, "Authentic Phony," on the *Boundless* webzine at http://www.boundless.org/2005/articles/a0001571.cfm (accessed January 11, 2012).

4. Aleksandr Solzhenitsyn, *The Gulag Archipelago* (New York: First Perennial Classics, an imprint of HarperCollins, 2002).

5. Psalm 34:8.

6. Psalm 102:9.

7. Psalm 24:1.

8. Psalm 88:18.

9. Luke 23:43.

10. Mark 15:34.

11. Quoted in Keller, *The Reason for God*, 30.

12. Frederick Buechner, *Telling the Truth: The Gospel as Tragedy, Comedy and Fairy Tale* (San Francisco: HarperSanFrancisco, 1977), 26, 21.
13. Curt Coffman and Gabriel Gonzalez-Molina, *Follow This Path: How the World's Greatest Organizations Drive Growth by Unleashing Human Potential* (New York: Warner Books Inc., 2002).
14. *Chariots of Fire*, directed by Hugh Hudson (Burbank, CA: Warner Home Video, 2005), DVD.
15. Charles Kraft, *Communicating Jesus' Way*, revised edition. (Pasadena, CA: William Carey Library, 1999), 26–27.
16. Willard, *The Divine Conspiracy*, 76.
17. Ibid.
18. *The Columbia World of Quotations* (New York: Columbia University Press, 1996); Bartleby.com, "Self-Reliance," Essays, First Series (1841), http://www.bartleby .com/5/104.html, from (accessed January 12, 2012).

CHAPTER 11—MAKING TRUTH TOUCHABLE

1. Although drawn from a variety of sources, the final telling of this story was refined with help from Dr. Little's wife, who also requested that her name not be specifically mentioned due to sensitivities with the ongoing work in Afghanistan.
2. See Mark 7:31–35.
3. Mark 4:39, NKJV.
4. John 11:43.
5. Exodus 3:5.
6. The one other place where God gives a similar instruction to take off sandals is to Joshua in Joshua 5:15, and for a similar reason.
7. "Song for the Waiting," sermon by Glenn Hoberg, December 6, 2009.
8. See Luke 13:34; Matthew 23:37.
9. See Ezekiel 37:4–6.
10. See Psalm 42:1.
11. Isaiah 55:8–9.
12. Psalm 19:1.
13. Romans 1:20.
14. 1 John 3:17-18.
15. Excerpt in *Knowing the Heart of God*, compiled by Michael R. Phillips (Minneapolis, MN: Bethany House Publishers, 1990), 96.

CHAPTER 12—CONCRETE GRACE

1. John 13:12–15; read the entire passage in John 13:12-17.
2. Joel Spolsky, "My Style of Servant Leadership," Inc.com, December 1, 2008, http://www .inc.com/magazine/20081201/how-hard-could-it-be-my-style-of-servant -leadership.html (accessed January 12, 2012).
3. Ibid.
4. See a virtual version of Thomas Clarkson's box at http://museumbox.e2bn.org/creator/ viewer/show/34 (accessed January 12, 2012).
5. "Slavery: Breaking the Chains," *The Economist*, February 24, 2007, 72, http://www .economist.com/node/8749406 (accessed January 12, 2012).
6. The Abolition Project, "What Did Clarkson Bring to the Campaign?" http://abolition. e2bn.org/box_136.html (accessed January 12, 2012).
7. John 7:37–38.
8. Luke 9:46–48.
9. See Matthew 22:15–22.

10. Mark 12:42–44.
11. George MacDonald, *Miracles of Our Lord* (London: Strahan & Co. Publishers, 1870).
12. Tom Davis, *Fields of the Fatherless* (Colorado Springs, CO: David C. Cook, 2008).
13. See Matthew 5:13–15.
14. John 6:35, 48.
15. John 4:10.
16. See Matthew 13:31.
17. See Matthew 13:33.
18. Matthew 13:44.
19. Charles Spurgeon, "Sermon in Candles," Lecture 1, http://www.spurgeon.org/misc/candles.htm (accessed January 12, 2012).
20. See note 1 from chapter 11.

CHAPTER 13—THE MARVELOUS POWER OF STORY

1. Patti J. Christensen, "Quotes About Story and Storytelling," http://www.storyteller.net/articles/160 (accessed January 12, 2012).
2. Walter Fisher, *Human Communication as Narration* (Columbia, SC: University of South Carolina Press, 1989).
3. Matthew 13:34, emphasis added.
4. Richard N. Ostling, "Born-Again Zeal Underlies TV's 7th Network," Associated Press, *South Coast Today*, October 2, 1998, http://www.southcoasttoday.com/apps/pbcs.dll/article?AID=/19981002/NEWS/310029932&cid=sitesearch (accessed January 12, 2012).
5. Quote from Os Guinness was spoken to small group gathering at Osprey Point, Maryland, in 2009.
6. Dudley Nichols, "The Writer and the Film," *Theater Arts*, October 1943.
7. Madelaine L'Engle, *Walking on Water* (Wheaton, IL: Harold Shaw Publishers, 1980), 54.
8. Carl Sandburg, *Abraham Lincoln: The War Years* (New York: Harcourt, Brace & World, 1939).
9. Annette Simmons, *The Story Factor* (Cambridge, MA: Perseus Publishing, 2001), back cover.
10. See Matthew 13:13–15.
11. John Muir, *My First Summer in the Sierra* (New York: Penguin Group, 1997), 61.
12. See 2 Samuel 12.
13. Charles Kraft, *Communicating Jesus' Way*, revised edition (Pasadena, CA: William Carey Library, 1999), 72.
14. Annemarie Caracciolo, *Smart Things to Know About Teams* (Milford, CT: Capstone USA, 2001), 212.
15. Francis Schaeffer, *Art and the Bible* (Downers Grove, IL: InterVarsity Press, 2006).
16. Isak Dinesen quote cited in Annette Simmons, *The Story Factor* (Cambridge, MA: Basic Books, 2001), 1.
17. See Luke 16:21.
18. Luke 15:9.

CHAPTER 14—STORYTELLING FOR COMMUNITY, CAUSE, AND CONVICTION

1. Alasdair MacIntyre, *After Virtue* (London: Gerald Duckworth & Co Ltd., 1981), 201.
2. For an excellent telling of this moving story, see the movie *Joyeux Noël*.
3. John 3:14.
4. Matthew 12:40.
5. Luke 17:26.
6. Howard Schultz, *Onward* (Emmaus, PA: Rodale, 2011).

7. This account, portrayed in the popular Broadway *The King and I*, is likely a historical embellishment. But it illustrates well how story can be such a significant form of argument through *enthymeme*. Even if *Uncle Tom's Cabin* played little role in the rejection of slavery in Siam, it indubitably did so in countries around the world.

8. As quoted in Donald K. McKim, *The Bible in Theology and Preaching* (Nashville, TN: Abingdon Press, 1994), 132.

9. Ibid, 131.

10. Isaiah 55:1.

11. Isaiah 65:2.

12. See Psalm 19:1–3.

13. Gary Haugen, *Good News About Injustice: A Witness of Courage in a Hurting World* (Downers Grove, IL: InterVarsity Press, 1999), 24.

14. From remarks at Idea Camp! conference in Little Rock, Arkansas, 2010.

15. Nicholas Kristof, "Nicholas Kristof's Advice for Saving the World," *Outside,* November 30, 2009, http://www.outsideonline.com/outdoor-adventure/Nicholas -Kristof-s-Advice-for-Saving-the-World.html?page=all (accessed January 12, 2012).

16. Ibid.

17. As quoted in Kirk Russell, *Decadence and Renewal in Higher Learning: An Episodic History of American University and College Since 1953* (South Bend, IN: Gateway Editions, 1978), 223.

18. C. S. Lewis, *The Discarded Image* (Cambridge: Cambridge University Press, 1964), 176.

19. Annette Simmons, *The Story Factor* (Cambridge, MA: Basic Books, 2001), 111.

20. Muriel Rukeyser, *The Speed of Darkness* (New York: Random House, 1968).

CHAPTER 15—HOW TO START A REVOLUTION

1. Jules Verne, *Journey to the Center of the Earth* (London: Penguin Books, 1965).

2. Thomas W. Benson, Michael H. Prosser, *Readings in Classical Rhetoric* (Davis, CA: Hermagoras Press, 1988), 24.

3. Ibid.

4. James D. Williams, ed., *An Introduction to Classical Rhetoric: Essential Readings* (Malden, MA: Wiley-Blackwell, 2009), 152.

5. Goodreads.com, "Patrick Henry Quotes," http://www.goodreads.com/author/ quotes/361839.Patrick_Henry (accessed January 12, 2012).

6. Martin Luther King Jr., "Letter From Birmingham City Jail," in William Bennett, *The Book of Virtues* (New York: Simon & Schuster, 1993), 262.

7. Milan Kundera, *The Unbearable Lightness of Being* (New York: Harper & Row, 1984), 254.

8. From Matthew 21:23–27, with a touch of creative license adding minor details not mentioned in the original story.

9. John 14:6.

10. Mark 8:29.

11. Matthew 20:32.

12. Mark 10:18.

13. Mark 9:33.

14. Matthew 15:34.

15. Roy P. Basler, ed., *The Collected Works of Abraham Lincoln,* volume 1 (New Jersey: Rutgers University Press, 1953), 273.

CHAPTER 16—DEEPER CHANGE THAN FORCE COULD BRING

1. See Luke 10:25-37.

2. See Mark 8:36.

3. See Matthew 6:27.

4. Matthew 6:25.

5. Thomas Clarkson, *The History of the Rise, Progress, and Accomplishment of the Abolition of the Slave-Trade by the British Parliament*, volume 1 (Fairford, England: Echo Library, 2006).

6. Saint John's College Library, "Papers of Thomas Clarkson," http://janus.lib.cam .ac.uk/db/node.xsp?id=EAD%2FGBR%2F0275%2FClarkson (accessed January 12, 2012).

7. Those who've seen the movie *Amazing Grace* may recall Clarkson's first meeting with Wilberforce. The details in the film may be a bit dramatized, but they accurately reflects Clarkson's way of communicating. As Clarkson seeks to persuade Wilberforce to take a bolder stand for abolition, he drops a set of iron shackles in front of Wilberforce upon an elegant dinner table. The well-crafted film carries other notable examples of efforts by the abolitionists to make their issue more tangible also. One of the most memorable is when Wilberforce leads a group of high society dames and dandies on a pleasant harbor tour, eating and chatting on the deck of a well-outfitted ship. Wilberforce has the vessel guided to a particular part of the harbor, where the high society crowd begin to wrinkle their noises, then cough and cover their faces at a horrific odor that begins to fill the air. Wilberforce announces that what they are smelling is the stench of death, disease, and suffering coming from a slave ship docked nearby. From the look on the faces of his fellow passengers, it is clear that Wilberforce has made the distant reality of slavery troubling present to their senses.

8. Thinkexist.com, "William Wilberforce quotes," http://thinkexist.com/quotation/god-almighty-has-set-before-me-two-great-objects/536942.html (accessed January 12, 2012).

9. 1 John 4:19.

CHAPTER 17—WE CANNOT GIVE WHAT WE DO NOT HAVE

1. George Crabb, *Crabb's English Synonymes* (New York: Grosset & Dunlap, 1917), 56; S. Austin Allibone, ed., *Prose Quotations From Socrates to Macaulay* (Philadelphia: J. B. Lippincott & Co., 1880); Bartleby.com, 2011, http://www.bartleby.com/349/authors/56 .html (accessed January 12, 2012).

2. A. G. Sertillanges, *The Intellectual Life: Its Spirit, Conditions, Methods* (Washington, DC: The Catholic University of America Press, 1987).

3. Kathryn Spink, *Mother Teresa: A Complete Authorized Biography* (New York: HarperCollins, 1997).

4. Mark 1:29–37.

5. Luke 5:16.

6. Dallas Willard, *The Spirit of the Disciplines: Understanding How God Changes Lives* (San Francisco: HarperSanFrancisco, 1988), 162.

7. Os Guinness, *Fit Bodies, Fat Minds* (Grand Rapids, MI: Baker Book House, 1994).

8. Henry Nouwen, *The Living Reminder: Service and Prayer in Memory of Jesus Christ* (San Francisco: HarperSanFrancisco, 1977), 11.

9. As quoted in Neil Postman, *Amusing Ourselves to Death* (New York: Penguin Books, 1986), 105.

10. Henri J. M. Nouwen, *The Way of the Heart* (New York: Ballantine Books, 1985).

11. Kundera, *The Unbearable Lightness of Being*, 94.

12. William Penn, *The Fruits of Solitude*. Public domain.

13. Mark 6:31.

14. Bartleby.com "Childe Harold's Pilgrimage," cto. 3, st. 90 (1812–1818) http://www .bartleby.com/100/368.63.html (accessed January 12, 2012).

15. See John 1:1.

16. Nouwen, *The Way of the Heart*, 13.

17. Richard H. Popkin, ed., *Pascal Selections* (New York: Macmillan, 1989).

18. Bonhoeffer, *Life Together*, 76–77.

19. Postema, *Space for God*, 20.
20. Willard, *The Divine Conspiracy*, 321.
21. Psalm 42:2.

CHAPTER 18—ONE UNCROWDED DAY EACH WEEK

1. Robert Isaac Wilberforce and Samuel Wilberforce, *The Life of William Wilberforce*, volume 3 (London: John Murray, 1838), 3.
2. See Mark 2:27.
3. Gabe Lyons, "A Candid Interview With Eugene Peterson," ChurchLeaders.com, http://www.churchleaders.com/pastors/pastor-articles/145302-a-candid-interview-with-eugene-peterson.html (accessed January 13, 2012).
4. Ibid.
5. Psalm 127:1–2.
6. Mom's Carelink, "Recover a Day of Rest," http://momscarelink.firstmbchurch.com/p/carelink-coordinators-corner.html (accessed January 13, 2012); Focus on the Family October 2010 bulletin.
7. Thomas Merton, *No Man Is an Island* (Singapore: Shamhala, 1983), 128.
8. Books such as Dallas Willard's *The Spirit of the Disciplines*, Richard Foster's *A Celebration of Discipline*, Henri Nouwen's *The Way of the Heart*, and Ruth Haley Barton's *Invitation to Solitude and Silence* can help guide in the practice of solitude and other disciplines. But remember, reading does not equal doing.

CHAPTER 19—WHEN WE GET OUR WISH

1. *Rolling Stone*, "500 Greatest Albums of All Time," http://www.rollingstone.com/music/lists/500-greatest-albums-of-all-time-19691231/nevermind-nirvana-19691231 (accessed January 16, 2012).
2. Eric Olsen, "10 Years Later, Cobain Lives on in His Music," MSNBC.com, April 9, 2004, http://today.msnbc.msn.com/id/4652653/ns/today-entertainment/t/years-later-cobain-lives-his-music/ (accessed October 20, 2011).
3. Ibid. See also Michael Azerrad, "Inside the Heart and Mind of Nirvana," *Rolling Stone*, April 16, 1992.
4. C. S. Lewis, "The Inner Ring," *C. S. Lewis Society of California,* http://www.lewissociety.org/innerring.php (October 20, 2011).
5. Randall Radic, "An Outsider in Latvia, America & Art: Mark Rothko," http://www.literarytraveler.com/authors/rothko_latvia.aspx (accessed January 13, 2012).
6. Max Wallace and Ian Halperin, *Love & Death: The Murder of Kurt Cobain* (New York: Atria Books, 2004), 146.
7. Angela Lu, "Francis Chan Leaves Megachurch for New Direction," *World Magazine,* April 2010, http://online.worldmag.com/2010/04/19/francis-chan-leaves-megachurch-for-new-direction/ (accessed January 13, 2013).
8. Tim Kizziar as quoted in Francis Chan's *Crazy Love: Overwhelmed by a Relentless God* (Colorado Springs, CO: David C. Cook, 2008).
9. "Books: *Bonjour, Tristesse*," *Time Magazine,* Friday, May 14, 1965, abstract viewed at http://www.time.com/time/magazine/article/0,9171,898848,00.html (accessed January 13, 2012).
10. *Historia Augusta* (Loeb Classical Library, 1921) http://penelope.uchicago.edu/Thayer/E/Roman/Texts/Historia_Augusta/Septimius_Severus*.html (accessed January 13, 2012). Public domain.
11. Ecclesiastes 2:11.
12. Cynthia Heimel, "Tongue in Chic," *The Village Voice,* January 2, 1990; thanks to Tim Keller for highlighting Heimel's column in *The Reason for God.*
13. Matthew 10:39.

14. Matthew 10:39.
15. Romans 12:1.
16. Luke 9:23 and other passages.
17. 1 John 3:16.

CHAPTER 20—THE BIGGEST DECISIONS WE'LL EVER MAKE

1. Chan, *Crazy Love*.
2. These studies are all referenced in "National Time Accounting: The Currency of Life," draft paper, April 2008 at Princeton University, by Alan B. Krueger, Daniel Kahneman, DavidSchkade, Norbert Schwarz, and Arthur Stone.
3. Jonathan Haidt, *The Happiness Hypothesis: Finding Modern Truth in Ancient Wisdom* (New York: Basic Books, 2006), cited in Nicholas Kristof's *Half the Sky* (New York: Knopf, 2009).
4. To learn more about Salomon and Mery Hernandez, and to assist their family's ongoing medical work with the poor in Guatemala, visit http://westmontbethel.org/ (accessed January 13, 2012).
5. Marcus Aurelius, *Meditations*, book 5, http://classics.mit.edu/Antoninus/ meditations.5.five.html (accessed January 13, 2012).
6. Oswald Chambers, "Where the Battle's Lost and Won," http://utmost.org/classic/where-the-battle%E2%80%99s-lost-and-won/ (accessed January 16, 2012).
7. Matthew 12:34 (NIV, 2011 revision).
8. Matthew 12:33.
9. Dallas Willard, *Renovation of the Heart in Daily Practice: Experiments in Spiritual Transformation* (Colorado Springs, CO: NavPress, 2006), 66.
10. See Psalm 127:2.
11. As quoted in Stephen R. Covey's *The 7 Habits of Highly Effective People* (New York: Free Press, 2004), 287.
12. Dietrich Bonhoeffer, *The Cost of Discipleship* (New York: Touchstone, 1995).
13. Bonhoeffer wrote to fellow theologian Reinhold Niebuhr, "I must live through this difficult period in our national history with the Christian people of Germany. I shall have no right to participate in the reconstruction of Christian life in Germany after the war if I do not share the trials of this time with my people." Quoted in Eberhard Bethge, *Dietrich Bonhoeffer: Eine Biographie* (n.p.: n.d.), 736. Source of English translation quoted at http://www.answers.com/topic/dietrich-bonhoeffer#cite_ref-20 is unknown (accessed January 13, 2012).
14. Dietrich Bonhoeffer, *A Testament to Freedom*, ed. Geffrey B. Kelly (New York: HarperOne, 1995).
15. Iris Murdoch, *The Sovereignty of Good* (London: Routledge Classics, 2001), 36.
16. "Water, Not Thunder" poem written by Jedd Mededfind.
17. Thomas J. Lueck, "Low Murder Rate Brings New York Back to '63," *New York Times*, December 31, 2007, http://www.nytimes.com/2007/12/31/nyregion/31murder.html (accessed January 13, 2012).
18. John Tierney, "The Holy Terror," *New York Times*, December 3, 1995, http://www .nytimes.com/1995/12/03/magazine/the-holy-terror.html?pagewanted =all&src=pm (accessed January 13, 2012).
19. Leif Enger, *So Young, Brave and Handsome* (New York: Atlantic Monthly Press, 2008), 199.
20. As quoted in "Nat Hentoff's Last Column: The 50-Year Veteran Says Goodbye," *The Village Voice*, January 7, 2009, http://www.villagevoice.com/content/printVersion/816040/ (accessed January 13, 2012).

CONCLUSION—LIFE BY A THOUSAND CUTS

1. Jean Giono, *The Man Who Planted Trees* (England: Random House UK, 2003).

2. Mark 4:31–32.

3. See Matthew 17:20.

4. Fyordor Dostoevsky, *The Brothers Karamazov* (New York: Bantam, 1981).

5. George Elliott, *Middlemarch* (New York: Penguin Classics, 2003), 735.

6. This episode is captured in the documentary *Olympia—Fest der Völker* by Leni Riefenstahl. Thanks, also, to the Wikipedia entry on Luz Long for sources and background.

7. Ibid.

8. Larry Schwartz, "Owens Pierced a Myth," ESPN.com, http://espn.go.com/sportscentury/features/00016393.html (accessed January 13, 2012).

9. Katie Davis, *Kisses From Katie* (New York: Howard Books, 2011).

10. John 7:17, emphasis added.

11. George MacDonald, "Salvation From Sin," http://www.online-literature.com/george-macdonald/hope-of-the-gospel/1/ (accessed January 13, 2012).

12. Shulamite Ministries, "The Wisdom of GeorgeMacDonald," December 1, 2002, http://www.shulamite.com/read/fresh-bread/1333/the-wisdom-of-george-macdonald/ (accessed January 16, 2012).

13. Davis, *Kisses From Katie.*

14. Ibid.

15. Ibid.

16. From Jon Tyson sermon at Trinity Grace Church on June 5, 2011, http://trinitygracechurch.com/wp-content/uploads/2011/06/Eastertide-_-06-Chelsea-5-June-2011.mp3.

17. Mother Teresa, *Everything Starts From Prayer* (Ashland, OR: White Cloud Press, 1998), 111.

18. Matthew 10:39.

19. Matthew 10:42.

AUTHOR BIOS

JEDD MEDEFIND

Jedd Medefind led the White House Office of Faith-Based and Community Initiatives as a special assistant to President George W. Bush. In this post he oversaw government-wide reforms that made local non-profits and faith-based groups the central partners in major initiatives to elevate the needy, from prisoner reentry to Global AIDS. As described by the *Harvard Political Review*, this initiative "fundamentally changed the government's strategy for improving the lives of the downtrodden."

Jedd now serves as president of the Christian Alliance for Orphans. The alliance unites a coalition of more than one hundred respected Christian organizations in joint advocacy campaigns that ignite and equip Christians for adoption, foster care, and global orphan initiatives.

Previously Jedd held a range of campaign and political posts in the California state legislature. He also helped establish the California Community Renewal Project, which strengthens nonprofits in some of the state's most challenged communities. He has worked, studied, and served in more than thirty countries, with organizations ranging from Price-Waterhouse in Moscow to Christian Life in Bangladesh.

Jedd has written numerous articles and two books. He and his wife, Rachel, love the great outdoors and live in California with their five children.

ERIK LOKKESMOE

Erik Lokkesmoe is founder and principal of Different Drummer, one of America's fastest growing, most forward-thinking entertainment marketing agencies Introducing a new strategy of "social mobilization," Different Drummer mobilizes fans and audiences within the movie, documentary, publishing, music, cause, and sports industries.

Erik began his career in entertainment with Anschutz Film Group/ Walden Media/Bristol Bay Productions as the project manager for the film *Amazing Grace*, the story of eighteenth-century abolitionist William Wilberforce. Erik's political experiences began in 1996 when he started a ten-year career in Washington DC, serving as a communication advisor for the National Association of Broadcasters, a press secretary on Capitol Hill, a speechwriter for American leaders, and the head of communications for the National Endowment for the Humanities.

Erik also launched the arts nonprofit organization Brewing Culture to fund artists and to create space for new conversations around the arts. Erik earned a MA in public communications from The American University in Washington DC and a BA in political science from Westmont College in Santa Barbara, CA. Erik lives in New York City with his wife, Monica, and three children.